T0331987

The Theory of *Guanxi* and Chinese Society

The Theory of *Guanxi* and Chinese Society

Jack Barbalet

OXFORD
UNIVERSITY PRESS

OXFORD
UNIVERSITY PRESS

Great Clarendon Street, Oxford, OX2 6DP,
United Kingdom

Oxford University Press is a department of the University of Oxford.
It furthers the University's objective of excellence in research, scholarship,
and education by publishing worldwide. Oxford is a registered trade mark of
Oxford University Press in the UK and in certain other countries

© Jack Barbalet 2021

The moral rights of the author have been asserted

First Edition published in 2021

Impression: 1

All rights reserved. No part of this publication may be reproduced, stored in
a retrieval system, or transmitted, in any form or by any means, without the
prior permission in writing of Oxford University Press, or as expressly permitted
by law, by licence or under terms agreed with the appropriate reprographics
rights organization. Enquiries concerning reproduction outside the scope of the
above should be sent to the Rights Department, Oxford University Press, at the
address above

You must not circulate this work in any other form
and you must impose this same condition on any acquirer

Published in the United States of America by Oxford University Press
198 Madison Avenue, New York, NY 10016, United States of America

British Library Cataloguing in Publication Data
Data available

Library of Congress Control Number: 2021933402

ISBN 978-0-19-880873-2

DOI: 10.1093/oso/9780198808732.001.0001

Printed and bound in the UK by
TJ Books Limited

Links to third party websites are provided by Oxford in good faith and
for information only. Oxford disclaims any responsibility for the materials
contained in any third party website referenced in this work.

For
Xiaoying

Acknowledgements

I am pleased to acknowledge my colleagues in the Sociology Department at Hong Kong Baptist University, with whom I worked over a very fruitful six-year period. Our frequent conversations regarding the sociology of China situated me perfectly for writing this book. I wish to thank (in alphabetical order) Kwok Shing Chan, Matthew Chew, Gina Lai, Hon Chu Leung, Yinni Peng, Danching Ruan, Day Wong, and Odalia Wong. During my time in Hong Kong I enjoyed supervising research students now embarked on their own academic careers, Chen Zetao, Du Yi, Gao Chunyuan, Zhang Linlin, Zhang Qing, and Tang Ling, who deserve acknowledgement for their contribution to my own education.

More directly related to my considerations of *guanxi*, I have enjoyed exchanges of many kinds with colleagues who have provided me with comments and advice in varying degrees of volume and intensity, written and verbal, over the past several years. I want to thank in particular those whose interactions have left their mark, namely Yanjie Bian, Cheris Chan, Xiangqun Chang, Tom Gold, Gary Hamilton, Nan Lin, Peng Wang, Xiaoying Qi, Ji Ruan, Alan Smart, Xiaoli Tian, Yunxiang Yan, Mayfair Yang, and David Wank. It goes without saying that none of them is responsible for what is written in the pages that follow. A quite different matter is whether they approve of what is presented here.

For accessing and providing me with an unpublished manuscript by Hu Hsien Chin, discussed in Chapter 4, I thank Edith A. Sandler of the Manuscript Division, Library of Congress in Washington.

No one is more directly responsible for the appearance of this book than my Commissioning Editor at Oxford. Adam Swallow is thanked for his singularly supportive contribution to this publication, and for his patience. Jenny King, also at Oxford, is thanked for taking the manuscript through production and turning it into a book.

It is necessary to acknowledge that two of the chapters were previously published, but in different form than they appear here. Chapter 2 borrows heavily from an article, 'The Analysis of Chinese Rural Society: Fei Xiaotong Revisited', published in *Modern China* in 2020, and Chapter 6 from an article, 'Tripartite *Guanxi*: Resolving Kin and Non-kin Discontinuities in Chinese Connections', published in *Theory and Society* also in 2020. A few pages from another article, 'The Structure of *Guanxi*: Resolving Problems of Network Assurance', which appeared in *Theory and Society* in 2014, have been used in writing Chapter 5. These journals, their editors, and anonymous reviewers are acknowledged and thanked for their contribution to this work.

Finally, for her love and support, I wish to acknowledge my wife, Xiaoying, to whom this book is dedicated.

Jack Barbalet
Melbourne

Contents

Introduction

Systematic, Historic, and Cultural Dimensions of *Guanxi*

This book is about 关系 *guanxi*, social connections prevalent in China and Chinese cultural areas. *Guanxi* is not simply a connection between two individuals, however. The connection in question is highly personalized so that those who participate in *guanxi* will experience both attractions between the persons involved and also emotional feelings about the relationship. As well as being a personalized connection *guanxi* is an instrumental relationship. Its instrumentality is not primarily utilitarian, though, because what *guanxi* provides access to is in the first instance important social goods, including a heightening of social esteem or status, summarily understood as face, in Chinese, 面子 *mianzi*, as a result of achieving a successful *guanxi*, and additionally access to the associates of a *guanxi* partner. The connection between the two people who share *guanxi* therefore lends itself to a fanning out of connections, or, to put it differently, to a network of interconnections. A person who has good *guanxi* will be particularly attractive to others as a prospective *guanxi* partner. This is because the social goods provided by *guanxi* can be mobilized to secure material goods in the form of a job, say, a business contract, or a loan, as well as opportunities to acquire other material goods through privileged access to facilitating others. It goes without saying that the favours provided by a *guanxi* partner go in both directions, so that *guanxi* involves reciprocity, indeed requires it, not immediately but at some future time when there is a need. In this sense, then, *guanxi* secures obligations from those who participate in it, as well as expectations concerning the behaviour of others, so that *guanxi* can be seen in terms of certain types of normative regulation, known in Chinese as 人情 *renqing*, to which it is subject. Given the lattice of bonding attachments through *guanxi*, the benefits it offers, and also the elements of compulsion that ensure its operation, *guanxi* relationships are typically enduring or long-term.

After this description of *guanxi*, with regard to its structure and the way in which it is conducted, it might be wondered if any more needs to be said about it. Indeed, a large number of studies of *guanxi* effectively spell out what has just been indicated when providing detailed accounts of specific cases of

The Theory of Guanxi *and Chinese Society.* Jack Barbalet, Oxford University Press (2021). © Jack Barbalet.
DOI: 10.1093/oso/9780198808732.003.0001

guanxi in a range of different settings. Such research may take the form of a descriptive ethnography, a statistical analysis, a policy study focused on business ethics, corruption, or organizational development and growth, or some other mode of exploration of the details of what is often referred to as 'instrumental particularism'. Whereas the generalized statement, as in the previous paragraph, may be brought to an enquiry, the factual details revealed by careful examination of actual experiences of *guanxi* clarify the causal connections between its elements, how established arrangements change as the context in which they operate is modified, and how different applications of *guanxi* may generate novel outcomes for participants and non-participants alike. The types of studies mentioned here are drawn on extensively in the chapters to follow.

As a social phenomenon *guanxi* raises questions in addition to those which may be answered by a detailed study of its application in social, political, or economic relations. In much of the discussion of *guanxi* in academic publications assumptions are made concerning its cultural background and endowments. For instance, there is a large constituency which supports, indeed advocates, the idea that *guanxi* has a foundation in Confucian social and ethical thinking and practice. In addition to this type of consideration, the general characterization of *guanxi* and its component dispositions and engagements requires relating this term to others, including, say, 'trust', 'network tie', and similar concepts drawn from social science discourse, in order to explain the operation of *guanxi*. While this may appear to be a straightforward matter, of incorporating into an explanation of *guanxi* terms drawn from the vocabulary of academic sociology, say, it raises questions about the suitability of applying concepts drawn from research primarily concerned with north American and west European experiences to accounts of Chinese practices which draw on social protocols and meanings dissimilar to those that inform the technical sociological terms in question. The point being made here is that any serious consideration of *guanxi* raises questions that go beyond the immediate relation itself, and invite investigation of how *guanxi* may be conceptualized, analysed, and explained in general terms.

Informed by these considerations, the purpose of the discussion in the six chapters to follow is to clearly identify what is meant by *guanxi*, to answer questions relating to the cultural and historical background of both the broad concept—which has had the label *guanxi* attached to it only relatively recently—as well as recounting the recent history of the term, and also to show how *guanxi* can be apprehended and also explained sociologically. Indeed, this book is the first to provide a sociological treatment of *guanxi* in terms of its broad context, historical, cultural and social; and, in doing so, provide a large number of novel assessments and findings, to be indicated below, which not only clearly illuminate the nature of *guanxi* but also indicate a great deal about the society in which it has currency, further explaining the character of instrumental particularism in China. The discussion to follow also indicates ways in which research on *guanxi* may most fruitfully proceed. It is for these reasons that the title of the book is *The Theory of Guanxi and Chinese Society*, because in its exploration of *guanxi* and the way in which it is theorized there is at the same time a significant discussion of Chinese culture and society, not only in the present day but from the late imperial period.

While this is the first book to comprehensively and critically examine the nature and background of *guanxi* it is only one of a large number of publications which address this particularly Chinese social relation. Since the 1980s when the Chinese economy drew the interest of foreign investors, *guanxi* has been of concern to the global business community. Indeed, a number of academic journals devoted to business studies, including the *Asia Pacific Business Review*, *Journal of Asian Business Studies*, and *Management and Organization Review*, are effectively dedicated to primarily reporting research on *guanxi*. It is not surprising, therefore, that the majority of single-authored or co-authored books about *guanxi* are located in this disciplinary area, including works by Ying Lun So and Anthony Walker (2006), Eike Langenberg (2007), Yadong Luo (2007), Chee-Kiong Tong (2014), and Barbara Wang (2019). While writers drawn from the disciplines of anthropology and sociology have collectively produced fewer books than management authors, the 'classics' of *guanxi* studies include the enduring monograph by Mayfair Yang (1994), *Gifts, Favors and Banquets*, and the collection, *Social Connections in China*, edited by Thomas Gold, Doug Guthrie, and David Wank (2002). More recently, Yanjie Bian (2019) has published a broad survey of the field, *Guanxi: How China Works*, that not only summarizes his own extensive contribution to the sociological study of *guanxi* but additionally overviews some key discussions. The present book augments this literature in its treatment of *guanxi* from the point of view of a critical sociological analysis.

It may be redundant to say 'critical' sociological analysis because it can be noted that sociology is inherently critical, in the sense that it is necessarily interpretive and evaluative. An earlier generation of sociologists emphasized the way in which a 'sociological imagination', to use C. Wright Mills's (1970) term, requires not only 'empirical studies of contemporary facts' but additionally held that these must be supported by 'historical' and 'systematic' investigation, in consideration of both the legacies of the past and the broad regularities of current social life (Mills 1970: 30–1). In this way, the practitioner of sociology must inevitably confront established 'truths' that defend given interests or persistent orthodoxies (Mills 1970: 206–14). This practice is described by Peter Berger (1966: 51–6) in terms of the 'debunking tendency in sociological thought'. In understanding *guanxi* it is necessary not only to examine its practice, including how *guanxi* is initiated and what it provides to those who participate in it, but also its historical background and cultural setting. The operative term here is 'examine' because representations are frequently made in the literature concerning the meaning and significance of *renqing*, for instance, that connect *guanxi* with Confucian principles. Claims regarding these matters are frequently repeated in studies of *guanxi* but almost never substantiated or seriously considered. Treatment of such questions requires going beyond *guanxi* to an investigation that is both historical and systematic, concerning cultural and linguistic aspects of Chinese practices, as undertaken throughout the present book.

The treatment of *guanxi* in Chapter 1 is introductory, in the sense that the practices associated with the formation of a *guanxi* between two people are set out and examined. After showing why *guanxi* can in general terms be described as a form of instrumental particularism, the chapter goes on to indicate on what basis two people may together participate as *guanxi* partners. It is not enough that they have a common purpose. It is shown in the chapter that in the first instance two people wishing to establish *guanxi* must recognize in each other a common identity, often described as a '*guanxi* base', the mutual acknowledgement of which permits the making of a connection between them. It is helpful to understand that a recognition of their common ground arises when two people realize the practical usefulness of their working together, so that the 'instrumentalism' of *guanxi* and its 'particularism' are seen as mutually supportive. This is important because in discussion of *guanxi* its expressive or particularistic element is sometimes seen as an alternative to its instrumental element. In this way some scholars separate 'rural' and 'urban' *guanxi* (Kipnis 1997: 147–8; Yan 1996: 226–9), even though the most instrumental business *guanxi* requires *renqing* decorum and village *guanxi* is in the service of beneficial social support. The chapter goes on to show how the *guanxi* connection is able to endure through elaboration of its particularistic elements, including the emotional involvement of the participants.

Two distinct types of emotion complex underlying *guanxi*, which consolidate the connection between participants, are identified in the chapter. These are 感情 *ganqing* and *renqing*; they are each described as an 'emotion complex' because they are not single emotions, such as hope or fear, but multifaceted feelings that express a person's affective disposition and at the same time convey a moral sensibility to which that person adheres.

Ganqing is usually translated simply as 'sentiment' or 'affect', and in the context of *guanxi* relates not only to the attraction between persons but more importantly to their mutual affective attachment to the relationship to which they are each committed. This aspect of *ganqing* in *guanxi* is not always properly understood, as addressed in this chapter. *Renqing* is more complex than *ganqing*, being a compound or composite disposition, usually translated into English as 'human feelings' or 'favour'. It is shown in the chapter that in Chinese culture what it means to be human is to engage in appropriate conduct, which varies with context and the status of the person one is relating to. Regarding its contribution to *guanxi*, *renqing* is the emotion of commitment to reciprocal obligation in exchange of favours.

The discussion in Chapter 1 goes on to consider how *guanxi* endures over time, in which a number of factors are identified. It is explained that self-disclosure, consideration of the other, and a sense of security and dependability, all work together through the *ganqing* and *renqing* shared by *guanxi* participants, and in turn reinforce them. But perhaps the most significant factor in the maintenance of an enduring *guanxi* is the way in which *guanxi* participants finesse the indebtedness between them. This is an aspect of *guanxi* that is a seldom discussed in the literature. Favour recipients in *guanxi* relations delay repayment of a debt, in order to avoid termination of *guanxi*; indeed, they tend not to acknowledge that a favour provided to a *guanxi* partner is discharging a prior debt to a person. Rather, such favours operate through a sense that they are to fulfil an obligation within a relationship, and it is the relationship rather than the persons participating in it that is the object of concern and to which a person's favour and commitment are directed. It is this orientation within *guanxi* that ensures that it is not exhausted or concluded by repayments of debt.

Consideration of *guanxi* debt, incurred by accepting a favour from another, raises the question, in a different register, of the costs and benefits of *guanxi*. When costs and benefits are thought of together, then the notion of 'efficiency' comes to mind, referring to a situation in which the lower the costs of an activity or relationship, relative to the benefits the activity or relationship provides, the higher the efficiency. The notion of 'efficiency' is invoked in Chapter 1 because less-efficient practices tend to be displaced by more-efficient, and this consideration relates to the persistence of *guanxi* and its changing form in a way that goes beyond the usual way of conceiving the prospects of *guanxi* in a changing China. The debate between Doug Guthrie (1998) and Mayfair Yang (2002), a hallmark exchange in the discussion of *guanxi*, is focused on only two alternatives, a decline in the incidence of *guanxi* or its persistence. The final section of Chapter 1, on the other hand, shows that it is more useful to conceive of the prospects of *guanxi* in terms of its efficiency in different areas of economy and society, so that while *guanxi* may decline in some domains it can become significant in others, and fail to appear at all in yet others. This novel approach is supported by a discussion of the incidence of *guanxi* in a number of sectors of Chinese society, including retail markets, the diamond trade, and scientific research. The chapter finishes by considering the way in which *guanxi* is associated with corruption. Because *guanxi* involves an informal if not irregular provision of a favour that is given with the expectation of a benefit in return, it may appear to be indistinguishable from a bribe, as discussed in the chapter.

After considering the nature of *guanxi* in Chapter 1, how *guanxi* might be theorized is addressed in the following chapter. Chapter 2 undertakes an investigation of an approach that has become an overarching influence on the conceptualization of *guanxi* and its broader meaning and significance. *From the Soil*, a book by a leading Chinese sociologist, Fei Xiaotong (1910–2005), was first published in Chinese in 1947 with an English translation appearing in 1992. Widely regarded as providing an architectonic model of *guanxi*, *From the Soil* is referred to in practically every published discussion of *guanxi*, no matter what the disciplinary background of its author. Fei (1992) raises a number of crucial questions core to an understanding of *guanxi*, including its cultural background, its structure as based on the strong ties of familial bonds, and its modus operandi in gift exchange. These are all brought together in a concept proposed by Fei (1992: 60–70), which explicates the flexibility, endurance, and differentiation of *guanxi* in a single term, 差序格局 *chaxugeju*, translated as 'differential mode of association'. Given the pivotal significance of *From the Soil* for an understanding of *guanxi* and the way in which it is portrayed in the broader scholarly discussion of it, the second chapter of this book considers Fei's account of the 'differential mode of association' and its context in the analysis of Chinese society and its contribution to the study of *guanxi*.

The purpose of Chapter 2, then, is to provide a distinctive appraisal of the notion of the differential mode of association as Fei (1992) develops it in *From the Soil*, whilst also paying attention to the broader claims regarding the nature of China's rural society and its cultural background, especially as it informs an understanding of *guanxi*. By drawing on Fei's other publications of the 1930s and 1940s, as well as contemporary research by Chinese and non-Chinese social analysts, it is shown that Fei (1992) develops a model of lineage reflecting the intergenerational and multifunctional form of the Chinese family that in fact represents an idealized vision in conformity with Confucian ideology. Indeed, it is shown that Fei's reliance on Confucian rather than sociological sources in *From the Soil* means that many of his perceptions and judgements depart from those presented in his village studies of the time (Fei 1939; Fei and Chang 1948). It is revealed in the chapter that not only does Fei (1992) primarily rely on traditional tropes but also that his concept of *chaxugeju* is original in name only, as it restates ideas drawn from the Confucian *Book of Rites*. It is also shown that by focusing on the family and lineage, on the one hand, and their village context, on the other, Fei's (1992) representation of Chinese rural society ignores the importance to villagers of social relations conducted within inter-village marketing areas, into which those relations extend and which significantly include non-kin ties. The chapter is unique in the discussion of Chinese sociology in demonstrating that the concept of *chaxugeju* is unhelpful for an analysis of *guanxi* in that it provides no purchase on the notion of instrumental engagement. The latter is shown to be readily explained with regard to *guanxi* through the notion of *mianzi*, face, a notion about which Fei (1992) surprisingly has nothing to say. It is also shown in the chapter that, in his discussion of *chaxugeju* as a category of sociological analysis, Fei (1992) conflates two distinctly different forms of obligation, relating to familial roles on the one hand, and favour exchange on the other. This is a matter that is taken up again in Chapter 6.

Questions regarding the theorization of *guanxi* and its cultural background continue to be discussed in Chapter 3, which addresses the notion of reciprocity in *guanxi*. The idea that key aspects of China's cultural heritage inform *guanxi* is supported not only by the idea that its structure is parallel with that of the Chinese family form, but also that *guanxi* expresses the traditional notion of 报 *bao*, reciprocity, as a number of leading scholars have claimed. The argument concerning the historical sources of *bao* is examined in the chapter. It is found that, while classical sources do indeed provide examples of a large number of forms of interaction that may be associated with the notion of reciprocity, many of them, however, are not identified with the term *bao*. Indeed, the idea that there is a unified notion of reciprocal relations in classical sources, implicit in *guanxi*, is at best an exaggeration. Some scholars have identified another term, 恕 *shu*, as also representing reciprocity and thereby similarly contributing to a legacy inherited by *guanxi*. For a number of reasons, this is an intriguing proposition.

It is shown in Chapter 3 that while *shu* is important in Confucian thought, a nineteenth-century missionary scholar, James Legge, mistranslated *shu* as 'reciprocity' in conveying Confucius's 论语 *Lunyu*, *Analects*, into English, an error repeated in frequently cited publications by the eminent Hong Kong Chinese sociologist Ambrose King. Rather than 'reciprocity', *shu* may be summarily understood as 'empathy', but more completely—as shown in the chapter—it refers to what is known sociologically as 'role taking'. It is of interest that this correct understanding of *shu* is not incorporated into the discussion of *guanxi* by any of the standard sources, and yet it relates to an important aspect of it. *Guanxi*, as a relationship cultivated by its participants, requires all of the attributes of role taking through which a person comes to know their own capacities and is orientated to the accessibility and capabilities of a potential or current *guanxi* partner. This neglected aspect of *guanxi* is indicated through the serendipitous correction in Chapter 3 of misunderstandings in key sections of the literature regarding *shu*.

The final part of Chapter 3 considers another aspect of the Confucian tradition that many associate with *guanxi*, namely the notion of *renqing* as its underlying ethical dimension. The argument proposing a classical source of *renqing* is typically based on its supposed link with Confucian 仁 *ren*, which is examined in the chapter. It is shown that, while *ren* is related to self-cultivation, among other things, *renqing* is connected with practices of favour exchange. It is shown how these are quite different enactments which practically and philosophically point in dissimilar directions. This part of the discussion concludes the examination of classical Chinese traditions as possible sources of *guanxi* principles and practices. The sceptical appraisals of Chapters 2 and 3 are not designed to imply that *guanxi*, as located in twentieth- and twenty-first-century China, is without historical sources. Instrumental particularistic behaviour and its associated utilization of gift-giving customs do indeed have a long history in China and its key elements are presented in Chapter 4.

In the discussion of *guanxi*, *renqing* is widely seen as an underlying element of it that provides an ethical orientation to its practitioners, crystallized in the obligation to return a favour. During the nineteenth century and the first half of the twentieth, the period covering the late imperial and the Republican eras in Chinese history, *renqing* was a term used to refer to instrumental particularism, as *guanxi* became the summary term from the 1980s. Chapter 4 opens with a discussion of *renqing* in two previously unexplored sources written in the late 1940s which reflect how the term was understood at the time. Having established the currency of *renqing* discourse and the nature of its practices in Republican China, the discussion turns to an account of the *renqing* practices of an imperial official of the mid-nineteenth century, Li Hongzhang. Two things emerge that contradict a good deal of what is currently assumed about *renqing*. First, money is today thought to be a difficult medium for *renqing* practice, but it was pivotal to Li's. The circumstances in which money can effectively serve *renqing* is outlined in the chapter. Second, it is shown that *renqing* gift-giving need not be part of gift exchange, that the provision of a gift may be a consummatory act rather than an element of reciprocal exchange. In this case *renqing* secures protection. It is shown in the chapter that in rural China, up until the establishment of the People's Republic, gift-giving was largely used as a means to offset envy and suspicion, a practice that continues today among rural Chinese. It was only since the collectivization of agriculture, from the 1950s, that villagers began to practise *renqing* not to buy protection but as part of an investment in reciprocal social support. The conditions under which these changes occur, in both the structure of rural China and in *renqing* practices, are identified and discussed in the chapter.

In considering the changes brought to *renqing* practices through the creation of the Communist state in 1949, Chapter 4 goes on to show that the enormous growth in the number of administrators, 干部 *ganbu*, cadres, meant that opportunities for favour seeking rose enormously in both rural as well as urban areas, and at all levels of society. Indeed, the largest change in the practice of instrumental particularism at this time was descent down the social scale in the practice of favour exchange, through which a significant lateral spread of the incidence of *renqing* also occurred. The chapter chronicles the changing vocabulary for instrumental particularism over a relatively short period of time, from the late 1950s to the early 1980s, from 拉弦 *la xian*, string pulling, and 走后门 *zou houmen*, going through the back door, to finally settle on *guanxi*. The final section of Chapter 4 is focused on a particular case of cultural meaning, in understanding *guanxi*. The discussion of *guanxi* in English-language sources provides a number of instances of incidental reference to 'friendship' in consideration of *guanxi*. It is shown, though, that the use of this term in the literature relates a culturally insular meaning of friendship which juxtaposes private and affective relations on the one hand with instrumental ones on the other. While this captures American and European mores, it fails to indicate the characteristics of Chinese friendship which is at the same time private and public, expressive and instrumental. It is the characteristically Chinese meaning of friendship that informs the practices of both *renqing* and *guanxi*, and which are discussed in the chapter.

While 'friendship' is occasionally brought to deliberation on *guanxi*, 'trust' is almost a constant. What these terms have in common, among other things, is the way in which their meaning is subject to significant cultural influence, and therefore variation. What 'friendship' or 'trust' mean in the United States, for instance, is markedly different from what these terms mean in China. The meaning of trust in *guanxi* is examined in Chapter 5. The chapter begins with a discussion of research which claims to demonstrate the centrality of trust to *guanxi*. Ambiguity in the English-language term 'trust', especially concerning the distinction between giving trust, on the one hand, and being trustworthy, on the other, is reduced somewhat in Chinese through the use of two distinct terms, 信任 *xinren*, meaning trustful, and 信用 *xinyong*, meaning to have credibility or trustworthiness. Whereas the default meaning of 'trust' in English is 'trustful', in Chinese it is 'trustworthiness'.

After discussing the place of trust in networks in general, in order to situate it in *guanxi* in particular, the chapter moves on to consider the cultural protocols of trust, and particularly *xinyong*, in Chinese society. Because of the mutual scrutiny, close familiarity, and propensity to demonstrate dependability in the maintenance of face for *guanxi* relations, it is shown in the chapter that the reputational component of trustworthiness in this context suggests the analytic value of the notion of assurance rather than trust in understanding the underlying mechanism of personal evaluation in *guanxi*. The incentive structure of trust is internal to the relation between two individuals, whereas that of assurance is external to the two-way connection because it is subject to the social appraisal of others. This is an important consideration not found in previous accounts of *guanxi*. The final section of the chapter returns to the network aspect of *guanxi* in considering the nature of influence in the practice of *guanxi*. Strong network ties are typically understood to imply high levels of trust between participants. In *guanxi* networks, on the other hand, the ties in question are not latent in pre-given structures but dependent on the instrumental value of the relationship, that is, they are cultivated. The consequences of this for understanding influence and also trust in *guanxi* networks are demonstrated in the chapter.

The final chapter provides a detailed sociological overview of *guanxi* by examining a number of conventions that arguably limit the development of a coherent theory of *guanxi*. Some issues mentioned in previous chapters are returned to in Chapter 6, in order to present a unified rationale for a model of *guanxi* that is both cognizant of its cultural setting in Chinese society and history, and also sufficiently rigorous to encourage future research. Three particular empirical issues are dealt with. First, the distinction between family and *guanxi* is clearly specified. It is shown that close family connections, between parents and offspring and between siblings, are based on principles of interaction that are fundamentally unlike those of *guanxi*. Family connections are closed to outsiders and provide support on the basis of need without any requirement of returned favour, whereas *guanxi* relations are open and based on obligations of exchange. Second, the idea that close friendship may transmute to a fictive kin relationship, bridging kin and non-kin ties and thereby strengthening *guanxi*, is shown to be based on a number of exaggerations and misunderstandings. Finally, the characterization of a distinction between friendship *guanxi* and acquaintance *guanxi*, variously described in the literature as 'savings' *guanxi* and 'investment' *guanxi*, or *guanxi* based on *ganqing* as opposed to *guanxi* based on 交情 *jiaoqing*, is shown to reify what are in fact not distinct types but different possible phases in the development of *guanxi*.

As important as identifying empirical suppositions that are in need of correction is the explanation of how such errors may occur. In Chapter 6 three sources are identified of what are described as category ambiguities concerning *guanxi*, especially related to the three issues of empirical analysis mentioned above. The first of these is the uncritical way in which everyday language terms are employed in treatments of *guanxi*. It is a feature of social analysis of all types that terms used by social participants themselves in describing or referring to their experiences are drawn on in explanatory accounts. It is for this reason that sociological analysis requires not only empirical investigation but also conceptual clarification and refinement. A failure to engage in the latter risks the possibility of simply repeating folk wisdoms rather than generating viable sociological accounts of what is studied. The claim here is that folk wisdom unfortunately populates a good deal of the accounts of *guanxi* published in academic journals. The fact that cultural and historical stereotypes are left unexamined in discussion of *guanxi* practices is a second source of category ambiguity in treatment of *guanxi*. The unexamined idea that China is a 'Confucian society' permits, indeed encourages, a number of assumptions concerning *guanxi* that cannot be sustained when subjected to serious investigation, as discussed in this chapter. Finally, methodological questions are raised concerning the tendency of social network analysis to privilege tie strength, when *guanxi* ties are strategically both strengthened and weakened out of strategic considerations of participants rather than being latent in the structure of their relations.

It can be seen that the six chapters to follow can be grouped according to the broad questions they consider. The first chapter provides a comprehensive introduction to *guanxi* as a social practice of instrumental particularism. The Chinese cultural context, frequently attributed to generating the character and development of these practices, is thoroughly examined in the second and third chapters. These chapter are designed to investigate and correct some conventional misunderstandings about the basis of *guanxi*, and in doing so have much to say about the society and culture of China as well as elements of its history. The fourth chapter continues both the systematic and cultural examination of instrumental particularism in China by considering the structure of *guanxi*-like practices in their institutional and historical setting from the late Qing period up to the reconstitution of social and political life in China from the perspective of the emergence of *guanxi* in the 1980s. The last two chapters consider how *guanxi* might be appropriately understood from the perspective of sociologically informed conceptual refinement, bringing systematic analysis to an operational understanding of *guanxi*.

In an account of *guanxi* that is not only empirically rigorous and historically informed, but also culturally sensitive, it is necessary in discussion throughout to refer to Chinese-language terms. In each chapter, as in this Introduction, the first mention of a Chinese word will include both 简化字 *jianhuazi*, simplified characters, as well as 拼音 *pinyin*, romanized transliterations. In subsequent statements within the chapter, though, only the *pinyin* will be indicated.

1
Making *Guanxi*

Anyone with even the vaguest awareness of Chinese business practices will know the term 关系 *guanxi*. From the time that China joined the globalized world in the early 1980s, when Western companies began doing business in China, the idea that special relationships are essential in order to deal with Chinese firms has been part of the sensibility of engagement in the international economy (Luo 2007; So and Walker 2006; Wang and Hsung 2016). *Guanxi* is generally understood to mean 'connection' or 'relationship' but it refers to a particular form of those things, a form in which the links between participants are enduring, involve informal exchanges of various sorts, operate in a framework of mutual obligation, and are voluntarily entered into in order to achieve benefits that arise from the relationship itself. The fact that the term is left untranslated indicates that *guanxi* is in some special sense 'Chinese', that it relates to a cultural heritage, and also that its complexity cannot be adequately captured by an English-language term, that indeed there is no equivalent term in English that could do justice either to the traditional background of *guanxi* or the intricacy of the relations indicated by the notion. While relevant in understanding Chinese business practices it is important to appreciate that *guanxi* is by no means confined to business but operates in all areas of social and political life in China and Chinese cultural areas. *Guanxi* is drawn on to ensure the adequate provision of health or medical care (Chan and Yao 2018), advantageous school placement (Ruan 2017), securing employment (Bian 2018), achieving military promotion (Wang 2016), reaching favourable legal decisions (Li 2018; Zhao 2019), and so on.

A person will go to the effort of establishing *guanxi* with another because it is beneficial for them to do so. The way in which *guanxi* is helpful is multifaceted; the fact that one can establish a *guanxi* indicates that the persons involved are regarded as resourceful and also reliable. To have such acknowledged qualities is registered in the relevant person's social standing or esteem, through which that person acquires 面子 *mianzi*, face. Not only is *guanxi* an expressive social resource in this sense, it has cumulative effect in so far as *guanxi* involves exchanges of favour and also gifts between

The Theory of Guanxi *and Chinese Society.* Jack Barbalet, Oxford University Press (2021). © Jack Barbalet.
DOI: 10.1093/oso/9780198808732.003.0002

participants which are generative of obligations to return the favour, and in that sense has instrumental value. Having *guanxi*, then, makes a person attractive—*guanxi* attractive—because a person who has *guanxi* with others is a person worth knowing. This tells us something else about *guanxi*. While *guanxi* is always dyadic in its basic form, that is it is always between two persons, any given individual may have *guanxi* with a number of different people and one of the benefits of a *guanxi* link is that it potentially gives a person access to the other *guanxi* partners of any single person with whom they themselves form a *guanxi*. So, while *guanxi* is dyadic these dyads may connect together into a lattice or web and thus form 关系网 *guanxiwang*, a *guanxi* network.

It has been mentioned that a characteristic feature of *guanxi* is that it is useful to the parties involved, something about which more will be said later. Of course, all relationships have some use to those who participate in them, at least potentially. The special quality of a *guanxi* is that it consists of two elements more or less fused together. The first of these is the 'particularistic' nature of *guanxi*, in the sense that it is not merely restricted to another person but in so being is affectively focused on the relationship between the persons involved. A *guanxi* relation, then, has an emotional dimension that is not incidental but is in many ways defining of the relation between participants. The other necessary element of *guanxi* is that it is 'instrumental'. It has already been noted that *guanxi* is useful or beneficial to the participants. Again, this is not an incidental aspect of *guanxi* but a core element in so far as *guanxi* only exists to advance the interests of participants. The combination of these two components of *guanxi* is captured in the idea that the favours exchanged between *guanxi* participants are 'social investments' as they are given with the expectation of 'something in return'; but unlike market exchanges these investments are not 'cold' but intertwined with 人情 *renqing*, human feelings or empathy as well as 感情 *ganqing*, emotional feelings or sentiment (Gold 1985: 660; see also Jacobs 1979: 263; Lin 2001: 156). It is these feeling states that elevate *guanxi* as significant for participants not simply in the rewards it provides but in the specially charged attachment to the relationship it evokes. *Guanxi* participants share a sense that their relationship possesses rightness, an ethical quality, that underlies feelings of responsibility to *guanxi* partners and to their relationship.

These and related issues will be examined in this chapter, which will outline the way in which *guanxi* is formed. We shall see that persons can share a *guanxi* only if they share a common identity, although the identity in question is not necessarily manifest prior to a connection being made between the persons involved. The identity underlying *guanxi* may not be noticeable until its usefulness is recognized, it may be latent or even constructed, as we shall see, but it is nevertheless essential in the formation of the connection. That a person recognizes a common identity with another is necessary for their *guanxi*, but it is not sufficient; if the significance of such common identity is to be realized and the relationship is to endure then some form of commitment between the persons and especially to their connection is required; this commitment is achieved through the emotional involvement of the participants, to be examined in the second section of the chapter. The third section considers how *guanxi* endures over time, in which a number of factors are identified including the special nature of debt between a favour giver and recipient, and the persistence of debt, so that *guanxi* exchanges are not exhausted or concluded. Finally, acknowledging the costs as well as the benefits of *guanxi* brings us to consideration of its 'efficiency'. The notion of efficiency is invoked because less-efficient practices tend to be displaced by more-efficient, and this consideration relates to the persistence of *guanxi* and its changing form, a theme that leads finally to the way in which *guanxi* is often associated with corruption, an association derived from the fact that an informal if not irregular provision of a favour given with the expectation of a returned benefit may appear to be indistinguishable from a bribe.

Making a Connection

While the process of making and conducting *guanxi* is necessarily complex, as we shall see, its beginning point is quite simple; those who share a *guanxi* connection must have a common 'identity', that is, a basis, premise or ground that they share; they must in some way belong together, each person recognizing and acknowledging that they are alike in some meaningful way, that they share 同 *tong*, a sameness. In his pioneering study of *guanxi* anthropologist Bruce Jacobs (1979) described this factor as a *guanxi* 'base'. There are many ways to achieve this property, of sharing a common identifying factor. The single most significant base for the *guanxi* of the small-town Taiwanese politicians Jacobs studied was locality of origin, the sharing of a 'native place' (Jacobs 1979: 244–5). The next most significant, he found, was kinship. Kinship is a term that covers a number of possibilities; Jacobs distinguishes between agnatic kin and affinal, referring respectively to kinship between male relatives on the father's side, on the one hand, and to individuals related by marriage, on the other. The most reliable of these kinship bases, Jacobs found, were agnatic kin, but as he notes regarding the case he studied, these were 'limited...in geographic scope' to 'one village' (Jacobs 1979: 245), and they therefore arguably overlap with native place or locality of origin. Another complicating factor regarding kinship as a *guanxi* base is that, for a number of reasons, 'fraternal conflict' may occur, and when it does it brings an element of competition which disqualifies kinship from being a *guanxi* base (Jacobs 1979: 246). The question of the relations between kinship and *guanxi* is a recurring issue that is taken up in other chapters of this book.

In addition to native place another *guanxi* base of significance identified by (Jacobs 1979: 247–9) is 'class mate'. This is also of two types, identified by Jacobs (1979: 248) as 'literal' and 'alumni', that is an actual class mate, on the one hand, and, on the other, a person who attended the same school but at a different time. Of particular interest in Jacob's case study is the political role of alumni associations, a factor that may have more general relevance in pointing to an organizational element of the *guanxi* base in certain instances. Being a co-worker, Jacobs (1979: 247) found, was also a frequently drawn on *guanxi* base for his respondents. In general terms, though, as with agnatic kin so with common workplace, the possibility of rivalry between co-workers means that this is not always a reliable source for founding *guanxi*. In a study of *guanxi* as a means of protection from allegations of corruption among senior cadres in China from 2012, it was similarly found that a common workplace provides an uncertain *guanxi* base:

> Informal ties established as a result of association with the same birthplace and same school affiliation played an important role in the bond-building between political and economic elites...By comparison, there is less certainty that common work experience will promote friendly ties among colleagues. It is true that many of the informal political networks in China...were formed around common work experience. Yet, work relations among colleagues can also engender jealousy, rivalry and bureaucratic infighting...[It is] not contended that former colleagues were more likely to be enemies and therefore become the targets of political revenge. Rather...while shared affiliations in birthplaces and educational background certainly always promote emotional bonding, ties arising from shared work experience contain greater uncertainty and ambiguity.
>
> (Zeng and Yang 2017: 49)

We shall return to the question of the nature of a *guanxi* base in various chapters to follow. These bases, as *tongs*, are of significance in so far as they provide a sense of commonality or sameness between persons so that they can begin to establish connections between them that are valued for the benefits they provide.

Given the limited scope and therefore availability of the different *tong* bases that encourage *guanxi*, and the difficulties associated with kinship and workplace for *guanxi* formation, it is necessary to consider what other means individuals may access in order to establish a shared link. Two previously unconnected persons may achieve *guanxi* through the intervention of a third party. There are different ways in which a third party may play a role in bringing two persons together. A third party may play a role in the achievement of *guanxi* between persons by accident. This possibility is described by Yanjie Bian (1994: 974) in his classic study of the Chinese labour market, when he notes that a latent possibility for *guanxi* may exist between people who up to that point 'may never come in contact with one another' even though they are in some way 'related to a common [third] person'; this is a *guanxi* that is activated when such people, when they do actually meet, 'recognize the pre-existing relationship'. Such a situation corresponds with the Chinese proverb, 一见如故 *yi jian ru gu*, which literally means 'familiarity at first sight'. Bian calls this *guanxi* through an 'indirect relationship'. Such an indirect relationship (间接 关系 *jianjie guanxi*) can, as a type, be contrasted with a direct relationship (直接 关系 *zhijie guanxi*). Once a contact is made through such an indirect relationship, as when the two persons in question recognize and acknowledge their common connection, then the relationship between them may become direct.

The same effect, of forming *guanxi* through an indirect link, can be achieved more candidly. A person wishing to establish *guanxi* with someone to whom they are not currently connected may seek the assistance of a friend or relative who already knows the 'target' person (King 1991: 74; Yang 1994: 124–6); this is to make *guanxi* by using 中间人 *zhongjianren*, literally a middle person, an intermediary, someone who knows both the *guanxi* seeker and also the person with whom they wish to establish a *guanxi* relation. This form of making a connection is an instance, simultaneously, of creating or forming a *guanxi* and also an application of an existing *guanxi*. The following narrative indicates how this works. Ling and Qin do not know each other but Ling has heard of Qin and wishes to get to know him. Coincidentally, Ling's friend Zhang is also a friend of Qin. Ling arranges to meet Zhang in order to gives him a box of persimmon, Zhang's favourite fruit, and during their conversation Ling asks his friend whether he could introduce him to Qin. Later that week Zhang invites Qin to dinner and over drinks tells him about Ling and asks whether he would agree to meet him. Toward the end of the month Zhang, accompanied by Ling, visits Qin. Ling brings a small gift for Qin, selected after discussing with Zhang what would be suitable. Ling and Qin now have a connection that either one of them can develop further.

In this case Ling has drawn on his existing *guanxi* with Zhang in order to establish a new *guanxi* with Qin.

A third general way of establishing the initial contact from which a *guanxi* may be built is more immediate and direct, namely through an indication by one person to another that they currently possess or in the future are likely to have a shared interest or concern. On the basis of an agreed acknowledgement of an existing or future interest, in the sense that they seek to achieve a similar or mutually supportive purpose, two people can directly establish *tong*, a 'sameness'. To show that a person shares with another the same enjoyments, curiosities, political or social endeavours on the one hand, or that they aspire to similar objectives in civic engagement, say, or in business, may be sufficient to provide a common ground from which a relationship can be developed. This has been described as an 'anticipatory *guanxi* base':

> In contrast to pre-existing shared social ties, 'anticipatory *guanxi* bases' refer to shared visions and aspirations that lead to new joint ventures and activities between parties who come into contact without pre-existing *guanxi*. Such new joint ventures, once initiated and accomplished, serve as substantive pre-existing *guanxi* bases for future *guanxi* building and exchange.   (Chen *et al.* 2013: 172)

In this way, the ground for establishing a *guanxi* between two people is literally manufactured through the means of an intention to form a relationship, without the benefit of pre-existing connections waiting to be activated. All three discussed forms of establishing a *guanxi tong* require such an intention, but this last case is not assisted by resources derived from past associations.

It will be clear from what has been said here that the basis of a connection between two persons who wish to be associated with each other for some useful purpose is not inherent in their individual situations and background. That there is a common 'sameness' between them arises through their utilization of opportunities provided by a range of possibilities that they themselves choose. Certainly, the possibilities vested in their coming from the same town or going to the same school are clear and strong in the way that a kin association or having worked in the same place may or may not be entirely reliable, depending on other factors. Similarly, drawing upon an existing connection to form a new one requires more than simply knowing another person because deliberation and negotiation are required. *Guanxi* connections do not simply occur, they are made by the participants and the acceptance of one by the other cannot be taken for granted. It is highly appropriate, then, that in her well-known exploration of *guanxi* Mayfair

Yang (1994) focuses on 关系学 *guanxixue*, the 'art' of *guanxi*, indicating that not only its practice but also its initial conceptualization or vision, its initiation, requires competence or 'technical' skill but also a flair or talent necessary for successful execution. In the case of *guanxi*, such artful creation meets the needs of the participants for an association that will have the possibility of enhancing their situation, whatever their particular circumstances may be.

Making the Connection Stick

The three means of establishing a common sense of shared identity described above, if successful, are only different footings from which a *guanxi* relationship between two people may be formed. Or, to put it differently, these are the patterns of emergent contact which create an opportunity to form *guanxi*. It is necessary that a person must know that they have something in common with another person in order for them to have *guanxi* together, but by itself it is not sufficient. A recognition between persons of a shared identifying factor may be sufficient to fix the attention of each to the other, but it is not enough to provide a sense of continuing involvement of one with the other. For this latter to occur, there must be a sense of shared complicity that invariably draws on their emotional attachment. The lowest level of such *guanxi* entanglement between two persons is 'acquaintance' and the highest is 'intimacy', at both ends of this range there exists a level of positive feeling between the participants. This is necessary for *guanxi* to emerge from their association. It might be thought that acquaintance is without affect or feelings, but *guanxi* acquaintance is infused with appreciative feelings and sentiments of obligation and expectation.

In a study of mature-aged university students in a city in China it was reported that a common situation of being under-resourced and marginalized by the regulations that govern the adult higher education system led these students to form *guanxi* relations that not only provided such instrumental benefits as making available learning resources that could then be shared between them, but also realize emotional resources of mutual self-validation and companionship (Guan and James 2020: 356–7). While relying on each other for learning material and mutual support, the students reported that they did not regard their *guanxi* partners as 'friends'. Guan and James (2020: 357) report the students as saying:

> *guanxi* with peers not only provides me with practical benefit, but also gives me company…although they are not my close friends.   (26 years, Year 3)

[W]e tell each other what the teacher says...[the peer] is an important resource
for me to have a higher score in exams...so we maintain our *guanxi* well although
we are not close friends.   (28 years, Year 1)

That the *guanxi* connections are not likened to those of close friendship
indicates not an absence of emotional feeling on the part of these *guanxi*
partners, but rather points to the circumscribed relations that these female
adult tertiary students share, confined to their university education and the
employment prospects associated with it. The *guanxi* in this case is specific
to coping with the limited provision of university resources and restricted to
this organizational sphere; but it is no less emotional for that.

It will be shown in Chapter 6 that different writers ascribe various specific
emotions to distinctive types of *guanxi* in distinguishing between
acquaintance and friendship. For our purposes here it is sufficient to follow a
prevailing convention and say that, on the basis of recognition of a shared
identity, *ganqing* will make an emergent *guanxi* ever more likely (Fried 1953;
Jacobs 1979; Smart 1999). The term *ganqing* literally means sentiment or
affect and refers to the emotional feelings of affection or attachment to a
person or a place; in principle, such a sentiment may be negative as well as
positive. In the context of *guanxi*, though, *ganqing* between two persons
means that their relationship will be enhanced by emotional commitment to
an enduring intimate bond (Yang 1994: 121). As a basis of personal
attachment *ganqing* emerges out of a person's direct experience with another,
especially if there is cooperation between them, as in a work situation or
through shared leisure activity, either innocent or licentious. In Chinese
communities toasting, competitive drinking, and drinking games are means
of not only relaxing inhibitions but explicitly encouraging *ganqing*
(Kipnis 1997: 53–7). The commercialization of Chinese society since the
1980s has encouraged the shared consumption of not only alcohol and
banquet meals but also commercial sex as a means of generating *ganqing*
among businessmen and between businessmen and officials (Barbalet 2015:
1047–8; Osburg 2013: 45–65). Such activities, explicitly constructed to
generate *ganqing*, 'would often end with declarations of friendship and
affection, plans for future forms of entertainment, and offers of mutual aid'
(Osburg 2013: 44, 57). While instrumentalism is at a premium in business
guanxi, it nevertheless requires the emotional component of *ganqing* for it to
operate effectively.

It can be seen from what has been said so far that *ganqing* is a means of
creating solidarity, of emphasizing an emotional connection between two
persons rather than necessarily indicating a forceful emotional state within

any single person. In this regard it is unlike the conventional notion of friendship, based on 'mutual affection and sympathy', because *ganqing* 'presumes a much more specific common interest' (Fried 1953: 226). It is this bond of attachment, generated through the situational manipulation of *ganqing*, that is primary in personalizing *guanxi* relations. The emotional commitment that operates in *guanxi* relations, through *ganqing*, is not merely to the other person, although this is necessary, but more significantly the attachment of each person must be to the connection itself that effectively binds them in *guanxi*. As indicated above, the emotional commitment of the adult university students to each other is present but muted because their relationship to each other is through the *guanxi* arising as necessary for them to cope with the disadvantages they experience in their university studies as atypical and marginalized students. The effective emotional commitment in *guanxi* is to the relationship between the persons involved, and the emotional commitment to the other person is an emotional commitment to that person as a *guanxi* partner.

The conclusion of the preceding paragraph is not frequently enough emphasized in discussions of *guanxi*, but it reflects an essential feature of this form of relation. *Guanxi* is a purposeful relationship to which participants are devoted because of the benefits it provides to them, so that their emotional attachment is primarily to the relationship itself. But, of course, the relationship is between persons and their involvement with the relationship each has with another is facilitated by affective bonds between the individuals in question. The complexity of the situation described here requires a distinction between a relationship on the one hand and those who participate in that relationship on the other. The importance of this distinction will be revealed when we consider how *guanxi* debt between participants operates to maintain the *guanxi* relationship. In simple terms, though, it might be said that relationships are constituted by the persons who participate in them, so that it could be held that the interactions between the persons involved are at the same time the relationship in which they are engaged. This form of reasoning, though, does not quite capture the nature of instrumental relationships.

Research student supervision, for instance, like *guanxi*, is an instrumental relationship. In such a relationship the student is committed to the relationship as a means of successfully completing a thesis, the academic supervisor is committed to the relationship as a professional practice that has a number of component elements including opportunities for joint publication, and so on. These commitments have emotional strands running through them related to the realization and satisfaction of particular interests of the participants. Indeed, for the supervisory relationship to succeed there must be a commitment to the relationship on the part of each party. In support of commitments to the relationship itself there are at the same time affective feelings between the persons involved, including, in the optimum cases, feelings of respect for scholarly performance, gratitude for support, and possibly an element of personal warmth through familiarity and recognition of certain commonalities. The emotional commitment to the relationship can be distinguished from the personal emotions between the participants in the relationship. The suggestion here is not that academic supervision is *guanxi* but that as each is a form of purposeful relationship, they are in that sense comparable.

In *guanxi*, the affective or emotion dimension of *ganqing* coexists with another type of emotion that is more directly focused on the mechanism of reciprocity or exchange that ensures the effective operation of the relationship. This emotion, which actually is more than an emotion, as we shall see, is known as *renqing*, which is often translated into English as 'human feeling' and sometimes as 'favour'. To be 'human' in Chinese society is to know how to behave appropriately, to know the rules of decorum, to be empathetic in relating to others, always giving to the other person what is due to them and showing respect to others, possibly by providing them with a gift or a favour. We shall refer to *renqing* throughout this book and explore it in more detail in Chapters 3 and 4. It is mentioned here because in discussions of *guanxi* the factor of *renqing* is typically taken to be normative in orientating the exchanges that occur within the framework of *guanxi*. In his influential discussion, Kwang-kuo Hwang (1987: 953) writes that *renqing* 'has three different meanings in Chinese culture', the first of which 'indicates the emotional responses of an individual confronting the various situations of daily life':

> If an individual can understand other people's emotional responses to various circumstances of life—feeling happy or sad when and as others do, or even catering to their tastes and evading or avoiding whatever they resent—then we may say that such a person knows *renqing*.

This first sense, then, is *renqing* as empathetic emotion.

The second meaning Hwang (1987: 954) identifies is that *renqing* is:

> a resource that an individual can present to another person as a gift in the course of social exchange. In Chinese society, when one has either happy occasions or difficulties, all one's acquaintances are supposed to offer a gift or render some

substantial assistance. In such cases, it is said that they send their *renqing*. Henceforth, the recipient will owe a *renqing* to the donors. By this, we see that *renqing* means a certain kind of resource that can be used as a medium of social exchange.

Finally, *renqing* also means:

> a set of social norms by which one has to abide in order to get along well with other people in Chinese society. This norm of *renqing* includes two basic kinds of social behavior: (a) Ordinarily, one should keep in contact with the acquaintances in one's social network, exchanging gifts, greetings, or visitations with them from time to time, and (b) when a member of one's reticulum gets into trouble or faces a difficult situation, one should sympathize, offer help, and 'do a *renqing*' for that person.   (Hwang 1987: 954)

According to this account, then, *renqing* is emotional empathy, an exchange resource, and also a moral code. Other accounts provide variations in interpretation of this complex notion (see, for instance, Yan 1996: 122–46; Yang 1994: 67–72). To give favour, as *renqing*, is emotional empathy subject to normative orientations in which reciprocity serves to maintain the relation between those who share *renqing*. The question that might be asked at this stage of the discussion is how are *ganqing* and *renqing* generated between those persons who share a connection.

Maintaining the Connection

The presentation of the discussion here is unavoidably sequential, one thing following another; in the reality of relations between persons, though, there is a good deal of simultaneous and directly interactive development, things not only more or less occurring together but influencing each other in doing so. In considering how a connection between two people is maintained it is necessary that we shall at the same time deal with additional or further detail concerning how the affective bonds of the connection between them are formed. In discerning the maintenance of *guanxi* between two persons, as we shall see, the focus is inevitably on the means whereby *ganqing* and *renqing* are acquired and enhanced. Indeed, these respectively are the first two of three broad strategies that operate in the building of affective relations between *guanxi* partners, namely the disclosure of personal information between associates, and second, the provision of a kindness, support, benefit, or favour from one associate to another. A third factor which serves to maintain *guanxi* between two people is the generation of a sense of security and dependability between them through each maintaining confidentiality regarding their relationship as it affects their *guanxi*.

One simple way of building a close personal bond with another person is for each to confide in the other, especially in giving 'privileged' information about themselves. Through each person providing aspects of their personal details to the other, there emerges between them a sense of 'lives shared'. While the mutual sharing of personal knowledge is not necessarily the basis of intimacy (Simmel 1950: 126–7), with the other aspects of reciprocity and confidentiality, to be discussed below, it serves to contribute to the consolidation of *guanxi* relations. Indeed, one means of bringing two people together is to enhance the empathy between them, to 'show mutual willingness to self-disclose as if [the participants] were old friends' (Chen and Chen 2004: 316). Self-disclosure is appropriately described as an 'operating principle' of *guanxi* (Chen and Chen 2004: 315). The activity of self-disclosure requires a context in which it can occur, and the relevant contexts not only provide opportunities for self-disclosure but associated practices which additionally contribute to *guanxi* production and maintenance. The contexts in which self-disclosure may occur include social eating and more focused or joint activities in which secrets between confederates are shared, and generated.

Social eating is a frequently referred to means of facilitating interpersonal bonding, not only with regard to *guanxi*, but in general. A study of social eating in the United Kingdom, for instance, concluded that:

> people who eat socially are more likely to feel better about themselves and to have a wider social network capable of providing social and emotional support...[In particular] evening meals at which laughter and reminiscences occur and alcohol is drunk are especially likely to enhance feelings of closeness.
>
> (Dunbar 2017: 206)

With regard to *guanxi*, a banquet is an acknowledged confirmation of a *guanxi* relation and a setting for the possible generation of future *guanxi* (Bian 2001; Kipnis 1997: 46–57; Tang 2020; Yang 1994: 137–9). The Chinese saying, 吃好了 喝好了 *chi haole, he haole*, which literally means 'eat well, drink well', captures a context the interior of which includes possibilities for personal disclosure, affirmation of warm feelings and high regard or face, as well as exchanges of favour or *renqing*. The practice of banqueting in China, in which multi-course meals are served, typically requires placement of seating which reflects social status and impression management. The host and principal guest, typically the provider of a *guanxi* benefit and recipient respectively, will sit at the head of a circular table around which are seated their associates, who are also to each other possibly current or prospective *guanxi* partners. Much toasting occurs at such banquets as well as other markers of esteem, both current and aspirational. More broadly, banqueting provides opportunities for conviviality and positive associations that tend to enhance affection and regard between participants.

In a highly marketized and mobile society, such as present-day mainland China, opportunities for self-disclosure in pursuance of building *guanxi* may need to be specially engineered as opportunities for more leisurely interactions which generate personalized knowledge of the other, that emerges over a long association, will be less frequently available than in earlier times. In business *guanxi* in particular, therefore, special means are applied. An ethnography of businessmen in the city of Chengdu, already referred to, reveals how the shared consumption of alcohol and commercial sex is used in the production and fulfilment of such bonding (Osburg 2013: 45–65). Because prostitution is illegal in China and the participants are typically married, these practices provide participants with shared secrets that are functionally equivalent to the personal bonding achieved by less pernicious self-disclosure. There are always risks in sharing privileged private information, especially with a newly encountered person. These include malicious use of such information or a failure to reciprocate. In either case, this will typically have the consequence that the relationship will not be pursued.

Self-disclosure, as suggested here, is a means of enhancing personal warmth between *guanxi* participants, and therefore contributes to the formation of *ganqing*. Another element in the development of a personalized and emotionally warm relationship is through the provision of caring gestures, including doing favours for the other, providing a gift, or sharing a meal. In a discerning account, the provision of a small gift is described as a 'disinterested rather than more instrumental *quid pro quo* exchange' through which 'emotional affect is imparted' (Wank 1996: 834). This is what Yunxiang Yan (1996: 61–7) might call an expressive gift, as opposed to an instrumental gift in which some benefit is expected in return for the gift rather than being given in expression of a pre-existing or ongoing relationship (Yan 1996: 67–73). In David Wank's account, though, there is an interesting distinction between a favour and a gift:

> Favours (*renqing*) differ subtly from gifts as they involve non-material exchange and suggest [the giver's] disinterest in calculated reciprocity. Whereas gift-giving induces obligation through gratitude, favours induce it by more genuine warmth

(*renqing*) and concern (*guanxin*). Furthermore, unlike gifts... a favour depends on the [giver's] shrewd observation of [the recipient's] unarticulated needs.

(Wank 1996: 835)

The last point in this quotation indicates that favours reflect a primary concern with the recipient, whereas a gift, as opposed to a favour, foregrounds the gift giver and their provision. The sense of personal obligation and gratitude that emerges through gift exchange is sociologically well understood (see, for example, Blau 1964; Komter 2005). But the possibility that a gift may be regarded as improper and thus refused (Bourdieu 1992: 98–111) means that the obligations that arise from gift exchange are always contingent and therefore that gift-giving may be problematic; as such it requires artful performance.

There is a broad consensus that gift-giving and the exchange of gifts underpins *guanxi*. At the same time, though, the instrumentality of a *guanxi* gift has to be distinguished from the blunt tool of a bribe, in which the exchange is to achieve some immediate objective:

In *guanxi*, immediate instrumental purposes are subordinated to the greater aim of developing relationships that may serve as resources for solving problems over long periods of time. A critical social capital of trust, not just obligation, is created through the repeated exchange of gifts and favors.   (Smart 1993: 403)

It could be added that the 'shrewd observation of another's unarticulated needs', which Wank associates with a favour, might also be required in finding a suitable gift, as he shows elsewhere (Wank 2009: 83–4). Indeed, carelessness in gift-giving is likely to have a marked negative effect. In an account of parents' use of *guanxi* in securing advantage regarding their children's school placement, Ji Ruan (2017: 84) reports a case in which a headmaster receives a gift of six apples, with which he is not satisfied:

Nowadays, apples are too cheap. If you want to give fruit you should buy expensive... [or] imported fruits. Besides, eight is a lucky number, why did she just save on buying two more apples? Ridiculous!

The problem here is not that the gift is too small but that it is regarded as thoughtless, and in showing that the gift giver did not think carefully enough about the gift, including its symbolic aspects—'eight is a lucky number'—suggests to the headmaster a lack of respect and therefore a failure to provide him with 'face' (Ruan 2017: 76–7, 95–100, 124–5).

Indeed, the status of a *guanxi* gift is complex. Not only must it be carefully considered as to its appropriateness, it must also be not really thought of at all. A feature of gift-giving between *guanxi* participants is paradoxically a ploy of disregarding the gift, of leaving it in an obscure location and not mentioning it after making sure that it is observed, and even tussling between the giver and recipient in gestures of refusal on the part of the recipient with the provider urging it on the recipient, in a show of disregard for the gift and high regard for the relationship (Fei 1992: 124–5; Ruan 2017: 83, 122; Yang 1994: 137). The offer of a gift in a *guanxi* relation, then, is notionally valued much higher than its receipt. The provision of a gift is to enrich the relationship rather than the recipient; the obligation of reciprocity that comes with acceptance of a gift is an obligation for exchanges of respect or face before it is a consideration of the material objects involved. We shall have more to say about this phenomenology of *guanxi* later.

The exchanges of gifts within *guanxi* relations are matters principally, even only, for the provider and receiver. If another person witnesses such exchanges, it is likely to be a *zhongjianren*, an intermediary, who is associated with the principals and is present in order to support their formation of a *guanxi* relation, otherwise *guanxi* exchanges are strictly confidential. In the same way, information relating to requests for or offers of favour are typically matters about which participants maintain the strictest confidentiality (Yang 1994: 129, 132–5). One possible reason for this may be that a *guanxi* favour is provided through improper influence. In his discussion of job allocation in the 1990s Bian (1997: 369, 371, 382) shows that information opacity is a consequence of the 'unauthorized' nature of attempting to influence control agents for job assignment. For this reason, according to Bian, information about job allocation through influence is not disseminated by the participants. But the suggestion here that the withholding of job search information is a consequence of the unauthorized character of the *guanxi* favour ignores the generality of information opacity in *guanxi*. The provision of even an innocuous favour or resource through *guanxi* is subject to confidentiality. In contradistinction to the argument that the use of *guanxi* in labour markets, and presumably in other 'black' areas (Wank 2009), leads to secrecy between participants, is the idea that confidentiality is a general property of *guanxi* exchanges.

Another explanation concerning confidentiality between *guanxi* participants, which accepts its generality, holds that there are social costs in failing to acquire a favour and also in refusing to provide one, in which case the interests of both parties are safeguarded by avoiding public disclosure or knowledge of their negotiations (Lin 2001: 158). This functional consideration is also important, relating to the risk of loss of face for unsuccessful negotiations of favour. But apart from the risk of failed negotiations are the prior personal ties between *guanxi* participants that puts them in a position to negotiate about significant favours. This strongly personal involvement in *guanxi* both facilitates and reflects the way in which the relations between participants are cultivated. In the quotation from Smart the 'social capital of trust' was mentioned. The nature and role of trust in *guanxi* will be treated in detail in Chapter 5. At the present time it can be noted that trust between *guanxi* participants relies upon mutual surveillance in dyadic interactions in which the trustworthiness of *guanxi* partners is based upon familiarity, and their reliability reflects a form of subordination in terms of dependence on another so that information about and associated with participants will in the course of things be internal to the relationship. The 'subordination' of *guanxi* partners is not necessarily pernicious as it is mutual, accepted by participants in order to receive the benefits of the relationship. In this way there are structural as well as social inhibitions preventing disclosure concerning *guanxi* favours. The confidentiality between *guanxi* participants testifies to the nature of intimacy within dyadic relations, classically treated by Simmel (1950: 125–8, 330–3), but as we have seen through a very particular formation.

If the *guanxi* a person has with another serves their purpose, if it is useful to the participants, then it is to their advantage to ensure that it persists. It has been shown that the emotional warmth between participants through *ganqing* operates to maintain their commitment to the relationship between them. We have also seen that *renqing* favours are granted or gifts provided in the maintenance of *guanxi*. A key element in the endurance of *guanxi* is the requirement that favours and gifts are not immediately reciprocated, indeed not reciprocated at all in any direct manner, as we shall see. It has already been noted that exchange relations in general are abrogated if a gift is immediately returned (Bourdieu 1992: 105). Relatedly, it is a feature of commercial or market transactions that payment for the provision of a product or service terminates the functional and episodic relation between buyer and seller. To avoid such termination in *guanxi*, it has been noticed that the recipient of a favour or gift may delay repayment (Yang 1994: 143–4). In this way 债 *zhai*, debt, that is not discharged serves to prevent the termination of the exchange, and the connection between the favour provider and the recipient is preserved and their *guanxi* endures. It is of particular interest, though, that in a *guanxi* exchange, the provision of a returned favour is not necessarily acknowledged to be the discharge or repayment for a prior debt.

It was shown above that to understand *guanxi* it is necessary to distinguish between a relationship, on the one hand, and, on the other, those who participate in that relationship. A *guanxi* favour may well have instrumental purposes that are highly significant to the participants. But what is more significant to them is the relationship through which such instrumental purposes may be achieved, not merely in a current and present moment but in the future, and repeatedly over time. Within this relationship favours are performed, gifts provided, and therefore debts incurred. To repay a debt is to provide a reimbursement to a person. But *renqing* is a relational form which together with the *ganqing* between participants addresses primarily not the involvement of persons, but the attributes of the relationship between them. This is partly captured by the discussion of *renqing* by the veteran Chinese sociologist Fei Xiaotong, but not quite:

> The unity of the intimate group depends on the fact that each member owes countless favors to the other members. This all seems so obvious to us that we take it for granted. Friends vie with each other to pay bills, each hoping to let the others 'owe them one' (*renqing*). Such debts are like an investment to the lender. When you owe another person a favor (*renqing*), you have to look for an opportunity to return a bigger favor. By repaying the favor with a bigger favor, you make others owe you more favors in the future. So it goes back and forth; the continuing reciprocation maintains the cooperation among people in the group.
>
> (Fei 1992: 124–5)

In this account the relationship between members of the group continues through a recurring cycle of debt that persists as a result of increases in the size of subsequent debt.

It is held by Fei here that the investment of lenders is in the form of a growing indebtedness of their *renqing* partners, and that the relations between them endure because of the impossibility of discharging the debts which become larger with each exchange. This model of continuous debt-growth is not convincing, however. The reciprocation between participants, of favour and gifts in *guanxi*, may involve growing debt in each successive exchange, but this cannot be the mechanism for the endurance of *guanxi* relations. The exchanges between participants in a *guanxi* relation do not primarily consist in the movement of services or goods that pass between persons; rather, the efficacious exchanges are of the sentiments and feelings that such utilitarian transactions may convey to participants; commitment to the relationship is through the feelings of *ganqing* and *renqing* not through the gravity of *zhai* or debt. Each *guanxi* debt exists in two forms; it is a burden on a person that has ultimately to be discharged, and at the same time a debt is a confirmation of a relationship experienced through *ganqing* and *renqing* which themselves are generated by the provision of favours and gifts. But this is not all.

Fei is correct to write that in *renqing* or exchange relations within a group 'each member owes countless favors to the other members'. Indeed, it is not the size of the debt that ensures unbroken and continuing *guanxi* but rather the overall distribution of debt or, rather, debts. Each *guanxi* relation of favour provision is dyadic, involving a giver and a receiver. But each participant in any given *guanxi* dyad will at the same time have *guanxi* relations with other persons, giving rise to a *guanxiwang*, a *guanxi* network. In such a network each member of a dyad potentially has access to the members of his or her associate's dyads. Within a *guanxiwang*, then, there will at any given time be undischarged debts. If expansion of debt supports the network, then, this is best conceived in terms of its lateral reach rather than the volume of debt. This resolves the issue raised by Fei concerning the relationship between debt and what he calls the 'unity of the intimate group'. There remains, though, the question of how *guanxi* participants regard and deal with debt. This is an issue because, as Fei intermates, the persistence of debt structurally contributes to the maintenance of *guanxi*. It is commonplace in discussion of *guanxi* to acknowledge that any debt incurred in the context of *guanxi* need not be immediately repaid:

> Chinese believe that *renqing* need not be returned immediately, as it can be stored and returned at the right time, when the other party needs it…Whereas a cash debt is easily repaid, it is almost impossible to repay the debts of *renqing*.
>
> (Wang 2007: 84)

The first part of this quotation is repeated many times in the literature. The second part of the quotation, though, deserves thoughtful reflection because it indicates something about *guanxi* debt, namely its persistence, that is less frequently articulated.

The basis on which a person receives a favour or gift is the *guanxi* that exists between giver and receiver. It is the *guanxi* between participants that is ultimately responsible for the provision of the favour; in this sense, then, the favour provider and the recipient each is an agent of the *guanxi* but respectively playing different although mutually supportive roles. The debt that a person incurs through *guanxi* enhances the value of the relationship. In a *guanxi* relationship, then, a person receives a favour rather than incurs a debt, and it is because of the relationship that a person who incidentally had previously received a favour will provide a favour to a *guanxi* partner. In this sense, then, there are only favours that are efficacious, and debt exists in the relationship as a maintenance cost in support of the relationship. Of course, the *guanxi* relations are between persons who are very aware of what they expend on others and conscious of the obligations that arise from their exchanges. In the phenomenology of *guanxi*, though, in the consciousness of its practices on the part of participants, there is nevertheless avoidance of a directly remunerative transactional orientation in which a provision generates a debt that must be discharged. Instead there is a sense of favour supporting a *guanxi* partner who, as a result of the *guanxi* relationship based on the effective factors of *ganqing* and *renqing* shall in turn support their *guanxi* partner. Sentiment is involved, and face. There is a tally in all of this, but the reckoning is submerged and secondary to the connection and the broader awareness of its value beyond any single exchange and any single debt.

The Efficiency of *Guanxi*

Having considered the fact that in providing favours *guanxi* participants necessarily incur debts, it is appropriate to acknowledge the costs of *guanxi* as well as its benefits; the balance of these two things, costs and benefits, can be regarded as the 'efficiency' of *guanxi*. In treating the costs and benefits of *guanxi* an account of its use in business is appropriate. Apart from the financial costs incurred in the lubrication of *guanxi* relations, including the provision of favours and gifts, two other types of costs are experienced. The cultivation of *guanxi* is a time-expensive activity requiring not only direct engagement with another in advancing the relationship through participation in social bonding practices, but also continuous monitoring of participants. Second, *guanxi* carries heavy opportunity costs that derive from the long-term reciprocal nature of *guanxi* obligations, through which participants are locked into relations with each other. These factors must qualify the often-repeated claim in the literature regarding the efficiency of business *guanxi* over market exchanges, which holds that transaction costs in the former are lower than in the latter because *guanxi* reduces the cost of legal contracts which become redundant as *guanxi* itself increases assurance between business partners (Boisot and Child 1996; Lee and Dawes 2005). This conclusion can only be accepted if the costs of cultivating *guanxi* and its locked-in form are ignored.

The benefits of *guanxi*, excepting its obvious instrumentality, largely derive from its connective form. First, *guanxi* participants 'are willing to sacrifice short-term interests for long-term favour exchanges, since they know that the benefit of group effort will be much greater than that of an individual endeavour' (Luo and Yeh 2012: 65). Second, the surveillance of partners, mentioned above as a cost of *guanxi*, at the same time provides participants with privileged information regarding the other's preferences, capabilities, and the quality and costs of their inputs and outputs. Such information imparts surety in any engagement between *guanxi* partners so that agreements between them will be self-enforcing. Finally, the cultivation of *guanxi* networks means that participants can enhance their benefits by strategically selecting new partners, in which case complementarity is achieved, in contrast with the constraints of formal contracts, as well as an extension of opportunities to acquire valued resources and support or services over an increasingly diverse range of items through *guanxi* network development and extension. The balance of these benefits and the costs mentioned in the preceding paragraph address the efficiency of *guanxi*.

It is often reported that *guanxi* is ubiquitous in Chinese society, that *guanxi* is necessary to get things done. The question, though, must be: which things? *Guanxi* gets things done when an informal provision of favour is effective, indeed more effective than alternate practices. Efficiency is technically expressed as a ratio, the ratio of input to output, of how much must be expended in order to achieve a sought outcome; the lower the level of input and the higher the level of output, the higher the efficiency of the performance in question. While it is possible to provide an abstract definition in this manner, the notion of efficiency is seldom invoked when considering social practices. The purpose here is not to measure the efficiency of *guanxi*. The question of efficiency is relevant to understanding *guanxi*, though, because it is reasonable to assume that, other things being equal, low-efficiency performances will be displaced by high-efficiency performances; if *guanxi* is not efficient, if the costs of engaging in *guanxi* are higher than the returns, then *guanxi* is unlikely to be practised.

Consideration of the efficiency of *guanxi* is not primarily about whether persons may choose to avoid *guanxi* (Hwang 1987: 964–7; King 1991: 76–8), although that is an important and neglected topic worth exploring; rather, it concerns the incidence or persistence of *guanxi*, whether and under what conditions *guanxi* is likely to be practised. In a well-known article Doug Guthrie (1998) argues that, as China experiences increased marketization and as economic enterprises are increasingly subject to legal regulation, then *guanxi* as a factor in Chinese economic society will become less important and the incidence of *guanxi* must inevitably decline. Directly responding to this argument Mayfair Yang (2002) questions both Guthrie's method and his conclusion. Rather than focus on responses of Chinese managers to interview questions, Yang recommends a historical approach to *guanxi*, which she regards as a 'repertoire of cultural patterns and resources which are continuously transformed in their adaptation to, as well as shaping of, new social institutions and structures' (Yang 2002: 459). According to Yang, then, *guanxi* is likely to persist in China's societal transformation and beyond by manifesting 'new social forms and expressions'. This landmark exchange between Guthrie and Yang is more or less universally regarded as resolved in favour of the continued presence of *guanxi* as a significant element of China's social economy.

The terms of this debate, though, are partly misleading in so far as *guanxi* becomes more or less efficient at different times in different social arenas under different sets of circumstances, so that the usefulness and therefore the significance of *guanxi* practice subsides for some purposes and may become more useful and so more significant for others. Rather than asking the broad general question of whether *guanxi* will persist, it more appropriately needs to be asked in what social areas is *guanxi* efficient? We shall see in the following that the changing balance of costs and benefits regarding *guanxi*, as changes occur in the circumstances of individuals and also in the social landscape more generally, means that for some purposes *guanxi* loses its usefulness and for others becomes increasingly attractive. For instance, during the so-called Mao era, from 1955 to 1978, China's households were subject to rationing and restrictions were placed on 'more than 20 items' of household goods, including 'grain and cloth...soap, tofu and good-quality bicycles' (Naughton 2007: 81). In these circumstances, then, the role of *guanxi* in the acquisition of household goods was widespread (Gold 1985: 662). The development of consumer markets in mainland China since the 1980s, however, has removed the need for *guanxi* in the acquisition and distribution of consumer goods. More will be said about consumer markets below.

While *guanxi* was useful in the acquisition of consumer goods under conditions of rationing in China, during the same period a reverse movement occurred with regard to job acquisition in which the role of *guanxi* declined during the Mao period only to rise with marketization of the economy after the death of Mao. Union membership data from the city of Wuhu in Anhui Province reveals that, during the period from the early 1950s, unlike the preceding period, job acquisition was principally through a formal job assignment system rather than through *guanxi* (Li and Tian 2020). This finding corresponds with data from Tianjin in north-eastern China, which shows that before 1949 58 per cent of urban workers' first job was acquired through *guanxi*, whereas for the period from 1953 to 1976 *guanxi* was implicated in less than 33 per cent of first job acquisitions (Bian 1994: 973). In the decade beginning 1977, however, the percentage of first jobs acquired through *guanxi* returned to 57 per cent (Bian 1994: 973). With the advent of economic reform from the late 1970s *guanxi* has become increasingly drawn upon in job attainment (Bian 2018). These contrasting trends in the distinct markets for commodities and employment suggest that the deployment of *guanxi* varies between different sets of circumstances.

Variation in the efficiency of *guanxi* and therefore distinctive patterns of its application is not simply between market sectors but may occur within a single broad market. While it is true to say that the acquisition of commodities no longer requires *guanxi*, as they are now freely available through market purchase, *guanxi* does remain a factor in the acquisition of particular goods. The prevalence of e-commerce is characteristic of markets for household commodities of all types in China today. Indeed, according to a World Bank report China is the largest e-commerce market in the world: the 'annual total e-commerce trade volume in China increased thirtyfold from RMB 930 billion in 2004 to RMB 29,160 billion in 2017, a compound annual growth rate of 30 percent' (Luo *et al.* 2019: 4–5). Internet shopping provides customers with increased information on merchandise and service and at the same time eliminates the 'need to put on a status performance to demonstrate their purchasing ability' and reduces the interaction cost of emotional labour (Tian 2018: 559–64). The life insurance market in China, however, operates against this trend in so far as personal sales predominate, and these are largely subject to *guanxi*. In a detailed exploration of the growth of the life insurance market in China since the 1990s it is shown that the mobilization or development of *guanxi* is significant in sales practices in this sector (Chan 2012: 118–32). While online sales in China are popular 'for car and accident insurance, the sales of life insurance products accounted for only a small part of the total online insurance revenue' (Jiang *et al.* 2019). Because of the cultural inhibition on discussion of death (Chan 2012: 6–9, 36–9) there is a high threshold of resistance in the marketing of life insurance that *guanxi* is particularly adept in overcoming (Chan 2012: 121–30; see also Kipnis 2018). While a vast range of commodities is purchased online and free of the need for *guanxi* facilitation, life insurance sales require the particularistic personalism of *guanxi* in order to be executed.

Certain new areas of activity, such as the market in life insurance, require the sales agents to have *guanxi* with their customers, while other emerging areas of the economy seem to lack any *guanxi* involvement. A study of the Chinese diamond processing trade shows that, except for its use between diamond traders and government agencies, in order to 'circumvent onerous regulations', *guanxi* is 'absent in the Chinese diamond industry' (Berger *et al.* 2018: 345). Diamond processing began in China in the 1980s and by 2000 China had become the second largest diamond producer in the world (Berger *et al.* 2018: 346). A characteristic feature of Chinese diamond traders is a business style that prioritizes short-term relations between operatives, and that is focused on cash transactions (Berger *et al.* 2018: 348). These are the practical obverse of what would occur through *guanxi*-driven transactions. The diamond trade in China has a number of features that explain why it is *guanxi*-free. The Chinese diamond trade is both chaotically organized and provides high returns to its participants. This situation encourages opportunistic behaviour, including a 'propensity to cheat with little possibility of legal redress' (Berger *et al.* 2018: 351). Under these circumstances, then, the prospect of quick—and large—profits implies that building long-term relations is unnecessary if not inhibitory of success in the diamond trade; also, market opportunism necessitates immediate returns of cash payment rather than recurring favour exchange. The Chinese diamond trade, then, is one area in which *guanxi* is not only without any efficiency but would be prohibitively repressive.

Perhaps unexpectedly, scientific research in China is an area in which *guanxi* plays a significant role. In a remarkably detailed study of training in and the practice of academic archaeology in China, Erika Evasdottir (2004) shows that relationship-building through reciprocity, gift-giving, rule manipulation, and banqueting serves the development of archaeological careers, as individuals negotiate university and department administrations, relations with the Chinese Academy of Social Sciences, transactions with peasants at excavation sites and the actual unearthing of artefacts, and finally, the preparation of reports and the publishing of findings. Although she does not use the term *guanxi*, Evasdottir's ethnography provides a comprehensive narrative of the centrality of *guanxi* in one scientific discipline in China. These findings are supported in a study, based on in-depth interviews conducted during 2013–14 with forty research physicists in eleven top-tier universities, which examine the relevance of *guanxi* for the conduct of scientific research in Chinese universities (Lewis *et al.* 2017).

The authors of the study of research physicists found that *guanxi* was relevant in two domains, namely in the distribution of government funding and in scientific collaboration. With regard to government funding, the authors found that researchers felt 'compelled to adopt *guanxi* when applying for government funding themselves' even though they regarded *guanxi* for this purpose with 'negative ethical connotations' (Lewis *et al.* 2017: 734).

Guanxi also played a role in building research teams; this study reveals that 'Chinese physicists are more likely to collaborate with scientists with whom they had close *guanxi* connections' (Lewis *et al.* 2017: 734). In the case of collaboration, as opposed to grant acquisition, the scientists 'attached neutral if not slightly positive ethical connotations to [*guanxi*]' (Lewis *et al.* 2017: 734). The difference in ethical evaluation, according to the authors, results from the fact that *guanxi* in grant acquisition is vertical, involving the physicist's *guanxi* with upper-level bureaucrats, in which case the scientist is necessarily subordinate and has little control over the outcome, whereas in scientific collaboration the *guanxi* is horizontal and the way in which it is exercised is subject to the scientist's own discretion (Lewis *et al.* 2017: 738). The conclusion drawn from this study, especially related to the use of *guanxi* in grant acquisition, is that 'Chinese physicists may practice *guanxi* not *just* because they receive actual benefits from the use of *guanxi* but because, as scientists in the physics community in China, they are constricted by the institutionalized *guanxi* culture in Chinese physics' (Lewis *et al.* 2017: 738). The idea of an 'institutionalized *guanxi* culture' warrants further exploration.

Lewis and his co-authors do not go beyond the incidence of *guanxi* in their sample of physicists and the way in which their interviewees morally evaluate their own use of *guanxi*. There is, though, an implicit assumption that the use of *guanxi* in the acquisition of research funding is distorting of the grant distribution process in so far as favour rather than merit seems to determine the allocation of research resources, and it should be the other way around. This issue is addressed directly in a careful and detailed examination of the allocation of science research funding in China which considers whether 'natural selection' or 'artificial selection' is principally responsible for the awarding of research grants (Zhang *et al.* 2020). Natural selection occurs when research funding is allocated on the basis of prior research performance, or merit, and artificial selection when it is allocated on the basis of good interpersonal relationships or *guanxi* between the grant provider and the recipient. In order to determine whether academic ability or social connections is responsible for Chinese scientists' acquisition of science research funding, Zhang and his colleagues analysed 274,732 publications identified in the Web of Science that had been authored by scientists in mainland China in the subject areas of chemical sciences, life sciences, health sciences, mathematical and physical sciences during the publication years 2010 to 2013. In spite of an acknowledged presence of *guanxi* in the peer-review systems for most science funding in China (Zhang *et al.* 2020: 435) it was shown that 'science funding allocation is mainly caused by "natural selection" rather than "artificial selection" in China, suggesting that scientists with better research performance would gain more funding' (Zhang *et al.* 2020: 443).

The findings of Zhang and his colleagues resonate with a qualitatively similar and even more counterintuitive finding in a very different arena of social life. In a study of the buying and selling of government positions in China it was found that, in the case of corrupt military promotions, the professional competence of an officer seeking advancement through a *guanxi* relation was necessary for the favour to be effective:

> As a government official pointed out, 'when a senior officer considers the promotion of...subordinates, [*guanxi*] is a major consideration, but [they still have] to consider the ability of subordinates'. Candidates whose professional competence is recognized by upper-level officials are more likely to be promoted. As a result, upper-level officials encourage candidates with high professional competence to pay bribes and build emotional bonds in order to gain promotion.
>
> (Wang 2020: 1296)

This finding is parallel with the one regarding the distribution of science research grants in China in so far as *guanxi* operates not regardless of professional competence but in concert or agreement with it. In the case of military promotion, the favour giver is concerned with the competence of the favour seeker, the officer seeking promotion, because government-set targets are monitored by external agencies to ensure that positions are filled by capable candidates, and additionally, the promotion of incompetent officers who perform poorly will diminish the influence of the favour provider who will ultimately be held responsible for any failures that result from his protégé's lack of capability (Wang 2020: 1296).

These cases do indeed suggest what might be called an 'institutionalized *guanxi* culture' that involves more than simply favour exchange. What is regarded as *guanxi* in both the case of applications for research grants and also military promotion implicates the favour seeker and provider in a vertical relationship, that is, a relationship between different levels of power. In these particular cases, then, of power disparity, a coercive element is inherent that sets it apart from relations governed by *ganqing* and *renqing* as these terms are normally understood (Barbalet 2018: 943–6). In an 'institutionalized *guanxi* culture' as described here, professional competence is by itself insufficient for success because those with power may extract from subordinates a levy that must be paid in order for them to be considered for a research grant or a promotion. In this context, then, an institutionalized *guanxi* culture is a corrupt arena in which bribery or extortion operate. The distinction between *guanxi* and corruption is frequently blurred, but it is necessary to maintain a separation between them:

> Because *guanxi* provides particular instead of general access to resources and operates through personal relations rather than formal structures, there is a tendency to associate it with corruption, bribery and malpractice [...but the] impropriety associated with *guanxi* is not inherent in it [...] While *guanxi* is not itself a cause of corruption, if corruption occurs *guanxi* is likely to be one of its mechanisms. The emphasis in *guanxi*, however, is on relationships, whereas in corruption it is on unwarranted material gain achieved through inappropriate means.   (Qi 2013: 311)

This statement captures something of the complexity of the relationship between *guanxi* and bribery. While *guanxi* is not in itself a type of bribery, should bribery occur in China it is likely that it will take a superficial form of *guanxi*, an exchange of favours in which benefits are provided.

There is another possibility to consider, though, when attempting to make sense of the notion of an 'institutionalized *guanxi* culture'. Institutional contexts may be distinguished in terms of the development of formality within them. In this case it is necessary to differentiate between cases in which formal structures are merely emergent or underdeveloped and those in which formal structures are well-established and central in both the organizational formation and the consciousness of participants. In the latter the duties and responsibilities of an official position are discharged without reference to any particular or personal relationship between persons because an official's provision of a service is primarily an obligation of their office, and attached to that office are integral benefits of adequate salary, opportunities for promotion on the basis of merit, and a culture of professionalism. When formal structures are underdeveloped, though, any receipt of official attention will typically be acknowledged through personal gratitude expressed as a gift of some sort, which is not regarded as a contravention of appropriate behaviour but, on the contrary, serves as an indication of appreciation. This situation is as representative of an 'institutionalized *guanxi* culture' as the description above of bribery, but is not so pernicious because etiquette rather than coercion is understood to be the principal driver. The association between *guanxi* and bribery cannot be regarded in a case-neutral manner because of the performative element which defies a clear legal or moral grasp of the distinction: 'For the gift to succeed as a gift, it must follow the social forms that usually prescribe that it be an unconditional offer of a prestation in which explicit recognition of instrumental goals is excluded from the performance'

(Smart 1993: 389; see also Bian 2019: 198–200; Ruan 2019). But this does not exhaust consideration of the relationship between *guanxi* and corruption.

A feature of the mainland Chinese market economy relates to the continuing role of the party-state in economic management and the consequences of that role for relations between enterprises and officials. First, the advent of the market economy has not led to differentiation from the political sphere; indeed, the Chinese state's regulatory, monitoring, economic enterprise, and planning roles have expanded as the private sector has grown from the beginning of the present century (Chu 2011; Heilmann and Melton 2013; Hu 2013). Second, the role of the Communist Party in state administrative functions has the consequence of creating an arena in which political capital plays a significant role in the market economy. The private sector is so circumscribed by administrative fiat and policy that a connection with political capital is crucial in order to obtain a licence, permit, or any other type of official product (Paik and Baum 2014; Sun *et al.* 2014). This situation encourages the particularistic relations between entrepreneurs and officials that are realized in *guanxi*. Third, family members of political and bureaucratic personnel are able to draw on the political capital of their kin, so that political capital translates to economic capital not only for officials but for members of their families, a situation exacerbated by the 1978 reforms in China through which the nexus of party-state and market economy was generated and strengthened. These relations are not necessarily vertical, between different levels of power, so much as involving conversion of one form of power to another, of political to economic capital and vice versa, in which gift performance predominates but in the provision of an underlying instrumental outcome.

The combination of the elements mentioned here, of market development in China during the period from the 1980s, has given rise to extensive irregular or corrupt practices interdependent with exceptionally high rates of economic growth (Wedeman 2012), the excesses of which have arguably been curtailed by the Communist Party's anti-corruption campaign inaugurated in 2012 by President Xi Jinping. This campaign has negatively affected aspects of *guanxi* efficiency in certain relations between entrepreneurs and officials (Yuan 2014). More generally, though, there is the unavoidable role of *guanxi* in accessing the attention of officials and the latter's satisfaction of business requirements. As marketization has progressed, business access to regional and local government and their administrative functions proceeds through patronage and clientelism in which business and state actors mutually cultivate *guanxi*. In this way mainland China can be described as having a *guanxi*-qualified market economy (Boisot and

Child 1996; Wank 2002; McNally 2012: 750–2) in which personalism is dominant over impersonality in legal, administrative, and business relations. This institutional context sets the parameters for the efficiency of a good deal of *guanxi* between entrepreneurs and entrepreneurs, and also between entrepreneurs and officials.

Conclusion

In examining the formation of *guanxi*, this chapter has summarized a good deal of what is generally understood by the term *guanxi* in the study of contemporary China's economy and society. In addition, a number of new approaches are introduced into the discussion that add to our existing appreciation of *guanxi*. By treating *guanxi* in the framework of its basic formation and how it is consolidated, the idea that *guanxi* combines affective, sentimental, or emotional elements on the one hand, with advantageous or beneficial purposes on the other, is placed in clear relief and points to the elemental constitution of *guanxi* as both expressive and instrumental, although these latter are sometimes regarded as alternative rather than complementary possibilities in *guanxi* (Hwang 1987: 949–53; see also Yan 1996: 226–9). This last-mentioned proposition derives from the claimed difficulty of locating self-interested action in what Hwang (1987: 949) calls 'congenial groups' of family and intimate friends, an idea whose limitations are discussed elsewhere (Barbalet 2014) and will be critically examined in following chapters.

It has been shown that, by seeking *guanxi* with another person, an individual selectively draws on and possibly constructs common markers of identity, what have been called *guanxi* 'bases'. This is to say that *guanxi* is initiated and actively shaped by its participants for their own self-chosen purposes, an idea that is summarized in the literature through the description of *guanxi* as a 'cultivated' relation or practice (Guo and Miller 2010: 267, 272, 280; King 1991: 73; Smart 1993: 400). In this regard *guanxi* stands in contrast to those associations that are latent in pre-existing structures of relations, especially familial or kinship relations. Whereas these latter can be described as closed, *guanxi* is open; where kinship might be characterized in terms of strong ties, the tie strength operative within *guanxi* is not pre-given but instead strengthened or weakened strategically by participants, as shown in detail in Chapter 6, so that in *guanxi* 'weak and strong ties are not permanently distinct categories' (Smart 1998: 561). To radically distinguish *guanxi* from kinship in this manner is in sharp contrast with some current standard understandings of *guanxi*, in which familial relations are seen as its archetypal form. This conventional perspective relates to an understanding of the family as institutionally dominant in Chinese society, a factor held to derive from Confucian ethics, itself often seen as essential for understanding China's history and social formation, and *guanxi* in particular. Core aspects of these matters are discussed in detail in the following two chapters and the last.

The fact that *guanxi* is cultivated by its participants has a number of corollaries in addition to the need to carefully distinguish it from kinship. One of these discussed above is the problem of exchange debt in *guanxi*. Debt constitutes a particular difficulty for *guanxi* insofar as the discharge of debt risks terminating the relations of exchange on which *guanxi* is based. A novel solution to this problem outlined in the chapter involves, first, the distinction between a relationship and the persons who participate in it, and, second, the possibility then of those who practise *guanxi* regarding debt as a residual contributor to the continuation of the relationship in which participants successively provide favours to each other. In this way the place of debt in remunerative transaction recedes to the background and *guanxi* participants experience their interactions as favour succeeded by reciprocal favour. The vibrancy of *guanxi*, then, is in the courtesy, esteem, benevolence, and benefit exchanged between participants. In being backgrounded, debt may continue as an underlying force encouraging a sense of obligation within the relationship, but without giving rise to a need for settlement through which the exchange underlying *guanxi* would be concluded.

Another corollary of the characterization of *guanxi* as a cultivated practice is the fact that through its maintenance *guanxi* participants incur costs as well as benefits. The considerable amounts of time devoted to working with others in building *guanxi* relations as well as the opportunity costs that derive from being locked into long-term relationships have been mentioned in the discussion, as are the benefits of participating in supportive networks. The reference to costs and benefits led to consideration of the efficiency of *guanxi*. Social practices are not normally thought of in terms of their efficiency, but this novel application of the latter term is justified in the present context as a way of addressing the question of the variable incidence of *guanxi*, an issue that arises through consideration of the future prospects of *guanxi* as a social practice resulting from growing formalization in China's market economy and organizational environment. The supposition that more efficient practices will come to or continue to operate while less efficient practices will decline provides a backdrop to consideration of the changing incidence of *guanxi* in commodity markets, for instance, in job markets and in scientific research. It was shown that, in some areas, including the distribution of scientific research grants and also the promotion of military officers, *guanxi* is 'institutionalized' in the sense that, while competence is necessary to achieve success in these areas, it is not sufficient as organizationally superior operatives may require a 'favour' from those seeking advancement in order for their applications to proceed. This discussion concluded with a consideration of the distinction between *guanxi* and bribery, and the role of *guanxi* in the corruption regarded by many as characteristic of marketized China.

A number of the things introduced in this chapter will be elaborated in subsequent chapters. The nature of *guanxi* and its place in Chinese society have been outlined here in order to provide an introduction to this particular form of social relationship and also to indicate some of the analytic and substantive issues that unavoidably arise in any consideration of it. The chapters to follow will provide more focused and deeper understanding of the nature of *guanxi* and how it can be properly appreciated. In making sense of *guanxi* the discussion to follow will also be concerned to contribute to our understanding of Chinese society more generally, including aspects of its history and reflective literatures.

2
Traditional Rural Society

A Model for *Guanxi*?

In the previous chapter the relevance to 关系 *guanxi* of kinship and family relations was briefly touched on. In mentioning the bases of *guanxi*, family was acknowledged to be one of a number of its possible sources, although not an entirely reliable one compared with some others. This empirical assessment of the link between kin relations and *guanxi* is mentioned here because it stands in sharp contrast to a theoretical appraisal of the role of kinship in *guanxi* formation that is now important if not hegemonic in the relevant literature. Sociologists from Ambrose King (1991) to Yanjie Bian (2019) argue that, as Confucian social theory holds that family is the basic unit of Chinese society, then kinship is the most compelling social relation for a Chinese individual. The most accessible source of this argument, and the most frequently cited by exponents of it, is a book by China's premier sociologist Fei Xiaotong, 乡土中国 *Xiangtu Zhongguo*, first published in 1947 and translated into English as *From the Soil: The Foundations of Chinese Society* (1992). Fei's considerable reputation was originally based on his pioneering village studies (Fei 1939; Fei and Chang 1948; see Celarent 2013), but today Fei is known principally for *Xiangtu Zhongguo*, referred to in what follows as *From the Soil*.

The strength of *From the Soil* and the basis of its sociological appeal is a concept developed in the book, 差序格局 *chaxugeju*, translated as 'differential mode of association', that is held by a number of writers to be central for understanding *guanxi*, and especially *guanxi* networks (Bian 2001: 275–8; 2019: 203–18; Chen and Chen 2004: 306; Herrmann-Pillath 2016: 40), an assessment encouraged by Fei's translators (Hamilton and Wang 1992: 21–2). It will be shown here that the application of *chaxugeju* to the analysis of *guanxi* is conducted beyond Fei's own intentions. The possibility of such an application of *chaxugeju* derives from a particular interpretation of Fei's account of contrasting likelihoods of the formation of strong ties and weaker ties, from the core of extended kin relations, on the one hand, to their outer edges, on the other. Fei (1992: 65) argues that a 'self-centered quality'

The Theory of Guanxi and Chinese Society. Jack Barbalet, Oxford University Press (2021). © Jack Barbalet.
DOI: 10.1093/oso/9780198808732.003.0003

of social relationships in China means that relations between persons are like 'ripples formed from a stone thrown into a lake, each circle spreading out from the center becomes more distant and at the same time more insignificant'. This is contrasted with 'the Western pattern [in which] all members in an organization are equivalent' (Fei 1992: 65). Whether this latter claim is correct need not be pursued here, but in any event the position that all, in theory, are equal before the law cannot itself inform a sociological apprehension of the unequal conditions and opportunities that arise out of organizational experience in Western society, to use Fei's term.

Fei's argument concerning *chaxugeju* holds that, when Chinese individuals are close to their family members, the bonds between them will be stronger, whereas the further the individual moves away from close kin in their social relations, to the outer 'ripples', then the associations will be 'more distant and at the same time more insignificant'. Some *guanxi* scholars have translated this assessment into the language of social network analysis: 'Strategic efforts at network building are made by the ego to increase the degree of particularism (shortening social distances) with resourceful alters and decrease the degree of particularism (lengthening social distances) with less-resourceful alters' (Bian 2018: 604). This is to say that the layers of concentric circles extending from ego, who stands in the centre of different orders of relationships, vary from strong ties at the core to weaker ties at the periphery. Through such network distance there are different expectations and responsibilities between family members, who share strong ties, and friends and acquaintances, who share weaker ties. It is ironic that Fei's supposition regarding Confucian relational protocols is regarded as equivalent to elements of social network analysis, the roots of which are in sociometry as developed by Jacob Moreno, a Jewish émigré working in the United States during the 1930s, and a number of researchers in various American universities during the mid-twentieth century (Freeman 2004). This sits uncomfortably with the distinction Fei draws between *chaxugeju* and the 'Western pattern' he calls 团体格局 *tuantigeju*, the 'organizational mode of association' (Fei 1992: 62–3), which in spite of Fei's characterization is the source and site of the development of social network analysis.

We shall see that the tendency to merge *guanxi* with close family relations is problematic. The difficulties with a Confucian grounding of the argument are discussed in this chapter while sociological and conceptual problems with the idea are treated more fully in Chapter 6. Reference to tie strength as a means of distinguishing types of relationships is also not accepted here. Network ties differ not only in terms of strength but also in kind. Network ties can be seen as bonds derived from distinctive forms of obligation, an observation that may serve as a basis from which a conceptual analysis of network ties can proceed, as indicated in Chapter 5 and argued more fully elsewhere (Barbalet 2020). In the present chapter these ideas are outlined with regard to the need to distinguish between role obligation and exchange obligation, applied to kinship and *guanxi* respectively. The strength of these bonds may vary internally, as when family disputes diminish the strength of the kin tie which they continue to share. Similarly, *guanxi* between acquaintances on the one hand and close friends on the other can be contrasted in terms of tie-strength, but in these cases the cultivated nature of the bond means that the strength of the tie can be strategically varied by the *guanxi* participants, and its explanatory value is low if not void.

These remarks are intended to convey the view that the ideas developed in *From the Soil* are an unsuitable platform from which to provide a viable and comprehensive account of *guanxi*. The purpose of this chapter is to demonstrate why this is the case. In doing so it is necessary to place *From the Soil* in its historical and literary context in order to more fully appreciate Fei's purpose and meaning. Relatively recent discussion of this work has been less concerned with its context and more with the respective authors' own endeavours to extract what they regard as Fei's enduring relevance for social science in general and analysis of Chinese society in particular (Feuchtwang 2015; Hamilton 2015; Herrmann-Pillath 2016; Yan 2015). These latter purposes are not neglected here; but an underlying supposition of the present chapter is that such purposes can best be achieved through familiarity with the historical setting of Fei's work, including related contemporary accounts. While the term *chaxugeju* was explicitly coined by Fei as a novel formulation, it will be shown here that the nature of the relations it refers to are conventional in Confucian thought and expounded by others during the late Republican period. It is also shown that, even from the perspective of Confucianism, Fei's account of rural social relationships is narrow in its neglect of non-kin relations because of his almost total focus on family and lineage. Additionally, the concept of *chaxugeju* remains opaque to understanding a necessary feature of *guanxi*, namely its mobilization to achieve the self-interested purposes of those who participate in it.

The following discussion, while focusing on *From the Soil,* is not confined to this source. Indeed, the treatment of this work and its concerns are set in the context of related writings published by Fei from the late 1930s to the late 1940s, as well as contemporary discussions by other writers of the late Republican period concerned with Chinese rural society. The present chapter also offers an original basis for a sociological conceptualization of *guanxi* as a characteristic form of social interaction in China. The following discussion is in seven parts.

The first part shows how Fei's (1992) apprehension of Chinese rural society is essentially Confucian, a proposition developed further in the second part of the chapter in which Fei's notion of *chaxugeju*, differential mode of association, is shown to derive from a particular conceptualization of the intergenerational and multifunctional form of family or lineage. The section closes with the claim that Fei's characterization of lineage is an idealization in conformity with Confucian ideology, as demonstrated in the subsequent part of the chapter in which social relations of lineage are treated. The fourth part considers Fei's village-centric view of rural society and begins to consider the importance of non-kin relationships that are barely acknowledged and not adequately theorized in Fei's account. The following section identifies a problem with the treatment of social obligation employed by Fei and provides a solution to it by distinguishing between obligations of role and obligations of exchange, related respectively to kin and non-kin relations. The penultimate part of the chapter explores the basis of non-kin friendship in rural China in the affective bonding of 感情 *ganqing*. The final section shows that the concept of instrumental self-interest, which underlies *guanxi* practices, cannot be located in *chaxugeju*. It also shows that the notion of 面子 *mianzi*, face, absent from Fei's account, provides a viable basis for an explanation of self-interested behaviour in *guanxi*.

Chinese Rural Society

In *From the Soil* Fei presents what he sees as the archetypical character of Chinese society, in both its own terms and compared with the general form of Western societies which he characterizes as *tuantigeju*, the 'organizational mode of association' (Fei 1992: 62–3). In this manner Fei contrasts what he regards as the foundations of Chinese society not only with a fundamentally different societal type but also with his understanding of a possible future for China, namely an impending modernity located not only in commerce without feelings (无情 *wuqing*) but also in motives based on cognition and knowledge rather than on ritual and custom (人情 *renqing*) (Fei 1992: 126–7, 138–40). The underlying point is that 'Chinese society is fundamentally rural', says Fei (1992: 1), and the 'basic unit of Chinese rural society is the village' (Fei 1992: 41). These simple statements are effectively Fei's response to fifty years of debate in China concerning the relevance and meaning of the notion 社会 *shehui*, society, a term introduced into China in 1898 from Japan, like so many other notions that transformed perceptions and engagements in China from the end of the nineteenth century. Fei's contrast of Chinese and Western forms of society is not in itself novel, as the newly arrived term, *shehui*, carried both an ancient Chinese meaning—which included 'gathering of village people'—and a new concept of the social, encapsulated in what Japan had learned from the West (Tian 2014: 48). Indeed, the notion of society as it was discussed during the late Qing and throughout the Republican period remained contested and served to provoke questions such as 'what constituted the essence of Chinese society…what groups could rightly see themselves as the core of Chinese society, both in the present and in the future?' (Sachsenmaier 2014: 61). In many ways Fei's answer to these questions constitutes a commitment to one element in the maelstrom of the intellectual and political currents of his day, but without explicitly declaring his allegiance.

Fei does not refer to the historical background mentioned above. The contrast he draws between Chinese relationalism and the individual-focused social system of the West owes an unacknowledged intellectual debt to the neo-Confucian rural reformer Liang Shuming (Arkush 1981: 150; Gransow 2001: 268; Lu and Zhao 2009: 55). Liang's ideas were first outlined in a book published in 1921, 东西文化及其哲学 *Dongxi wenhua jiqi zhexue, Eastern and Western Civilizations and their Philosophies*, a work described as the 'first to defend Confucianism and the Chinese tradition theoretically and systematically' (Chow 1960: 330). The relations both Liang and Fei believe to constitute the basis of Chinese society are those of family filiality within the framework of Confucian principles. While Liang's discussion is not mentioned in *From the Soil*, even though the comparative elements of their respective arguments are very similar, Fei (1992: 65) does acknowledge a debt to the approach to 论 *lun*, cardinal relations, developed by Pan Guangdan. Fei was taught sociology by Pan at Tsinghua University in the early 1930s and they remained lifelong friends. In addition to a common appreciation of Confucianism shared by Fei, Liang, and Pan (2015), Fei shared close political ties with both Liang and Pan through their common involvement in the Democratic League (Arkush 1981: 183; Gransow 2001: 278 n. 6). The projection of the image of family filiality in terms of Confucian principles as an enduring basis of Chinese culture emerges from a particular historical context that has to be understood in order to appreciate the limitations of the approach taken by Liang and repeated by Fei.

The cultural fabric of Chinese imperial society over many dynasties could be regarded as non-exclusive and polycentric, comprising intellectual and ritual spaces in which Confucian, Daoist, Buddhist, and local cults coexisted and on occasion and in various ways engaged in mutual borrowing. The changes that are relevant to understand the orientation of Liang and the elevation of Confucianism to a Chinese cultural 'essence' in part arises with the defeat of China in the Opium Wars of the mid-nineteenth century. It is from this time, in attempting to defend itself from Western incursion, that the Qing court, Confucian literati, and reformist intellectuals became engaged in a struggle that led to the identification of Chinese culture with Confucianism in both positive and negative terms. During 1898 the court-led 'Hundred Days' Reforms introduced two concepts borrowed from Japan into Chinese consciousness that had not previously existed in these forms, namely 宗教 *zongjiao*, religion, and 迷信 *mixin*, superstition. On this basis the Confucian literati came to regard Daoist, Buddhist, and local cult doctrines and practices as mere superstitions, providing a pretext for sacking their temples and confiscating their properties in order to fund a new national education based on Confucianism as a civic faith expressing what they regarded as the Chinese national essence (Barbalet 2017a: 65–70; Goossaert 2006; Kuo 2008).

A paradoxical elevation of Confucianism continued in the subsequent New Culture Movement of the early twentieth century in which reformers regarded China's ills and its weakness as an inevitable consequence of the conservatism of literati Confucianism (Chow 1960: 327–32). Both the defenders of tradition and their critics thus came to agree that Confucianism was the effective representative of China's cultural heritage. In reaction to what he regarded as the excesses of the New Culture Movement Liang, as we have seen, contrasted Confucian China with the Christian West in order to defend aspects of the former. The partial and reified view of Chinese culture that emerged in these strained debates and defensive posturing had an additional sustaining basis in that it satisfied the interests of the rural gentry, who relied on family and kin networks, taken by them as emblematic of Confucianism, to safeguard their privileges, an assessment that Fei (1946) in fact shares.

The background to Fei's apprehension of the Confucian character of Chinese society is dispensed with when, in a simplifying move, he points to the distinction between *Gemeinschaft* and *Gesellschaft* drawn by the late nineteenth-century German sociologist Ferdinand Tönnies. These terms are generally understood to distinguish 'community' and 'association', although the designation of them as 'rural' and 'urban' is also acceptable. Fei's identification of China as a 'rural society' (Fei 1992: 41) cites Tönnies, but it is likely that he in fact borrowed the term from the American anthropologist

Robert Redfield, who developed the rural–urban conceptual distinction during the 1930s. Redfield and Fei knew each other from the mid-1940s, and Redfield spent a year in China during 1947–8; they remained in contact until the end of the decade. There is a problem for Fei, however, in conceiving of traditional China as a 'rural society'. In acknowledging the 'egocentrism' (Fei 1992: 67) of Chinese family and village life, Fei (1992: 66) notes that a 'path runs from the self to the family, from the family to the state', thus effectively avoiding any reference to 'society' if not eliminating it. This latter idea is explicit in a parallel late Republican source: 'the word "society" does not exist as an idea in Chinese thought' as the Chinese 'are family-minded, not social minded' (Lin 1939: 172). Lin Yutang, whose book represents an endeavour to introduce China to an English-reading audience, goes on to say that these dispositions correspond to elements of Confucian philosophy in which there is 'direct transition from the family, *chia* [家 *jia*], to the state, *kuo* [国 *guo*]...[so that the] nearest equivalent to the notion of society is...*kuochia* [国家 *guojia*], or "state-family"' (Lin 1939: 172).

The Confucian classic 大学 *Daxue*, *The Great Learning*, to which Fei and Lin each allude, recounts that personal self-cultivation leads to the regulation of families which in turn leads to states being rightly governed (Legge 2001b: 358–9). The political nature of Confucian philosophy is not only in its focus on the regulatory force of kin relations but more generally in its concern with the 'rectification of names', the maintenance of a strict correspondence between office or rank and conduct, an absence of which would threaten state security and possibly risk the very collapse of the state. The necessity of adhering to familial roles, in this schema, functions in terms of a normative political framework that does not require an underlying social analysis. If adherence to these enforceable norms is pervasive then the requisite corresponding behaviour would simply emerge, as Fei (1992: 65–6) appreciates. This is not a sociological account but its obverse. Fei (1992: 71) does say, however, that different 'patterns of social organization give rise to different types of morality' and explains Chinese or Confucian ethics in terms of the 'differential mode of association' (Fei 1992: 78). The difficulty, though, is that the differential mode of association is itself explained by Fei (1992: 65–6) in terms of the precepts of 礼记 *Liji*, the Confucian *Book of Rites*, and, in particular, the 'order based on classifications' that is generative of the 'hierarchical differentiations [on which] traditional Chinese social structure rests' (Fei 1992: 66).

From the first chapter of *From the Soil* Fei draws on Confucius's 论语 *Lunyu*, *Analects*. This text and related sources are deployed by Fei in describing and explaining relationships, norms and practices. In the core chapters 4 and 5 of *From the Soil*, namely, '*Chaxugeju*: The Differential Mode of Association' and 'The Morality of Personal Relationships', Chinese classical sources (the Four Books of the Confucian canon, the *Analects*, *The Great Learning*, 中庸 *Zhongyong* or *The Doctrine of the Mean*, and 孟子 or the *Mencius*) are the exclusive basis of discussion. Indeed, it is probable that the Confucian complexion of *From the Soil* was primarily responsible for its popularity in Hong Kong and Taiwan, where it has been republished many times. Fei's extensive reliance on Confucius in explaining Chinese society, not only in *From the Soil* but also in the contemporary *China's Gentry*, drew the comment that it left Fei 'open to criticism' (Redfield 1953: 14–15). Indeed, Fei's Confucianism placed him in an ambiguous position relative to the major social scientific currents of the period in China, in which the legacy of the anti-Confucian New Culture Movement remained significant in construct- ing sociology as an instrument of China's modernization (Chiang 2001). At the same time, the Christian missionary origins of sociology in China led from the 1930s to a reactive interest in the Sinification of Chinese sociology (Wong 1979: 19–36) which for Fei took the form of an appropriation of Confucian concepts.

Fei was in fact involved in both currents of Chinese sociological development, the scientific and, for want of a better term, the nativistic. With regard to the latter, Fei's advocacy in his later years of 'cultural self-awareness' in sociology (Chen 2018: 123–4) is arguably continuous with his endeavours to indigenize Chinese sociology through Confucian tropes during the period stretching from the Japanese war of the late 1930s through to the Civil War in the 1940s, especially in his newspaper writings that formed the basis of both *From the Soil* and *China's Gentry*. He wrote in 1947 that sociologists should 'not devote themselves to the systematic introduction of Western theories... [nor] simply enumerate the facts of Chinese society; but rather... use the scientific method, transmitted from the West, and *pre-existing social theories* to observe and analyze actual social life in China' (quoted in Cheng and So 1983: 476; emphasis added). Needless to say, the 'pre-existing social theories' are those of the classical canon and while Fei's use of Confucian texts and terminology is explicit in works of this late Republican period, and acknowledged in recent discussion of Confucian philosophy, in which Fei is recognized for his exposition of Confucian concepts and modes of analysis (Ames and Rosemont 2014), there is a curious shyness in the sociological literature about the traditionalist foundations of Fei's understanding of rural China. Yet without explicit awareness of the Confucian basis of Fei's theoriz- ing in *From the Soil* its argument, and especially its idealization of family and kinship, cannot be properly understood.

Chaxugeju

Chinese rural society is schematically depicted by Fei (1992: 80) through a neologism, *chaxugeju*, 'in order to conceptualize clearly [a] context… currently absent from sociological terminology'. It refers to a 'pattern of oscillating but differential social circles' (Fei 1992: 69). *Chaxugeju* is made up of four characters, 差 *cha*, meaning difference and indicating horizontal differentiation; 序 *xu*, meaning order as in rank order or moral order and therefore implying vertical differentiation; and 格局 *geju*, meaning structure or framework, such that horizontal and vertical dimensions operate within a common formation. This is not an ideal-type concept in a Weberian sense, as some have claimed (Hamilton 2015: 110, 113; Gransow 2001: 267; Yan 2015: 40, 41, 50–1) and which Fei himself came to accept (see Hamilton 2015: 113–14). The concept of ideal-type derives from a neo-Kantian sense of cultural knowledge (Weber 1949: 106; see Barker 1980), not entertained by Fei, and constructs the point of view of the researcher rather than directly depicting empirical evidence as it is 'formed by the one-sided accentuation of one or more points of view and by the synthesis of a great many diffuse, discrete, more or less present and occasionally absent concrete individual phenomena' (Weber 1949: 90; see Eliaeson 2002: 46–56; Parkin 2002: 28–35). *Chaxugeju*, on the other hand, is an abstraction of familial relationships broad enough to encompass the extensions of kinship found in rural China.

In order to understand *chaxugeju* as an abstract summary of family relations in rural China Fei's (1992: 81–5) distinction between two senses of the term 'family' is signal; family may refer to the unit of procreation, consisting of parents and their children, or it may refer to what he calls a lineage. The family in this latter sense comprises not only the horizontal conjugal relationship between two adults of the same generation together with their offspring but vertical consanguine or intergenerational relationships which incorporate and are served by the conjugal relations of sexual reproduction. The family as a lineage is thus not limited to the function of procreation but has additional functions—political, economic, and religious—and therefore, depending on which of these is dominant and on how it performs them, has an enduring quality and structural flexibility that the merely conjugal family lacks (Fei 1992: 84). It goes without saying that the possible relationships that are available to an individual in a lineage family are much greater and more variable than those of a conjugal family. It follows, then, that the 'pattern' underlying Chinese rural society 'is composed of distinctive networks spreading out from each individual's personal connections' (Fei 1992: 71).

In *From the Soil* Fei makes much of his conceptualization of 'family' and 'lineage'. Fei (1992: 81) reports that he wishes to revise the terminology he employed in his earlier study, *Peasant Life in China*. In this work, under the influence of Malinowski's functionalist anthropology, Fei (1939: 27) defines the family as 'the procreative unit consisting of parents and immature children', but he goes on to note that the Chinese family may include 'children even when they have grown and married' and may also include 'relatively remote patrilineal kinsmen'; the Chinese family is thus an 'expanded family'. On this basis the difference between Chinese and Western families is one of size; but this is not sufficient because, as Fei (1992: 82–3) came to appreciate, Chinese and Western families can be distinguished more significantly in terms of differences of structure and function. Whereas 'Western families have strict boundaries...[and thus are] able to manage few things beyond raising children' (Fei 1992: 82), Chinese rural families have no strict organizational boundaries and can incorporate 'ever more distinct categories of relatives' on the basis of patrilineal affinity; in this sense, then, 'Chinese families are lineages' (Fei 1992: 83).

This distinction between the conjugal family of sexual and limited social reproduction and the consanguineous lineage serving political, economic, religious, and other functions is familiar in nineteenth-century Western social science (Durkheim 1972: 185; Maine 1905: 117–18) as well as in the early discussion of the Chinese system:

> Kinship ties necessarily begin within the family as a procreational unit. These primary ties... are biologically the same in all societies though functionally they may differ from culture to culture. But kinship ties do not rest within the reproductive family. They are extended to a much wider circle of individuals who are actually or reputedly related to those of the procreational family. In this process of extension certain groups of related individuals are emphasized and certain others minimized, although their degree of relationship may be exactly the same... The character of the kin groups emphasized likewise reflects the wider ranges of the social structure of which the kinship system is part. In the Chinese kinship system, relatives in the male line receive emphasis; the formalized basis of which is the exogamous patrilineal sib [lineage].   (Feng 1937: 173)

Relevant for the discussion here is Fei's idealization of the consanguine or lineage form of the Chinese rural family in conformity with Confucian formulations. Fei (1992: 84) holds that:

> The Chinese family is a medium through which all activities are organized. The size of the family depends on the extent of the activity being organized. If an

activity is small enough for husband and wife to handle, the family can be as small as a single household; but if the enterprise goes beyond what the couple can manage, then brothers and uncles may join in to form what now becomes a large family. In Chinese rural society, therefore, the size of the family varies a great deal. But no matter how much the size may vary, the structural principle, the patrilineal pattern of differential relationships, always remains the same.

The idea in this statement, that family size varies in terms of the activities undertaken and that lineage relationships are cooperative and mutually supportive, invites examination.

Lineage

The idealization of lineage, as a multigenerational and multifunction social formation, is not in the proposition that ethical norms govern relations between members (Fei 1992: 73–5); rather, it is in the disregard of the role of property in lineage and of the privilege, based on inequalities of wealth and power, it generates (see Baker 1979: 49–70; Stover 1974). Fei does, of course, acknowledge the centrality of land in rural China; but in doing so he refers more to attachment to the land as soil rather than to the role of land as property (Fei 1992: 38–40). Indeed, his treatment of land is in a rather different register than that of an earlier sociological account of Chinese lineage which recognized that Chinese familism is based on both blood and land, that membership and obligation in the sib or lineage are linked with land as an economic resource (Kulp 1925: 138). Again, Fei (1992: 124) observes that 'rights over the land are protected by lineages' but he creates an impression of rural egalitarianism in which 'everyone earns his or her own living from the land' (Fei 1992: 71). The claim here is not that Fei was ignorant of landlordism, inequalities of wealth and power, and exploitation (see Fei 1992: 64), but that in *From the Soil* he suspends reference to these things in his exposition of Chinese lineage and its supposed Confucian foundations. He is able to do this in part because he regards absentee landlords in terms of an opposition between village and town, between rural and commercial life (see also Fei 1939: 181–91; Fei and Chang 1948: 219–35), ignoring the fact that the residency of landlords in towns was a consequence of their economic role, not its cause (Elvin 1996: 8–13).

While membership of a lineage did provide protection of various sorts to even poorer members in their relations with other lineages and to state power, within any given lineage a poor member experienced both subordination and exploitation at the hands of powerful and rich members (Freedman 1979: 339–40). Because of the corporate nature of ownership in lineages of economic resources, especially land, the fortunes of poor members were in many ways subject to the decisions of lineage leaders who could redistribute lineage resources to disadvantaged members or instead deploy those resources for investment (Gates 1996: 113). In situations in which the obligations of lineage welfare were deemed burdensome, a lineage could simply 'displace the weaker and poorer lines from its midst' (Faure 1986: 64). Fei (1992: 122), on the other hand, regards lineage segmentation as a consequence of ecological factors of population growth and land productivity. A contemporary source notes that members of the same family or lineage may not provide mutual support to each other, that there may be 'little solidarity' within families, and that the self-interested behaviour of a 'few powerful and self-fattening families in the clans…add causes for much intra-clan hatred' (Hsu 1948: 129–30). By 'clan' Hsu (1948: 122) means 'a unilateral descent group', which is what Fei (1992: 83) refers to as 'lineage'.

The Confucian ideal, summarized in the folk saying 'five generations under the same roof' (Fei 1992: 83) was seldom realized, attained at any one time in no more than 7 per cent of Chinese families (Eastman 1988: 16). Indeed, the conjugal family form, at most two generations consisting of two parents and their unmarried children typically comprising between three and six persons, was the norm in late Republican China and probably in earlier times as well (Hsu 1943: 555; Freedman 1979: 235). It is estimated that approximately 60 per cent of families were of this type (Eastman 1988: 16). The prevalence of the conjugal family form in China's villages at this time derived from economic necessity, resulting from the incapacity of family estates to support all of their members. Indeed, in an earlier study Fei (1939: 192) reports that approximately 90 per cent of the population in a village in the Yangtze Valley owned less than ten 亩 *mu* or one and a half acres, insufficient to support a family. In his slightly later study of a Yunnan village Fei found that 'a minority of the population holds most of the land, and the majority is landless or has insufficient land for its support' (Fei and Chang 1948: 54). In each case tenancy and wage labour were required to support the majority of families.

Given the prevalence of the conjugal form of family structure it is not out of place to consider relations between husband and wife. In his account of spousal relations, Fei (1992: 85–6) indicates that there is psychological 'separation' and 'obvious indifference between husbands and wives' that operates in both 'wealthy' and 'rural village' families. But there are relevant structural differences between rich and poor families that this account ignores. The traditional Chinese household had a membership not confined to kin and spouses; it could also include non-kin members who provided labour of various kinds, including concubines. Concubines were ostensibly purchased to provide a family with an heir. The sons of concubines were legitimate as the concubine's consort's wife was their 'official' mother; but unlike wives, concubines had no ritual relationship with their consort's ancestors. Possession of a concubine primarily symbolized the consort's social status (Watson 2004: 176–7). At the same time, in reducing a man's interest in his wife, possession of a concubine effectively supported the axis of consanguine relations against the conjugal: a man who finds 'other pleasures than his interest in his formal wife...is much less likely to side with [her] against his mother' (Hsu 1943: 561).

The situation in poor families was different than in wealthy families, leading to different concerns and behaviour. A wealthy family had no difficulty securing and replacing wives for its sons. This was not true for poor families. The loss of a wife and daughter-in-law was much more greatly felt in a poor family than in a wealthy family, and especially for a husband; in these circumstances 'It is therefore in the interest especially of the husband that he should side with his wife' (Hsu 1943: 561). Additionally, in rich families 'married brothers...[stood] together, refusing to listen to their wives' complaints...because they were posed against their father...whose power rested on the economic resources he controlled' (Freedman 1979: 246). In wealthy families, then, consanguinity encouraged father–son relationships with corresponding heightened interest in sibling relations and a reduction of a husband's interest in his spouse. In poor families, on the other hand, the 'father's control was weak and the brothers highly individualized among themselves [with each] brother [standing] close to his wife' (Freedman 1979: 246). These patterns do not necessarily produce greater affection between spouses in poor families than in rich, but while family relationships generated indifference between rich husbands and their wives, in poor families there was increased reliance of a husband on his wife.

As the various roles or positions within an intergenerational family or lineage have attached to them particular expectations, so a corresponding set of norms can be identified which in Confucian philosophy are understood as governing ethical principles. It is in this sense that Fei (1992: 78) says that each 'knot' in the 'webs woven out of countless personal relationships' within a lineage has attached to it 'a specific ethical principle', so that while personal relationships form out of individual 'social influence' (Fei 1992: 63) that influence is not unprincipled. Fei (1992: 66–7) follows Confucius in holding that one's ethical development leads to extensions in one's human relationships, with a 'basic path' through 'relations between parents and children and among siblings' drawing upon the 'ethical values' of 'filial piety and fraternal duty', with an 'additional route out from the self...through friends', governed by ethics of 'loyalty ([忠] *zhong*) and sincerity [or trust] ([信] *xin*)' (Fei 1992: 74). While friendship is mentioned here Fei holds that family and kinship are dominant in Chinese rural society. It is appropriate therefore to consider his statements regarding friendship.

In addition to this reference Fei mentions friendship in *From the Soil* in the context of it being one of the 五伦 *wu lu*, five relations, of the Confucian classic *Doctrine of the Mean* (Fei 1992: 66–7, 76). He also mentions friendship in terms of its particular Chinese as opposed to Western character, including its significance in same-sex relationships (Fei 1992: 65, 92, 124). Fei's most theoretically interesting reference to friendship is in an acknowledgement that cooperative credit associations 'included friends with whom members had no kinship relations' (Fei 1992: 125). This is explained in terms of two factors: first, lineage members are obliged 'to take care of each other's needs', so that cooperative credit associations are unnecessary between kin. Fei (1992: 125) notes such provision of care is in reality 'fairly rare', however, and that, although 'relatives are concerned with each other', that concern 'goes only so deep'. Second, family *renqing* prevents defaulting relatives being forced to repay loans and, on this basis, cooperative credit associations between kin cannot properly function (Fei 1992: 125). The significance of friendship and the limitations of kin relations mentioned here are not explored further in *From the Soil* (but see Fei 1939: 267, 269; Fei and Chang 1948: 121), except insofar as it is noted that it is necessary that the 'intimacy' of kinship 'does not turn into resentment [and therefore that] too many favors, too much *renqing*, should be avoided' (Fei 1992: 125). The suggestion here, that friendship may be a safety-valve against burdensome kin relations, is not developed. These brief remarks do show, though, why the disadvantage of poor lineage members, mentioned above, is unassailable within the relations of kinship themselves, though Fei fails to address this issue as well.

This account of friendship returns us to Fei's (1992: 63) insistence in *From the Soil* that kinship 'is the most important relationship' in Chinese society, that 'the basic path' along which personal relationships are extended 'is through kinship' (Fei 1992: 74), and that 'the most basic group in Chinese rural society [is] the family (*jia*)' (Fei 1992: 81). According to Fei (1992: 84) 'Chinese rural society took on a differential mode of association when kinship was successfully used as a medium to create social groups and to manage all kinds of activities'. Indeed, an elaboration of this last point adumbrates the concept of *chaxugeju*, suggesting that *chaxugeju* refers only to family or kin relationships (Feuchtwang 2015: 132–5; Hamilton and Wang 1992: 31). As we have seen, the notion of *chaxugeju* is represented as figuratively 'similar to the concentric circles formed when a stone is thrown into a lake' and stands for Chinese social structure in general because it portrays the 'most important relationship' in particular, namely 'kinship' (Fei 1992: 63). The waves or circles of these relationships become weaker as they extend from the centre; ego's tie with kin similarly weakens through dispersal as kinship forms become more tenuous, moving from the strong bond of the parent–child relation in the centre to the much weaker connections in the outer ripples of clan, composed of same-surname lineages (Fei 1992: 82–3). Two issues can be noticed in this discussion; first the overarching significance of the family or kin and therefore its variable form, and secondly the idea that there are different ethical principles distinguishing its core and periphery. The first issue will be discussed in the section to follow and the second in the section following the next. Before proceeding to these matters there is another requiring consideration here, namely the originality of the concept of *chaxugeju* if not its name.

Western scholars have typically held that there is no place in Chinese society for the individual, that China has a 'collectivist' culture, an assessment that has not gone unchallenged (Barbalet 2013; Herrmann-Pillath 2016). Fei's account of the 'egocentric' dimension of Chinese society draws upon Confucian appreciations of the moral significance of the self and self-cultivation. Indeed, underlying Confucian morality is an emphasis on the uniqueness of each person in the performance of the roles he or she occupies; an understanding of the basis of the person in sharp contrast with the notion, associated with 'Western' ethics, namely that one's individuality derives from one's autonomy from prescribed positions in relationships (Ames 2011: 87–157; Rosemont 1991). This is essentially the difference referred to by Fei (1992: 65–6) when he says that egocentric selves operate in a system of qualitatively different categories, classifications, or roles, whereas individualistic or Western selves operate in formal organizations that are characterized by equivalence, equality, and therefore constitutionality. The discerning appreciation of Chinese selfhood outlined by Fei is a restatement of the Confucian contextualization of relations between individuals.

In an article first published in 1949 the philosopher Feng Youlan (Fung Yu-lan) wrote that in traditional Chinese philosophy 'the emphasis is upon the individual...[insofar as it] is the individual who is a father or a son, a husband or a wife' (Fung 1998a: 634). Persons exists as individuals in this sense through their role compliance and performance. It is therefore 'quite wrong', Fung (1998a: 636) holds, 'that there was no place for the personality of the individual' in traditional Chinese society. Indeed, Feng adds a further dimension to his recognition of the significance of the individual self in traditional Chinese society when he says that, according to *Liji*, the Confucian *Book of Rites*, 'every individual is the center of a social circle which is constituted of various social relationships' (Fung 1998a: 635). These relationships radiate in both vertical and horizontal directions, according to Feng, and '[w]ithin the radius there are different degrees of greater and lesser affections and responsibilities' (Fung 1998a: 635). Here is a complete description of the concept of *chaxugeju*, but without the name.

A Village-Centric View

Fei's idealizátion of lineage in *From the Soil*, and his idea that kinship dominates Chinese rural social life to the exclusion of practically all else, is reinforced by his claim that 'the basic unit of Chinese rural society is the village' (Fei 1992: 41). He goes on to say: 'Villagers restrict the scope of their daily activities; they do not travel far; they seldom make contact with the outside world; they live solitary lives; they maintain their own isolated circle' (Fei 1992: 41). Traditionally, then, 'every family regards its own household as the center and draws a circle around it... [which] facilitate[s] reciprocation in daily life' (Fei 1992: 64) so that, in this sense, according to Fei, the rural family is more or less self-sustaining: the 'Chinese family is a medium through which *all* activities are organized' (Fei 1992: 84, emphasis added; see also Fei 1946: 2). On this basis 'kinship' is coterminous with 'spatial relationships', in rural society kinship and spatial relationships are subject to the 'same pattern of organization' (Fei 1992: 63) because 'where the population is static, lineage groups actually imply a geographical location' and thus 'native place' is inherited in the same manner as 'a family name... [or] blood relationship... [so that] native place is only the projection of consanguinity into space' (Fei 1992: 122). Thus, family and lineage denote spatial limitation and the village is circumscribed by and confined to the family and lineage relationships interior to it.

Fei does not ignore the space beyond the village. This space, though, is necessarily not only one in which non-kin relations predominate but in which those relations are only commercial. There seems to be nothing between lineage and commerce so that, while friendship is mentioned in passing in *From the Soil*, the possibility of relations that are both non-kin and non-commercial seems not to be available for the villager Fei describes and if such relations did form, they would not be explicable in the terms he employs. Regarding the mutual exclusiveness of family and commerce Fei (1992: 126) says that 'Commerce cannot exist in an intimate consanguineous society' because here 'people exchange with *renqing*' whereas commercial exchanges are settled on the spot '"without human feelings" (*wuqing*)'. In this sense, according to Fei, markets operate in contradistinction to rural society and to the family relations that constitute it. The relevance of *renqing* in exchange will be taken up later.

It has been mentioned that Fei (1992: 84) holds that the 'Chinese family is a medium through which all activities are organized'. While it is true that the traditional Chinese peasant household produced, either directly or indirectly, much of what it consumed, it is not true that the rural family was able itself to satisfy all of its needs. In his previous empirical investigations Fei (1939: 129, 141, 240–62; Fei and Chang 1948: 47–8, 170–2) demonstrated that, while rural 'self-sufficiency was highly developed…it was not complete', because external trade was necessary to provide 'some of the necessities of life of the villagers' (Fei 1953: 100). Not only does Fei (1953: 101, 103–4) acknowledge the integration of village economies with temporary markets and market towns, he also indicates that rural industry or handicrafts were an essential part of China's agrarian economy, providing a necessary element of farm income and therefore a reliance on regional markets (Fei 1953: 114–15), discussed extensively in *Peasant Life in China* (1939). Indeed, the situation described here in which the reliance of village economies on regional markets was a characteristic feature of Chinese society has a long history, going back at least to the eleventh century (Elvin 1973). This situation was noted to apply during the Republican period by an astute foreign observer, drawing upon contemporary studies, who said that 'Chinese villages are not self-sufficient units, though some larger areas are' (Tawney 1932: 54). Tawney goes on to say that: 'rather more than a quarter of the goods consumed by agricultural families are purchased [such that] farming is carried on for the market, rather than subsistence, to a greater degree than is sometimes suggested' (Tawney 1932: 54). Indeed, *From the Soil* provides an incomplete representation of Chinese rural society, not because Fei underestimates the significance of what Stephen Feuchtwang (2015: 135) calls the 'territorial neighborhood' but because the market spaces were not simply arenas of commercial exchanges for villagers but also spaces in which non-kin social relationships occurred.

The significance to peasant households of the social space beyond their village, that is, in marketplaces, is demonstrated in fieldwork in Sichuan in the late 1940s. In his report of this research, William Skinner (1964: 32) shows that 'anthropological work on Chinese society, by focusing attention almost exclusively on the village, has with few exceptions distorted the reality of rural social structure'. This is a limitation for which Fei has been frequently criticized (Chun 2012: 264; Freedman 1979: 389–90; Wang 2012: 180), and which was discussed by contemporary sources (Cheng 1939; Lee 1949). Skinner (1964: 32) writes that:

> Insofar as the Chinese peasant can be said to live in a self-contained world, that world is not the village but the standard marketing community. The effective social field of the peasant...is delimited not by the narrow horizons of his village but rather by the boundaries of his standard marketing area.

Skinner (1964: 33) shows that in the modal case marketing areas occupy just over fifty square kilometres and that in this space are a variety of settlement types, including market towns that are less than eight kilometres apart, and that the maximum walking distance to such towns for any villager is approximately four and a half kilometres. He goes on to say that the mean population of the standard marketing community 'is somewhat over 7,000 [persons]' so that in 'the case of the typical [market] community—1,500 households in eighteen or so villages distributed over fifty square kilometres—we are not dealing with a cozy primary group structured through bonds of great intimacy or intensity' (Skinner 1964: 33).

The social knowledge and acquaintance of Chinese villagers, according to Skinner (1964: 35), extends well beyond the circles of family and kinship:

> The peasant in Kao-tien-tzu's marketing community had, by the age of fifty, attended his standard market more than three thousand times. He had, at least one thousand times on the average, been jammed into a small area along one street with the same male representative of every other household in that community. He made purchases from peasant vendors whose homes lay in all directions from the town, and more to the point, he socialized in the teahouses with fellow peasants from village communities far removed from his own. Nor was the peasant alone in this, for in Kao-tien-tzu there was a teahouse for everyone, and few persons who went to market failed to spend at least an hour in one or two. Codes of hospitality and sociability operated to bring any community member who entered the door quickly to a table as somebody's guest. Inevitably an hour in the teahouse enlarged a man's circle of acquaintances and deepened his social knowledge of other parts of the community.

Skinner (1964: 36) goes on to say that services required by households, including those of midwife, tailor, rotating-credit society, or hired worker, 'will be sought for the most part from [other] households within the [standard marketing community], thereby building up a modest network of patron-client relationships all contained within [it]'. In addition, this 'community' provided access to membership of secret societies, prevalent during the Republican period, and a variety of voluntary associations, including those linked with town temples as well as organized recreation (Skinner 1964: 37–9). It is of interest that in *Peasant Life in China* Fei provides a practically identical description of villagers' social dependence on the market town: 'Men will use [periodic intervals in agricultural work] to enjoy themselves in teashops. Teashops are in the town. They bring together people from different villages. Business bargainings, marital negotiations and arbitration of disputes take place [there]' (Fei 1939: 129, see also 141). In *From the Soil*, however, the supposed antipathy of village and market as kin and commerce reinforces the Confucian gloss on lineage.

From the perspective of extra-village neighbourhoods or marketing communities, there is much more than family and kin in the social relationships and social circles of Chinese rural society. It is of interest that Fei (1992: 124) implicitly and unwittingly acknowledges this fact but in a confusing manner when he notes that the 'unity of the intimate [kinship] group *depends on the fact* that each member owes countless favors to the other members' (emphasis added). This is a curious claim given that family and kinship intimacy, as Fei (1992: 74) indicates elsewhere, is based on obligations of role structured by normative constraints, especially filial piety and fraternal duty. Within these relationships are interactions of various kinds, including mutual support, possibly provided in the form of favours and gifts, described by participants as *renqing*, about which more will be said later. While these latter are no doubt routine within the framework of kinship ties, such favours cannot be the basis of these bonds, as Fei claims. This is to confuse context and what might occur within it.

Obligations of Role and Exchange

The notion that the 'unity of the intimate group depends on the fact that each member owes countless favors to the other members' Fei (1992: 124) says is 'so obvious to us that we take it for granted'. Such 'continuing reciprocation maintains the cooperation among people in the group' and if accounts were to be settled then the relationship would cease 'because if people do not owe something to each other, there will be no need for further contact' (Fei 1992: 125). This part of Fei's account has been understood to clearly suggest that *chaxugeju* is an analogue of *guanxi*, as it is widely and correctly appreciated that *guanxi* is formed on the basis of favour exchange. But it is precisely this part of Fei's account that deserves the most critical attention. In his discussion Fei (1992: 124) associates favour exchange with *renqing* and in doing so inextricably links kinship ties with exchange obligations. But to proceed in this manner is to conflate two quite distinct principles of obligation which the notion of *renqing* masks, partly because *renqing* is a multifaceted concept that if treated as referring to a unitary phenomenon covers and hides diverse practices.

Familial obligations are the obligations of roles, roles which define the kinship links and assign social resources and expectations to them; as Fei (1992: 127) says: 'Blood ties provide the foundation for status in Chinese society'. The obligations that arise from exchange of favours between persons, on the other hand, are of an entirely different order based on non-binding expectations of a returned provision that may be ignored, avoided or subverted (Bourdieu 1992: 89–101; Hwang 1987: 963–7; King 1991: 75–9; Komter 2007). The distinction between role obligation and exchange obligation is fundamental (Barbalet 2020). Its character is clear in the distinction Coleman (1990: 427–8) draws between a 'social structure of positions in relation' and a 'social structure of relations among persons'; in the first of these, persons 'take on the obligations and expectations . . . associated with their positions', whereas in the second the obligations arise out of mutually beneficial transactions that exist in exchanges as 'self-contained pairwise relations'.

The association of favour exchange and kinship obligation, in the Chinese context, is frequently explicated in terms of *renqing* (Fei 1992: 124, 126). In one sense *renqing* is the feeling underlying the obligations inherent in 'natural' human relations, especially those of family life, based on principles of seniority and gender (Hwang 1987: 953; Yang 1994: 67). More broadly, though, it refers to feelings connected with appropriate behaviour, such as showing respect for others, providing sympathy where it is due, acknowledging a favour, repaying a debt, and so on. These latter can be described as giving *renqing* and the actual gifts given in such circumstances can also be called *renqing* (Hwang 1987: 953–4; Yang 1994: 67–70). In this sense, then, there is no necessary association of *renqing* with kinship, as when 'friends vie with each other to pay bills, each hoping to let the others "owe them one" (*renqing*)' (Fei 1992: 124). In discussing exchange between kin Fei uses the term in the latter sense but draws on the connotation of the former. In this way, through the elasticity of the term *renqing*, the concentric circles of obligation in rural Chinese society, including kinship and, at the outer circles, what might be described as friendship (Fung 1998a: 635; Ames 2011: 114–18), are brought within a single framework. Such usage hides the fact that the relations in question are subject to quite different bases or principles, even though they may share elements of affective connection, typically characterized respectively as 亲情 *qinqing* (family feeling) and *ganqing*, which may refer to feelings arising from favour exchanges between non-kin.

Many writers bridge kin and non-kin relations in Chinese society by invoking the notion of 'fictive kinship' (Baker 1979: 162–7) or 'pseudo-family' (Lin 2001: 154–5), a matter that will be examined more fully in Chapter 6. While Fei (1992) does not explicitly engage the notion of fictive kinship, his account of *chaxugeju* facilitates such a manoeuvre and possibly encourages it. Such conflation of roles through the notion of fictive kin is typically justified in terms of the overarching dominance of family and its kinship extensions in Chinese society, and in doing so not only is Fei's work drawn on but also contemporary sources, including Liang (1949) and Morton Fried (1953), among others (Bian 2019: 13). This and similar readings of Fried (1953) implicitly testify to the dominance of Fei's analysis and his model of *chaxugeju* as a conceptualization of hegemonic familism (see also Feuchtwang 2015: 139), through which other accounts, including Fried's, are read or rather, in this particular instance, misread.

Contrary to the assessment just indicated Fried (1953) provides an entirely alternative view to that presented by Liang (1949), Hsu (1948), and especially Fei (1939; 1946; Fei and Chang 1948), as noted by contemporary reviewers (Hsu 1954; Redfield 1954). While Fried's study does not depreciate the significance of kinship in Chinese society, it does show that the structure of relations in this society are not exhausted by kinship and that other forms of relationships, summarized in large part as non-kin friendship, operate alongside kinship. Friendship, Fried (1953: 67) says, 'at times...serves as a complement to pre-existing kinship rights and obligations [though] it often challenges kinship for prior loyalty...[when it] furnishes avenues by which familial pressures may be avoided and introduces elements which are potentially subversive of familial unity' (see also Fried 1953: 218, 230). Fried highlights, therefore, that a comprehensive and meaningful understanding of Chinese society, both rural and urban, needs to give due regard to non-kin relationships in their own right. Second, he identifies an independent basis of non-kin relations in *ganqing*, which will be explored here.

Non-Kin Relations through *Ganqing*

Morton Fried's research was conducted over an eighteen-month period in Zhu Xian in Anhui; it is particularly relevant to a discussion of *From the Soil* because it was carried out in 1947–8, which is the same time that Fei's book was published. Fried (1953: 230) goes beyond Fei's and similar analyses in recognizing that the 'complex design of Chinese society becomes more comprehensible when systematic study of extra-familial relations is added to the research on Chinese familial organization'. Indeed, the idea of fictive kinship and pseudo-family reifies a folk attribution which 'does not necessarily involve an extension of specific privileges and obligations... [or] a real extension of kinship relation' (Fei 1939: 91); rather, it obscures the distinctive form of non-kin ties and in doing so limits sociological apprehension of social roles and relationships. In addition to underscoring the centrality of kinship in traditional Chinese cultural identity, then, Fried (1953: 199–206) documents the cultural significance of non-kin friendship, including the qualified depreciation of kinship relative to it, as in the Chinese proverb: 'Nearby neighbours are worth more than distant relatives' or 'Distant relatives are not as valuable as nearby friends' (Fried 1953: 91, 181). The significance of friendship over kinship is indicated in another well-known Chinese proverb: 在家靠父母在外靠朋友 *Zaijia kao fumu zaiwai kao pengyou*, 'At home you depend on parents, outside the home you rely on friends'. Indeed, against the idea of self-sustaining kin relations Fried (1953: 129) shows that non-kin relations supplement the family farm, and also that partnerships in commercial relations are formed to avoid the inefficiency and nepotism of the family firm (Fried 1953: 139–42).

Whereas Fei (1946: 12) recalls visits of poor clan (lineage) uncles to his family home, where they were given 'a handsome amount of money as a present' by his grandmother, Fried (1953: 91) documents cases in which 'Not only did nearby friends respond to his [informant's] needs with more alacrity than distant relatives, but they outdid nearby relatives as well'. Certainly, 'family connections grow in importance' when a need arises, but in practice there is 'no hard and fast rule which dictates the help which flows along kin lines' (Fried 1953: 82; see also Fei 1992: 125). Fried (1953: 214) goes so far as to suggest against the established stereotype that kin ties 'are not the main binding force...in Chinese society at large, a generalization that may well apply to the past two millennia of Chinese history, as well as the present'. Representations to the contrary, Fried suggests, derive from a gentry bias (Fried 1953: 214), a point independently proposed by Skinner (1964: 43) and in effect confirmed by Fei (1946: 4–5) when he explains that 'among the peasants the basic social co-operative group is small…Chinese peasants usually live with their parents who are too old to work and depend on the younger generation for support' but 'Among the gentry it is different [as here] big kinship groups are found'. This difference arises 'when a person does not earn his living by his own labor but depends on rent [for then an] absentee landowner needs political power for his protection…[typically provided by] a strong kinship organization…[It follows, then, that] to maintain close relationships among the kin is necessary for the gentry'.

Fried shows that the basis of friendship is *kan-ch'ing* (*ganqing*), a relational quality of affective bonding derived from shared activities or experiences and mobilized by persons in order to achieve a common purpose. *Ganqing* is distinguished by Fried (1953: 153, 221) from both bribery and nepotism, and he says that it operates in the absence of kinship (Fried 1953: 227). He writes that *ganqing* 'not only recognizes exploitation but is a technique of ameliorating it' (Fried 1953: 224), and that friendship is 'a relationship between two or more persons based on mutual affection and sympathy and devoid of the object of exploitation…[whereas *ganqing*] presumes a much more specific common interest' (Fried 1953: 226). This latter juxtaposition has been understood to mean that 'Fried strongly distinguished between friendship and *ganqing*' on the grounds that *ganqing* is a technique for reducing class differences between non-kin whereas friendship tacitly assumes equality (Smart 1999: 121–2; see also Jacobs 1979: 259). But this reading is unnecessarily literal and by ignoring context misunderstands the relations Fried outlines.

Certainly, *ganqing* and friendship are not identical; *ganqing* is not friendship but an affective basis of friendship, and it may be the basis of other relations as well. When Fried (1953: 224) writes that *ganqing* 'not only recognizes exploitation but is a technique of ameliorating it' he refers to the situation of rural gentry who 'through the repeated extraction of local surpluses…circumscribe the development of friendships'. In these circumstances 'the best the gentry can do is establish good *kan-ch'ing* with a few persons while relationships with others deteriorate'. Between a tenant and his landlord, on the other hand, an underlying relationship of *ganqing* 'if properly conducted, can strengthen the friendship' between them (Fried 1953: 126). The idea that *ganqing* supports friendship is suggested also with regard to relations between non-kin farmers (Fried 1953: 129), and between a young landlord and a young geomancer, 'based on mutual affection and sympathy'; indeed, their 'friendship…was used by the geomancer to help establish his own business' (Fried 1953: 145) in which case affection and interest coincide. As Fried elaborates, friendships which 'cross-cut status lines…prove [to be] of great benefit to the junior man…[who may] actively cultivate' them (Fried 1953: 161). Such friendships may be achieved or enhanced by the performance of 'many small favors and services' (Fried 1953: 161). Indeed, *ganqing* is promoted, according to Fried, by exchanges of gifts and favours (Fried 1953: 153, 193) as well as common experiences in school (Fried 1953: 184–5). In this sense the notions of friendship and *ganqing* may be interchangeable (Fried 1953: 155). It is of particular interest that Fei (1992: 88) explicitly rejects any role for *ganqing* in 'stabilizing social relationships', preferring instead 'understanding (*liaojie*)' of status mutuality and therefore distinction. This arguably is the obverse of friendship, both in terms of Confucian principles and in general.

The Paradox of Self-Interest in *Guanxi*

The role of *ganqing* in *guanxi* is extensively recognized in the literature. Fried does not use the term *guanxi* but he does indicate instances of friendship supported by *ganqing* in which some extrinsic benefit obtains for at least one if not both of the participants; these are clear references to *guanxi*-type relations. Jacobs (1979: 255) regards Fried's *Fabric of Chinese Society* a 'classic study' which 'found [that] friendship clearly exists on all levels of…society' and he goes on to recognize that Fried's 'classic analysis of *kan-ch'ing* [*ganqing*]' provides an account of the 'affective component of *kuan-hsi* [*guanxi*]' (Jacobs 1979: 259). At the same time, Fei's concept of *chaxugeju*, entailing the idea of flexible networks structured by ego in the process of 'making personal connections' (Fei 1992: 61), also appears to be a fitting model for *guanxi* as numerous commentators observe, as already noted. That Fei conceives *chaxugeju* as entirely kin-based is problematic, however, not simply because of the exclusion of *ganqing* from *chaxugeju* but also because *guanxi* resources are more highly embedded in non-kin ties than in kin ties (Bian 2001: 292). To put the point slightly differently in terms that are familiar in the literature, *guanxi* cannot be dependent on kin ties as kinship at best is only one of a number of possible *guanxi* bases (Chen and Chen 2004: 311–12; Jacobs 1979: 243–56). The position adopted here is that kin relations and *guanxi* relations are fundamentally distinct. Kin ties are by their nature closed, confined to blood relatives, whereas *guanxi* ties are necessarily open; obligations of kin are role-based whereas *guanxi* obligations derive from exchanges of favours between persons who are or may become friends. The major problem for *chaxugeju* as a proxy for *guanxi*, however, is additional to and distinct from these concerns. *Guanxi* is mobilized to achieve ego's particular purposes that alter either supports or contributes to, but there is no place for the notion of personal interest in *chaxugeju*.

The question of self-interest is typically regarded as difficult to articulate in Chinese social relationships, partly because persons are egocentric but dependent in hierarchical relations of various sorts so that, while there is selfishness, it is 'impossible to prove that someone is acting selfishly' (Fei 1992: 68–9). In following Fei's argument Yunxiang Yan (2015: 52) writes that 'the hierarchal nature of dyadic relations and the duty-oriented life course make it almost impossible to find open and naked egoism in traditional China' so that 'self-interest *per se* never gained public legitimacy in traditional China; the pursuit of self-interest must be disguised as work for the collective interest of a given entity'. In fact, 'open and naked egoism' is difficult to find not only in traditional China but in any society, as a failure to 'humble the arrogance of self-love' detracts from rather than realizes one's purposes in a context comprising other persons, as Adam Smith put it in his eighteenth-century classic (Smith 1979: 83, 173). It is possible, nevertheless, to meaningfully discern self-interest in traditional China, even in a context to which Yan alludes where 大我 *da wo*, a 'greater self' of family or network, tends to subordinate 小我 *xiao wo*, a 'lesser self' of individual persons (Barbalet 2013, 2014). With reference to *guanxi* in particular, there is a path to self-interest that overcomes these concerns raised by Fei and Yan.

Yan (2015: 45) notes that, even though 'interpersonal relationships remain hierarchal in nature' it is nevertheless possible in *guanxi* networks that the person at the center 'can manipulate the boundaries and functions of the network in accordance with personal interests and strategies'. In this case Yan refers to 'bribing a superior or exploiting a subordinate'; but in the most general sense *guanxi* can be connected with self-interest irrespective of whether *guanxi* is corrupt or oppressive, as in Yan's case here, or benign. This is because the intrinsic benefits of *guanxi*, for both the provider of a *guanxi* favour and also for the recipient, are enhanced public recognition or gaining *mianzi*, face (Lin 2001: 157). Face, the formation of self or ego implicated in the perception of others, is something in which each person has an abiding interest, not only in *guanxi* relations but in social relations in general.

The significance of the underlying face mechanism in the formation and mobilization of *guanxi* in order to achieve an extrinsic purpose can be explicated in terms of *renqing* (Hwang 1987). Such an approach provides a cultural framework for understanding *guanxi* but it is sociologically unnecessary, not only because of the ambiguities in the notion of *renqing* mentioned above but primarily because it is sufficient to indicate that *mianzi* or face is the register of successfully achieved *guanxi* and the social currency of its operation. The connection between *mianzi* and *renqing* is a separate philological or philosophical concern. The importance of face to Chinese social relations was discussed extensively during the Republican period, including by the literary author Lu Xun and the anthropologist Hu Hsien Chin (Hu Xianjin) (Qi 2014: 148, 152), as we shall see in Chapter 4. It is of particular interest that consideration of face is absent from Fei's writing, with the exception of a reference to the necessity of hypocrisy in a society 'ruled by the paternalistic power of elders' which can be managed by distorting 'their wishes while giving them face, that is, outward compliance' (Fei 1992: 132). Face is pivotal, however, in a work that in many ways offers a parallel account to Fei's *From the Soil*, and was published prior to it.

Lin Yutang's chapter on 'Social and Political Life' in *My Country and My People* is half the length of *From the Soil*; it discusses many themes treated in the latter and in a similar manner. Lin (1939: 172) begins with Chinese selfishness and goes on to show that the root of Chinese society is the family system and the village, which is the family 'raised to a higher exponent' (Lin 1939: 175). The importance of this work in the present context is its account of face, 'the most delicate standard by which Chinese social intercourse is regulated' (Lin 1939: 200). An individual's personal interest in their face is paramount, and in relations with others attention will accordingly be paid to their face so that officials, for instance, may attend a number of banquets in a single night in order to maintain face-based relations (Lin 1939: 201). The terms *guanxi* and *renqing* do not appear in the text but behaviour associated with them is clearly reported by Lin. While the officials in Lin's example are not rural characters their concern with face is not confined to urban experiences.

Conclusion

The supposition that *chaxugeju* may serve as a model for *guanxi* has been critically examined in order to show that not only was it not Fei's intention to outline an abstract form of *guanxi* but also that the content of *chaxugeju* lacks the essential ingredients of *guanxi* even though its egocentric animus and the flexibility of its structure are characteristic of both *guanxi* and also the Chinese lineage relations to which Fei applied the term. Perhaps the most pertinent element of Fei's treatment of *chaxugeju*, however, that deflects its viability as a model for *guanxi*, is his prognosis mentioned earlier in this chapter, that with the development of market society in China the days of *chaxugeju* are numbered. This reflects the way in which Fei juxtaposes rural society and market society, in which the underlying relations of *renqing* and *wuqing* are mutually incompatible; such a dichotomization, as we have seen, allows no place for non-kin friendship supported by *ganqing*. Lin (1939: 196), on the other hand, projects a continuing presence for face, and by implication *guanxi*, well into the future.

In considering the argument of *From the Soil* a number of issues have been highlighted, including its underlying Confucian assumptions and the narrowness of its focus on family or lineage and village. The present chapter has additionally indicated three considerations relevant for understanding Chinese society which also have general significance. First, following the important but neglected work of Fried (1953), non-kin friendship and related ties must be treated in their own terms and not assimilated as a form of pseudo-kinship; second, the very different types of obligation, deriving from role and exchange respectively, can be used to distinguish between types of social bonds and the relationships associated with them. Finally, purposive associations and relationships—including *guanxi*—reveal the multifaceted nature of self-interest in which esteem or face as well as utilities or material values are pursued. Something about each of these can be said in conclusion.

References to friendship in the context of Chinese society typically regard it as a secondary form of relationship if not irrelevant for understanding social dynamics. This is because of the notion that family and kinship are the primary and dominant relationships underlying social forms of all kinds in China, and that these are continuous and interdependent with another concept, *guanxi*, which has come to characterize bonding relations in realization of cooperation and purposive achievement. These presuppositions are challenged in the present chapter. Through discussion of the findings of Skinner (1964) and Fried (1953) the significance of non-kin relations in late Republican China's rural society is indicated. It is of particular interest that these and associated writers do not refer to *guanxi* as it is understood today. And yet Fried's account of the continuities of friendship and *ganqing* suggest a fundamental connection with *guanxi*. In a rare discussion of the notion of friendship in China, which includes a survey of previous accounts of friend-ship and an assessment of the association between the concepts of *guanxi* and friendship, Alan Smart (1999: 129) argues that 'Friendship is simultaneously a base on which *guanxi* ties can be built, and a cultural resource for criticism of (certain kinds of) *guanxi*'; between friendship and *guanxi*, he adds, 'there are no sharp and uncontested boundaries' (Smart 1999: 132). On similar grounds the present chapter effectively reverses the assumption that *guanxi* may be regarded as a realization of kin ties either directly or indirectly through the notion of 'pseudo-family', a proposition to treated in much more detail in another chapter.

The discontinuity between kinship and *guanxi* has been indicated in the discussion by showing the fundamentally different bases of obligation between kin on the one hand and between non-kin friends or *guanxi* participants on the other. Kin obligations are based on role expectations while *guanxi* obligations arise through favour exchange. This is not to say, of course, that kin do not exchange favours; but such favour exchanges cannot be the primary bases of the obligations of kinship. Kinship roles and their obligations are prior to the exchanges that take place between kin and provide the context in which they occur. The obligations of *guanxi*, on the other hand, derive from favour exchanges between participants; and what brings those participants into a common orbit of durable connection is the affective component of *ganqing*, through which the porous ties of friendship and *guanxi* are possible. What is necessary for *guanxi*, and also incidental in friendship, is the mobilization of the relationship for a purposive outcome through which interests are realized. Consideration of the factor of interests brings us to the third thing mentioned, namely the interest persons have in *mianzi*, face, and its connection with the realization of benefits achieved through *guanxi*.

Self-interest is conceived in terms of the satisfaction of a desire or need for personal benefit or advantage. Confucian-inspired discussion may insist that self-interest in this sense is difficult to achieve in Chinese society because the individual, the 'lesser self', is necessarily subordinate to the 'greater self' of kinship groups. The application of *guanxi*, a social relational form, to achieve an individual purpose presents analogous problems of conceptualization and the identification of operative mechanisms. It is widely understood that the purpose of *guanxi* is to achieve an outcome for individual participants that provides benefit or advantage for them. At the same time, the costs of *guanxi*, in the form of gifts, time spent in cultivating *guanxi* partners, and the opportunity costs of being locked into long-term obligatory relationships, are balanced against the benefits of collective effort that affords higher yields than any individual effort might achieve if a person were to act alone on their own behalf, as discussed in the previous chapter. The interest that motivates the cooperative effort that is *guanxi*, as opposed to the individual or personal benefit or advantage, is the social esteem or face that comes from the appreciative recognition of others. This is not an exclusively Chinese phenomenon (Brennan and Pettit 2005; Qi 2014: 143–64).

Through a discussion of social connections in late Republican writings it has been shown that the widely accepted focus on the overarching significance of relations of kinship, as exemplified in Fei Xiaotong's celebrated *From the Soil*, provides a Confucian ideological representation of rural Chinese society rather than an adequate sociological understanding of it. It has been shown here that a key to the analysis of the structure and process of social relationships in late Republican China must include non-kin friendship. In his detailed account of *ganqing* and its ambiguous connections with friendship Fried (1953) points the way to an understanding of *guanxi* that avoids the confusion and errors of Fei's notion of *chaxugeju* that informs, or arguably misinforms a number of recent accounts of *guanxi*.

3
Reciprocity in Chinese Traditions

The previous chapter was focused on Fei Xiaotong's interpretation of Chinese rural society in order to address the prevalent understanding of 关系 *guanxi* as morphologically similar to the Chinese family form, including its extension through lineage formations. This particular apprehension of *guanxi*, which operates through an elucidation of Fei's account of 差序格局 *chaxugeju*, the differential mode of association, derives from an understanding of Confucian ethical thought, which is held to be the basis of China's cultural personification both historically and as a continuing influence. This argument, from the supposed societal pre-eminence of kinship in China, is not the only course through which Confucian thought is brought to explaining the origins and operation of *guanxi*. There is also an argument that the language of Confucian ethics, and especially particular key concepts drawn from it, provide the ground from which *guanxi* practice may emerge. These two arguments, of family and language, are by no means mutually exclusive. They provide complementary rather than alternative support for the idea that *guanxi* is based on traditional protocols. This chapter will examine the idea that *guanxi* is informed by the Confucian or traditional Chinese notion of 报 *bao*, reciprocity, together with related concepts.

In two foundational applications of Confucian thought to sociological analysis, Ambrose King (1985, 1991) points to the centrality of the notion of 'reciprocity' in Confucian ethics and its coterminous significance for the practice of *guanxi*. King (1985: 57) writes that '*shu*, or "reciprocity"', is the 'architectonic concept in Confucian ethics', its 'cornerstone'. In a footnote King (1985: 66 n. 3) explains that 'Reciprocity as a moral principle has been applied to social relations of all kinds', and he refers to an article by Yang (1957), 'The concept of *pao* [*bao*] as a basis for social relations in China', which we shall consider in this chapter. In a later article King (1991: 73) reiterates that, within Confucian social theory, the individual self is 'a dynamic and reflexive entity at the center of relation construction'. Apart from blood relations between parents and siblings, then, social 'relations are voluntarily constructed with the individual self as the initiator'. In this sense, 'Chinese *kuan-hsi* [*guanxi*] building can be characterized as an ego-centered social engineering of relation building' (King 1991: 74). Underlying the building of

The Theory of Guanxi *and Chinese Society.* Jack Barbalet, Oxford University Press (2021). © Jack Barbalet.
DOI: 10.1093/oso/9780198808732.003.0004

guanxi, King continues, are 'Confucian norms of interpersonal relationships' that are 'fundamentally based upon the concept of *shu*, or reciprocity'. It must be noted that the concepts 恕 *shu* and *bao* are in fact quite different terms and refer to different activities, a matter taken up later. At this stage of the discussion, though, only King's reference to the relevance of reciprocity for *guanxi* requires attention, and the idea that reciprocity is the 'cornerstone' of Confucian ethics.

The position King outlines that is described here, regarding the importance of reciprocation to *guanxi* and its basis in Confucianism, is now common-place in discussions of *guanxi*. A characteristic statement holds that '*Guanxi* is based on reciprocity, the traditional concept of *bao*, where one does favours for others as "social investments", clearly expecting something in return' (Gold 1985: 659–60; see also Bian 2018: 603; Chen and Chen 2004; Hwang 1987; Yang 1994: 218). In an extensive discussion, the Chinese soci-ologist Jar-Der Luo (2005: 439) holds that 'an indigenous Chinese concept called *pao* [*bao*], (translated as the norm of reciprocity in English), is a highly appreciated basis of morality in China'. He goes on to write that it is 'the prin-ciple of *pao* in long-term favor-exchanging processes that enhances the probability that all parties of the *guanxi* will come to trust each other' as the meaning of *bao* corresponds with the idea of 'obligations and expectations' (Luo 2005: 440). Given the Chinese cultural qualities of *bao*, Luo (2005: 455) asks in 'what ways is *pao* similar to or different from the concept of reciprocity, which is presumed to be universal in sociological literature'. The answer to this question is provided in a subsequent article in which it is claimed that the indigenous Chinese concept, *bao*, is both a basis of morality in China and equivalent to a universal sociological 'norm of reciprocity' (Luo and Yeh 2012: 335–6).

It can be seen, then, that a number of researchers agree that *guanxi* is a characteristically Chinese social form, expressive of traditionally based norms of reciprocity, that are derived from a Confucian cultural heritage. In this sense, then, like Confucius himself as revealed in 论语 *Lunyu*, the *Analects* 7:1, *guanxi* in modern China is effectively a 'transmitter' of the traditional culture (Legge 2001a: 195). In consideration of these and related issues the present chapter will show, on the other hand, that such claims regarding the basis of *guanxi* in traditional sources of normative ethics, derive from a num-ber of misunderstandings both linguistic and sociological. The following sec-tion of the chapter will examine the claim that there are Chinese traditions in which 'reciprocity' is represented by *bao*. It will show, on the contrary, that a large number of concrete forms of interaction discussed in classical sources are not represented by the concept of *bao*, and that those identified in the important discussion by Yang (1957) do not gravitate to a unified notion of reciprocal relations. The section following the next considers the notion of *shu*, another Chinese character located in the Confucian tradition that King, as we have seen above, interprets as reciprocity. It is shown that this term has been mistranslated in leading sources and that rather than clearly pointing to 'reciprocity' it more appropriately relates to another notion known to sociologists as 'role-taking'. In the literature role-taking is seldom associated with *guanxi*, although an exploration of the connection between them is useful in shedding light on certain aspects of *guanxi* practice. The connection between the concept of *shu* and the Confucian notion of *ren* is addressed in the third section of the chapter. The tenuous link between *ren* and *renqing*, the latter term central for an understanding *guanxi*, is explored in order to more clearly situate the cultural sources of *guanxi*.

Bao in Chinese Traditions

It was shown in Chapter 1 that, in the context of social analysis, the term *guanxi* indicates connections between those who have an affective commitment to the relationship and a sense of obligation between its participants in their provision of support or benefit to the other. Given the affective basis of these connections it can be assumed that the associated commitments between participants will be sustained over time only if the support or benefit accorded to one participant by the other is repaid or reciprocated. In this sense, then, the notion of reciprocity is a core element of *guanxi*, as it is to practices of favour exchange in general. As already indicated, this facilitating factor of *guanxi*, reciprocity, can be characterized through the Chinese-language term *bao*. Nevertheless, if reciprocity entails a response in the sense of 'mutual action or influence' or 'mutual correspondent concession of advantages or privileges' (*Shorter Oxford English Dictionary*), then *bao* is an inexact equivalent of 'reciprocity'. In modern Chinese, *bao* can be translated as 'reciprocity' but it is also used to indicate unilateral or separate actions such as 'report', 'announce' or 'inform', and 'judgement', as well as what might be construed as negative exchange, including 'revenge' and 'vengeance'. This is not to say that *bao* does not mean 'reciprocity', but as we shall see not only is it a term with a meaning that goes beyond reciprocity as it is normally understood in English, it is not the only or necessarily the most appropriate term to indicate reciprocity in a number of its manifestations. Indeed, the generic 'reciprocity' has a number of particular and dissimilar manifestations, not all of which are captured by *bao*.

In consideration of the argument regarding the Confucian basis of *bao* as reciprocity in *guanxi*, it can be noticed that it is difficult to locate this particular character (报) in Confucius's writings. When it does appear, however, as in *Analects* 14:36, it offers little direct support to the idea of reciprocity normally associated with *guanxi* as a practice of favour exchange. Confucius is asked how should injury be recompensed, to which he responds 以直报怨 以德报德 *yi zhi bao yuan, yi de bao de*, translated by Legge (2001a: 288) as 'Recompense injury with justice, and recompense kindness with kindness'. This is not exactly 'reciprocity' underlying favour exchange as required of *guanxi*. The Confucian tradition, it will be argued more fully below, does not provide support to the idea that *guanxi*, through *bao*, can be traced back to classical sources of Chinese thought.

The most detailed account of the traditional basis of *bao* is the essay written by the Chinese-American economic historian Lien-sheng Yang (1957). Yang (1957: 291) holds that the concept *bao*, as 'the principle of reciprocity', is 'marked by its long history [in China], the high degree of consciousness of its existence, and its wide application and tremendous influence in social institutions'. Yang's argument, which will be examined here, has exerted a discernible influence on the sociological understanding of *guanxi* (see Chen and Chen 2004: 317; Hwang 1987: 956; King 1985: 66 n. 3; King 1991: 74; So and Walker 2006: 27–8; Wank 2001: 94 n. 1; Yan 1996: 18). Yang (1957: 291) begins by quoting from 礼记 *Liji*, the *Book of Rites*:

> In the highest antiquity they prized (simply conferring) good; in the time next to this, giving and repaying was the thing attended to. And what the rules of propriety value is reciprocity. If I give a gift and nothing comes in return, that is contrary to propriety; if the thing comes to me, and I give nothing in return, that is also contrary to propriety.

The original, from which this translation by James Legge is taken, does not use the term *bao* but rather 往来 *wang lai*, literally 'go back and forth', so the statement could more correctly read: 'What the rules of propriety respect is to receive and return'. Of course, receiving and returning is one specification of reciprocity. As we shall see, 'reciprocity' is an abstract or summary term for a large number of concrete forms of interaction, so that insistence on a singular representation, as with *bao*, is misleading (see Chang 2009: 449–50). We shall return to this issue. Yang's purpose here is to identify the Confucian tradition as one of three sources of the principle of reciprocity in Chinese culture, the other two being the 'knight-errant' tradition and the Buddhist.

The Warring States period of early Chinese history (475–221 BC) provided opportunities for the emergence of what Yang (1957: 294) regards as a new social category, 游侠 *youxia*, the so-called 'knight-errant'. These Chinese knights, unlike European knights, were not members of a religious order, and neither were they organized as a social caste, as were Japanese samurai; knights-errant were neither professional warriors nor rural bandits. On the basis of literary sources James Liu (1961: 30) writes:

> The essential qualifications of a knight errant were not so much outstanding physical strength and military skill as a spirit of altruism and a concern for justice. In short, knight errantry was not a profession but a way of behaviour, and a knight errant was simply a man who sought to right wrongs and help people in distress, often by the use of force and in defiance of the law.   (See also Liu 1967.)

Yang (1957: 294–6) believes that this tradition informed development of the concept of *bao* because a knight-errant would unfailingly return the kindness of others, even though they expected no reward for the favours they performed and would reject any that was offered. While the knight-errant responds to an injustice, he will block the expression of gratitude from the recipient, something Yang (1957: 296) describes as 'righteousness'. Righteousness, in Chinese 义 *yi*, suggests a quality of a person, underlying their response to the circumstances they witness, rather than an exchange or reciprocal conduct. The knight-errant practice of rejecting returned favours is in fact an abrogation rather than an expression of reciprocity (see Bourdieu 1992: 98–106; Coleman 1990: 309–10; Komter 2007: 99–100; Simmel 1950: 392–3). The third tradition in which Yang (1957: 298–300) finds the principle of *bao* is that of Chinese Buddhism, through which natural retribution is explained in terms of *karma*; in Chinese, 业 *ye*. Although Yang does not draw attention to the fact, *bao* is incorporated in the Chinese term for retribution, 报应 *baoying*.

After surveying these three traditions and their contribution to the Chinese principle of *bao*, Yang (1957: 301) considers the 'influences of the concept of *pao* [*bao*] over Chinese institutions'; he identifies three 'noticeable' cases, namely, '(1) familism, (2) worldly rationalism, and (3) ethical particularism'. With regard to Chinese familism or 孝 *xiao*, filial piety, Yang (1957: 302) notes that 'the basic virtue of filial piety has a ready justification in the concept of response', insofar as parents invest in their children's upbringing and are in turn cared for by their sons (and daughters-in-law) in their old age. Indeed, the Chinese family system is frequently discussed sociologically in terms of intergenerational exchange (Croll 2006). The reciprocity of *xiao* is a particular form of *bao*, traditionally hierarchical and ascending with regard to age and gender. Worldly rationalism, the second institution he refers to, is described by Yang (1957: 302–3), as indicating ret-ribution, both divine and worldly, and especially the descent of the former into the latter. As shown above, this is readily assimilated into *bao* as 'reci-procity' insofar as 'retribution' in Chinese is *baoying*. Finally, 'Chinese par-ticularism' means that even an officially provided service in China will generate a personal debt:

> In traditional China, even in a case of fulfilment of an official duty, if it happened to be beneficial to a particular person, he would be expected to cherish a sense of indebtedness to the person who was instrumental in the outcome.
>
> (Yang 1957: 303)

Irrespective of whether this type of practice is best understood as an expres-sion of a cultural form, in which 'cherish[ing] a sense of indebtedness' comes from a pattern of values, or is a consequence of institutional practices, in which officials' salaries were by design lower than their living costs and in which supervision of officials was minimal (Balazs 1964: 10–12, 42, 223; Stover 1974: 188–95), it is manifest as asymmetrical reciprocity. In that sense, then, it can be regarded as an instance of *bao* in so far as it involves 回报 *huibao*, paying back a consideration provided by an official. The type of indebtedness Yang refers to here could also be regarded as an instance of 人情 *renqing*, and is likely to be described as such by the participants in this particular form of exchange.

The three different traditions identified by Yang (1957), as supporting the cultural presence of *bao* in Chinese historical consciousness and social prac-tices, in fact only incompletely and unevenly sustain the idea of a Chinese norm of reciprocity in the way he describes it. Indeed, Yang concedes that at best the Confucian tradition provides limited support to the idea of *bao* as a basis of social relations because he says that this tradition has both 'a realistic as well as an idealistic' aspect, and only the former supports his argument (Yang 1957: 293). The terms 'realist' and 'idealist' are borrowed from Fung (1998b: 266–79, 349–61), who uses them to characterize the interpretations of Confucius in the writings of later philosophers, Xunzi and Mencius respectively. In the *Analects*, Confucius has practically nothing to say about *bao*, but much to say about *shu* and also 仁 *ren*, none of which supports Yang's argument, as will be shown shortly. The knight-errant tradition pro-vides poor support to Yang's argument because, as indicated above, the 'righteous' practice associated with this tradition, of refusing a gift, is a threat to rather than a realization of *bao*. An additional problem with Yang's argument is the absence of a linguistic and etymological discussion of *bao*. As indicated above, many instances of what could arguably be represented as reciprocity are not clearly located in *bao*.

Yang, then, arguably fails to demonstrate a pervasive and coherent cultural appreciation in Chinese traditions of *bao* as a clear reference point for practices of reciprocity. There is another aspect of his argument that warrants attention. Yang accepts that, while 'the principle of reciprocity is required in practically every society', it is especially pertinent to the understanding of social relations in China:

> The Chinese believe that reciprocity of actions (favour and hatred, reward and punishment) between man and man...should be as certain as a cause-and-effect relationship, and, therefore, when a Chinese [person] acts, he normally antici-pates a response or return.   (Yang 1957: 291)

If the principle of reciprocity is required in all societies, then the reference to what a Chinese person anticipates *vis-à-vis* reciprocity is possibly unneces-sary and at best incomplete. What needs to be articulated here is how the scope of the application of the notion of reciprocity is culturally prescribed, so that in different societies reciprocity attaches differently to different rela-tionships; a statement of what underlies such differences is also required. But Yang does not go this far. A first approximation of such an explanation is provided by the classical German sociologist Georg Simmel (1950: 387):

> Gratitude, in the first place, supplements the legal order. All contacts among men rest on the schema of giving and returning the equivalence...In all economic exchanges in legal form, in all fixed agreements concerning a given service, in all obligations of legalized relations, the legal constitution enforces and guarantees the reciprocity of service and return service social equilibrium and cohesion do not exist without it. But there also are innumerable other relations, to which the legal form does not apply, and in which the enforcement of the equivalence is out of the question. Here gratitude appears as a supplement. It establishes the bond of interaction, of the reciprocity of service and return service, even where they are not guaranteed by external coercion.

In this account then, the types of reciprocity identified by Yang (1957) are based on what Simmel calls 'gratitude', in contradistinction to the 'legal order'.

Simmel's discernment, between exchanges governed by law and those gov-erned by gratitude, accepts the universality of reciprocity and at the same time the conditionality of its different forms in terms of institutional setting. This idea is developed further, without reference to Simmel, by Alvin Gouldner (1960: 171):

> In the Philippines, for example, the *compadre* system cuts across and pervades the political, economic, and other institutional spheres. *Compadres* are bound by a norm of reciprocity. If one man pays his *compadre's* doctor's bill in time of need, for example, the latter may be obligated to help the former's son to get a government job. Here the tendency to govern all relations by the norm of reciprocity, thereby undermining bureaucratic impersonality, is relatively legitimate, hence overt and powerful. In the United States, however, such tendencies are weaker, in part because friendship relations are less institutionalized. Nonetheless, even in bureaucracies in this country such tendencies are endemic, albeit less legitimate and overt. Except in friendship, kinship, and neighborly relations, a norm of reciprocity is not imposed on Americans by the 'dominant cultural profile', although it is commonly found in the latent or 'substitute' culture structure in all institutional sectors, even the most rationalized, in the United States.

It is often observed that *guanxi* operates in the absence of a framework of regulatory institutions (Bian 2018: 600–2; Jiang *et al.* 2012: 211–12), in which case Simmel's 'gratitude' and Gouldner's 'latent' relations of friendship, kinship, and neighbourliness govern exchanges through informal reciprocity.

Shu and its Mistranslations

As already noted, King (1985: 57) observes that '*shu* … is the architectonic concept in Confucian ethics' and he claims that *shu* means reciprocity (King 1985: 57; 1991: 74). It will be shown here that, while King is correct to see *shu* as core to Confucian ethics, he is incorrect in his claim that *shu* can be translated as 'reciprocity'. The meaning of *shu* is pursued in the following discussion not principally to correct King's misunderstanding but because the concept does have relevance for an appreciation of the operation of *guanxi*, although this aspect of it is unexplored by writers who regard the latter as having a basis in Confucianism as well as those indifferent to the thesis that *guanxi* derives from Confucian or other traditional foundations. The source of King's apprehension—more correctly, misapprehension—of *shu* as reciprocity, is drawn from a passage in *Analects* 15:23 which he quotes: 'Tsze-kung asked, saying, "Is there one word which may serve as a rule of practice for all one's life?" The Master said, is not reciprocity such a word?

What you do not want done to yourself, do not do to others' (King 1985: 66 n. 4). King here quotes the authoritative translation by James Legge (2001a: 301), who puts the word 'reciprocity' in capital letters. But Legge mistranslates *shu* as 'reciprocity', as we shall see, and the passage in *Analects* 15:23, 己所不欲 勿施于人 *ji suo bu yu wu shi yu ren*, translated appropriately by Legge as 'What you do not want done to yourself, do not do to others', does not itself suggest reciprocity.

In fact, King's own confusion is clear in that while he maintains that *shu* means reciprocity, as indicated above, he at the same time writes that *shu* refers to the 'emphatic [empathetic?] capacity to take the role of others' (King 1985: 57). This latter understanding makes sense of his important observation that, as an individually constructed 'personal relational network', *guanxi* is based on a 'kind of social communication' that depends on 'the Confucian norm of *shu*' such that one can 'infer another's wants and desires from one's own wants and desires' (King 1985: 64). Internal to this passage King repeats his claim that *shu* means 'reciprocity', which is discordant with his understanding outlined in the quotation here in which *shu* means, rather, using oneself as a means through which the requirements of others may be inferred, so that *shu* may loosely be rendered as 'empathy'. In his translation of *Analects* 15:23, King's colleague at the Chinese University of Hong Kong, D. C. Lau (1979: 135) leaves the term *shu* in the English-language text. He writes that, in response to the question regarding a single word for a lifelong guide for one's conduct: 'The Master said, "It is perhaps the word '*shu*'. Do not impose on others what you yourself do not desire."' Lau (1979: 135 n. 7) explains that *shu* means 'using oneself as a measure in gauging the wishes of others', a translation agreed by the cultural historian of early China Paul Goldin (2008: 169).

By accepting Legge's mistranslation of *shu* for reciprocity in *Analects* 15:23, King, in an endeavour to be consistent, renders another key passage of *Analects*, correctly translated by Legge, in a manner that is incorrect. To recount these errors risks what in Chinese is regarded as 画蛇添足 *hua she tian zu*, literally to 'draw legs on a snake', a picturesque way of pointing to how excessive elaboration ruins the effect that an exposition seeks to achieve. With that risk of overdoing it in mind it is interesting to see that, after following Legge's mistranslation of *shu* as reciprocity in *Analects* 15:23, King (1985: 66 n. 4) changes a passage from Legge's translation of *Analects* 4:15, which states how his disciples understand the unifying principle, *shu*, of Confucius's doctrine. King's adaptation has 'the doctrine of our master is loyalty and reciprocity—this and nothing more'. The original passage, on the other hand, in Legge (2001a: 169–70) reads: 'The doctrine of our master is to be true to the principles of our nature and the benevolent exercise of them to others,—this and nothing more'. This latter is a fair translation of the master's doctrine, in the original source, 忠恕 *zhong shu*. Legge's translation of *zhong* as 'principles of our nature' could at the margins be King's 'loyalty', although, as we shall see, in the context it is inappropriate; but Legge's 'benevolent exercise of [those principles] to others' for *shu*, which is appropriate, could not meaningfully become King's 'reciprocity'. Before we go on to say more about *shu* and its relevance for understanding *guanxi* it is necessary to ask an obvious question. How could Legge have translated *shu* in *Analects* 15:23 as 'reciprocity', when his translation of the term in *Analects* 4:15 is accurately 'the benevolent exercise of [the principles of our nature] to others'?

The probable answer to these questions can be found in Legge's experience as a Protestant missionary in China from 1840 until 1873. During this time Legge became ably equipped with extensive knowledge of Chinese language and culture, factors that facilitated his appointment as Professor of Chinese at Oxford University in 1876, a position he held until his death in 1897 (Girardot 2002). The missionary interest in China was not only to convert the Chinese to Christianity but also to interpret Chinese traditions in such a manner as to make the Chinese amenable to conversion, finding 'equivalent' Chinese terms for Christian notions and personalities or roles (Wong 2005). A tenet of Christianity, given in Jesus's Sermon on the Mount, is the injunction: 'whatever you want men to do to you, you also to them, for this is the law and the prophets' (New King James Version, Matthew 7:12); that is, treat others as you want to be treated by them, a tenet known as the Golden Rule.

In a controversial paper delivered in Shanghai in 1877 to the Protestant missionary community in China, Legge (1877: 8–9) indicates his belief that Confucius advocated the New Testament's Golden Rule. He writes that 'If a hall were somewhere to be erected to contain the monuments of the sages and benefactors of mankind, on the statue of Confucius there should be engraved his conversation with Tze-kung, related in the 23rd chapter of the 15th book of "The Analects"' (Legge 1877: 9). In a later work, Legge (1880: 137, 138) notes that Confucius enunciated the Golden Rule 'repeatedly in the *Analects*, the *Doctrine of the Mean*, and the *Great Learning*', and acknowledges that he arrived at it through his 'analysis of human nature, and laid it down without a divine sanction'. Legge (1880: 262) notices that Confucius always 'delivered the golden rule...in the negative form', but that 'his countrymen are as familiar with it as we are with the form in which it is presented in the Sermon on the Mount; and...they understand it not only as a negative, but also as a positive rule'.

There is a sense in which the injunction of the Sermon on the Mount does imply reciprocity, namely that behaviour towards another should be in the spirit of one's desire for the other to behave similarly towards oneself. The principle of exchange in the Golden Rule has a form designed to avert the vengeful reciprocity set out in the Old Testament of 'an eye for an eye' (Exodus 21:24) by insisting on a premise of initiating behaviour: treat others as you would want them to treat you. Jesus addresses this issue earlier in his Sermon on the Mount through a direct rejection of the requirement of 'an eye for an eye' by advocating the idea that an appropriate response to a wrong is to 'turn the other' cheek (Matthew 5:38–42), that is, treat others as you want to be treated by them, in this way, an initial provision of a favour leads to the formation of an obligation to reciprocate with a similar provision, an idea that is central not only to New Testament Christianity but in a quite different context to modern social exchange theory (Blau 1964: 98). In this way a norm emerges to reinforce what Peter Blau (1964: 92) describes as the 'existential conditions of exchange'. The norm of reciprocity, thus, is as central to Christian faith as it is to present-day sociology. The sixteenth-century Protestant theologian, John Calvin (2002: 779) defines a sacrament, a rite ordained by Christ, as:

> an external sign, by which the Lord seals on our consciences his promises of good-will toward us, in order to sustain the weakness of our faith, and we in our turn testify our piety towards him, both before himself, and before angels as well as men. We may also define more briefly by calling it a testimony of the divine favour toward us, confirmed by an external sign, with a corresponding attestation of our faith towards Him.

But it is a mistake to assume that the reciprocity implicit in the Golden Rule can also be located in the negative form of Confucius's explication of *shu*, 'What you do not want done to yourself, do not do to others'. The idea that *shu* is 'reciprocity' in the sense of the Golden Rule, as claimed by Legge—and by King—is, ironically, a Christian not a Confucian attribution. The negative form of the Confucian instruction prevents it being understood as implying reciprocation, it is about not doing and therefore an absence of action. Indeed, it is important to appreciate that, for Confucius, *shu* has a fundamentally non-reciprocal character, a matter to be developed later.

Confucius's understanding of *shu* is clear in *Analects* 4:15, which claims that the Master's principles are *zhong shu*. The character *zhong* can be taken to mean 'considering the centre of one's own mind', sometimes rendered as 'being conscious'. The present-day translation of *zhong* is 'loyalty', as we saw in

King's (1985: 66 n. 4) usage; but, as Lau (1979: 16 n. 6) points out, this was 'not the meaning at the time of Confucius'. The interpretation Lau (1979: 16) proposes, 'doing one's best', is described as 'anachronistic' by Goldin (2008: 170), who instead, paying regard to the historical context, defines this particular use of *zhong* as 'being honest with oneself in dealing with others' (Goldin 2008: 170). Turning to *shu*, Goldin (2008: 169) says that '*shu* is placing oneself in the position of others, and acting toward them as one imagines they would desire... [that is] by taking oneself as an analogy'. It is necessary to clarify, though that Confucian *shu* must take account of the social status of the actor in question. Confucian *shu* does not 'require fathers to treat their sons in the same manner that their sons treat them' but rather 'for a son to consider... how he would like his own son to treat him', because *shu* is 'a relation not between two individuated people, but between two social roles' (Goldin 2014: 16). *Shu* is often translated as 'forgive' or 'altruism', which may encourage an association with reciprocity. According to Goldin (2008: 170), though, *zhong* 'bespeaks a scrupulous self-analysis necessary to ensure the integrity of *shu*'. The combination *zhong shu*, in Confucian terms, thus indicates:

> that we must relate to other people by taking ourselves as an analogy, by placing ourselves in the position of our comrades. However, this requires that we be vigilantly self-aware, lest we come to pretend that what is immediately and unreflectively advantageous to us is somehow advantageous to those whom we deal with.   (Goldin 2008: 170)

The underlying engagement here is not reciprocity but a particular type of extension; rather than expressing an expectation of a return or reciprocal action, *shu* is a moral principle that transcends individual purposes.

In an extensive discussion of *shu* in Confucian thought philosopher Roger Ames indicates a number of its special qualities. In particular, Ames (2011: 195) notes that by putting *shu* at the centre of his approach Confucius indicates 'the unparalleled importance that imagination plays in the productive correlating of one's conduct and in the refining of one's moral judgement'. He goes on to say:

> *Shu* contrasts sharply with more abstract and calculative analytic or theoretical strategies for determining moral conduct. Understood as 'putting oneself in the other's place', it is the most fundamental gesture of a concrete, contextualizing moral disposition. It entails the importance of 'deference' both in the sense of deferring action until we overcome uncertainty in our moral inquiry, and in the sense of taking under consideration the interests of others in that process.
>
> (Ames 2011: 195–6)

This is essentially the position indicated by historian Daniel Gardner (2007: 141):

> *Shu* 恕 ('empathy')...is to treat others as one wishes to be treated oneself. This requires that one be keenly sensitive to others and their particular circumstances, that one be able to put oneself in their place and to take a measure of them and how to treat them using one's own feelings as the standard.

The notion of 'putting oneself in the other's place' is known sociologically as role-taking, an aspect of sociality associated with the work of the American classical sociologist and philosopher George Herbert Mead (1934). Indeed, it is remarkable how closely Confucius's *shu* anticipates Mead's analysis of role-taking.

Mead (1934: 254) says that, in taking the role of the other person, one is 'able to direct his own process of communication', an engagement that provides the individual with 'control...over his own response' and in that sense facilitates the 'development of cooperative activity'. The means by which this occurs, Mead (1934: 366) says, is 'sympathy'. But while the instrumental aspect of role-taking is enhanced communication, its broader implication is the development of 'a self in the fullest sense' (Mead 1934: 154) through which individuals are not only integral beings but socially functioning in both the moral and institutional sense because the 'ideal of human society cannot exist as long as it is impossible for individuals to enter into the attitudes of those whom they are affecting in the performance of their own peculiar functions' (Mead 1934: 328). Meadian role-taking, then, like Confucian *shu*, involves strictly empathic activity rather than overt behaviour; imaginatively putting oneself in another's situation not only provides insight into the other person's probable intention and likely behaviour, but also is necessary in developing one's own self-awareness and is the basis for reflecting on moral possibilities.

What Schwalbe (1988: 426) says of the relation between role-taking and elaboration of social structure is directly analogous to the relation between role-taking and an individual's moral development:

> Role taking is essential to establishing stable patterns of action and interaction. It is necessary to coordinate joint action and to sustain community life. The very existence of social structure is thus premised on role taking. Role taking is also essential to the alteration of social structure. When habitualized patterns of interaction prove inadequate for guiding joint acts to successful completion, conduct must be realigned through role taking. The periodic need for such realignments is inescapable, because novel events and the unforeseeable products of human

creativity call forth conflicting tendencies to act, and so bring action to a halt. In reconciling these conflicting tendencies to act, social structure is simultaneously preserved and modified.

It is clear that role-taking is quite distinct from the reciprocities of favour exchange; indeed, it is more affective and cognitive than behavioural as it is an engagement of sympathy and the formation of understanding of one's own self through imaginatively constructing the other's situation, disposition, and purpose or intention. It is a characteristic element of morality through trans-subjectivity.

In describing role-taking in this way, the form and content of Confucian *shu* is captured. It remains at some distance from 'reciprocity'. It does connect with reciprocity, though, insofar as *shu*, as role-taking, will inform the sympathy of an exchange partner regarding the other's needs and intentions. Given the affective basis of *guanxi*, and its cultivated nature, discussed extensively in Chapter 1, the significance of *shu* as role-taking is in its enhancement of the orientation of *guanxi* participants in more readily sensitizing them to both their own capacities as participants and to the accessibility, requirements, capabilities, and potential of the other participant in *guanxi*. All of this is prior to any exchange between *guanxi* partners, and distinct from such exchange, but at the same time it is prerequisite to the successful formation of *guanxi* and to its continued practice. This aspect of *guanxi*, highlighted through a correct understanding of *shu*, is not found in other treatments of *guanxi* even though it is fundamental to the formation and practice of such relationships.

From *Shu* to *Renqing*

It is of particular interest that the Confucian disposition of *shu* relates to enactments of the much better-known Confucian principle of 仁 *ren*, generally translated as 'benevolence', 'virtue', or 'humanity' (Fung 1998b: 239; Goldin 2008: 169). This coupling of *shu* and *ren* is documented by Fung (1952: 71) when he notes that Confucius, in *Analects* 6:28, describes *ren* as the ability 'to draw a parallel for the treatment of others' from 'one's own self', so that the practice of '*chung* and *shu* [*zhong shu*] is genuinely to practice *jen* [*ren*]'. The connection between Confucian *shu* and *ren*, on the one hand, and *guanxi*, on the other, is only loosely specified in the literature:

Confucian social theory proceeds from neither the society nor the individual, but from interpersonal relations. This point of departure leads logically to the emphasis on exchange behavior to concretize and nurture social relationships, and thus [to] the notions of reciprocity and empathy…With this concern for the proper and ethical conduct of social relationships and its stress on obligation and indebtedness, *renqing* discourse is the popularized version of the classical Confucian textual tradition.   (Yang 1994: 70; see also Bian 2019: 7–11)

Acknowledging that the term *guanxi* cannot be located within the Confucian classics, King (1991: 65–6) argues that the Confucian notion of 伦 *lun*, 'relationship' or 'order' (as in 'social order') is a functional equivalent of the term *guanxi*. In the Confucian tradition *lun* is conceived in terms of five variants relating to five distinct social roles, each characterized by an affectual-moral orientation:

These five relationships and their appropriate tenor are *ch'eng* [*qing* 情] (affection) between parent and child; *i* [*yi* 义] (righteousness) between ruler and subject; *pieh* [*bie* 别] (distinction) between husband and wife; *hsu* [*xu* 序] (order) between older brothers and younger brothers; and *hsin* [*xin* 性] (sincerity [or trust]) between friends.   (King 1991: 66)

In the relations between individuals, then, the focus in the Confucian matrix, as indicated in this summary, is role compliance animated by the appropriate affectual-moral orientation.

While social roles are prescribed by social structure, role performance, in exercising affectual-moral orientations, is always subject to variation depending on the role occupant's opportunities and resources, including past experience and what has been learned from that experience. In a loose interpretation of the Confucian tradition, the practice of learning to conform to the appropriate standards of behaviour associated with each role, which is understood as the attainments of 礼 *li*, propriety, is expressed through *renqing*, literally 'human feelings', and more fully, human feelings regarding the obligations associated with a social role (see King 1991: 73–5). The problem here, though, is that *renqing*—in so far as the term relates to social exchange practices and behaviour—departs from and is not equivalent to the Confucian concern with acquiring particular role capacities. The Confucian focus in *lun* and *li* is primarily developmental, in the sense of self-cultivation; the focus of *renqing* in social exchange considerations, on the other hand, is regulatory. The differences between these is arguably one of emphasis, but as we shall see, what is emphasized in each case points in quite different directions.

These differences are apparent in the Confucian notion of *ren*, made of two characters, 人 *ren*, meaning 'person', and 二 *er*, meaning the number 'two'. From this King (1991: 65) draws an obvious albeit misleading conclusion:

According to Confucianist philosophy, the individual is never an isolated, separate entity; man is defined as a social or interactive being. It is no accident that the Chinese character *jên* [*ren*] (benevolence) means two men. Indeed, there is no concept of man as separate from men.

On the most conspicuous level 仁 does indicate two persons; but, given the Confucian focus on moral improvement, the two persons in question can be seem as consisting of a person at one level of self-cultivation and, second, the same person at a higher level of self-cultivation. In a real sense, then, at different levels or stages of self-cultivation a person is not the same; hence, two persons. As the relationship implied in Confucian *ren* is the relation of moral development then *ren* must be seen first as a generic term for 'cultivated virtuosity in role-specific dispositions that conduce to making any particular action optimally elegant and appropriate, and thus rendering such an action a source of significance for all concerned' (Ames 2011: 181). Herein lies the virtue inherit in *ren*, as the successful execution of an action as it relates to the performance of a social role. Social roles necessarily involve relations between persons as bearers of roles. Self-cultivation is therefore directed to attaining distinctive capacities realized in relations with others, the other—and more obvious—sense in which *ren* implies 'two men'.

Confucian *ren*, then, first and primarily relates to practices of self-cultivation. Cultivating oneself, through and for role performance, is linked, in the Confucian lexicon, with virtuous relations with others. According to *Analects* 6:28.2, 'Now the man of perfect virtue [*ren*], wishing to establish himself, seeks also to establish others; wishing to enlarge himself, he seeks also to enlarge others' (Legge 2001a: 194). It is through self-cultivation that virtue is achieved, and the endeavour for self-cultivation is attained and consummated in relations with others. The object of the relation is the achievement of virtue, of acquiring the status of the Confucian 'superior man'—a *ren*. *Analects* 4:11 reports Confucius saying: 'The superior man thinks of virtue; the small man thinks of comfort. The superior man thinks of the sanctions of law; the small man thinks of favours which he may receive' (Legge 2001a: 168). According to this statement, then, there is a fundamental disjuncture within social relations between role as a medium of self-cultivation, on the one hand, and exchange as a basis of self-satisfaction, on the other. Indeed, the injunction here is clear that the achievement of Confucian *ren*, on the one hand, and favour exchange directed to mundane comfort, on the other, relate to respectively distinct discourses and practices. This is to say that Confucian *ren* and the *renqing* underlying *guanxi* are not continuous but different and contrasting if not opposed practices.

The term *renqing*, invoked in all accounts of *guanxi*, is as we saw in Chapter 1 typically acknowledged to have a number of different meanings (Chang 2009: 461–2; Yan 1996: 145–6). These differences arise from variation in the connotation or implication of the term as a consequence of change in the context in which it is used and how it is applied. The oldest meaning of *renqing* refers to the feelings inherent in 'natural' human relations, especially those of family life (Hwang 1987: 953; Yang 1994: 67). Family life in traditional China is governed by hierarchically organized roles and ritual relations between them. In this context *renqing* means feelings appropriate to human relationships in which harmony and order in descent and intergenerational relations are maintained, based on principles of seniority and gender. *Renqing* thus refers to feelings connected with how to act appropriately, including those feelings associated with a sense of proportionate relational expectation and the moral or normative patterns of social life and a person's sensibility to such norms. Feelings in this context are both affective and cognitive, both emotions and thoughts, understood in the Chinese classical tradition as 心 *xin*, heart-mind (Ames 2011: 59–61; Qi 2014: 165–90).

In conventional Chinese-language usage, *renqing* is relatively free of philosophical entailments, referring to actions and engagements that primarily contribute to concurrent and conforming relationships, such as being sympathetic to others and showing respect where it is appropriate. Also, properly acknowledging a favour and repaying a debt, central to the practice of *guanxi*, are understood as performing *renqing*. The behaviours referred to in these everyday contexts can be described as giving *renqing*. The actual gifts or favours given in sympathy, out of respect, and in repaying a consideration by others may also be called *renqing* (Hwang 1987: 953–4; Yang 1994: 67–70). *Renqing* thus captures a broad spectrum of 'human feelings' concerning what is behaviourally appropriate for a given situation involving persons occupying particular roles. It includes those feelings expressive of custom and social etiquette. Earlier in this chapter we saw Yang (1957: 291) begin his discussion of *bao*, reciprocity, by quoting from the *Liji*, the *Book of Rights*.

The social protocols of gift-giving and exchange are mentioned a number of times in the *Book of Rites*, an ancient anthology reporting administrative, ceremonial, and social practices of the 周 Zhou dynasty (1046–256 BC). The following observations are representative statements of the discussion of exchange in this source:

> At meetings of rejoicing, if there were not some gift from the ruler, they did not congratulate one another…When the ruler sent (to an officer) the gift of a carriage and horses, he used them in going to give thanks for them. When the gift was

of clothes, he wore them on the same occasion...Whenever a gift was conferred on a man of rank, nothing was given to a small man on the same day.

(Legge 1885: 21–2)

The description in this work, of practices and their qualifying requirements, is in places quite detailed, as when the reader is informed: 'If (only) his mother were alive, he did not lay his forehead to the ground. Where such a prostration should have taken place, as in the case of one who brought a gift with his condolence, an ordinary bow was made' (Legge 1885: 140). These are reports of courtly practice and arcane exchange *rituals* informed by prevailing conventions at the time. They are mentioned here because, while Yang (1957: 191–2) believes they constitute the basis of Confucian ethics, it is much more likely that they represent reports of mundane practices in the same way that today *renqing* conduct relates to prevailing conventions rather than enduring principles.

Failure to express the situationally appropriate feelings and to behave accordingly, in both the Zhou court and in present-day China, would be seen as a demonstration of an absence of *renqing*. To show that one lacked *renqing* would have the likely consequence of withdrawal of approval and therefore lead to loss of face (Hwang 1987: 960–1; Yang 1994: 69). In this sense *renqing* functions to maintain the expectations associated with favour exchange, of instrumental particularism, including *guanxi*; it provides both a sense of the codes of conduct appropriate to the social exchanges that constitute *guanxi*-like relations and also the feelings that are the means of personal commitment to their practices. This notion of *renqing* is not based on and does not require Confucian affirmation, then, and can be seen as operating independently of Confucian heritage or sanction.

Conclusion

The discussion in the present chapter is focused on the possibility of locating the principles underlying *guanxi* practice in classical Chinese traditions, especially but not only those associated with the Confucian legacy. Taking as points of departure three key sources that have exerted significant influence on the sociological understanding of *guanxi* (King 1985, 1991; Yang 1957), the basis and nature of 'reciprocity' in Chinese culture have been examined through analysis of the notions of *bao* and *shu*, and also *renqing*. It has been shown that the concept of *bao*, drawn from a number of literary and institutional settings, provides a less than coherent ground from which a singular notion of reciprocity can be inferred. It is also shown that the notion of *shu*, while more consistently applied than *bao*, in fact relates to cognitive, affective, and imaginative practices, of role-taking, rather than to the more concrete enactments of exchange. The concept of *renqing*, widely regarded as both derived from the Confucian tradition and centrally important for *guanxi*, is shown to relate to everyday practices in which Confucius was uninterested, and which in any event do not require traditional endorsement. Indeed, as standard sociological analysis accepts, following the pioneering work of Peter Blau (1964), among others, reciprocity in social exchange, including in *guanxi*, does not require a traditional or externally provided ethical framework.

In sociological accounts, the norms of social exchange are held to be emergent in the acceptance of a favour and it is through such acceptance that an obligation emerges requiring the recipient to return the favour at some future time. These are the 'existential conditions' (Blau 1964: 92) of favour exchange, rather than cultural forces that operate prior to the actual enactment of exchange. Thus, a form of obligation widely acknowledged in sociology arises from receipt of a favour or gift. The force of this compulsion, the obligation inherent in social exchange, can be located in those expressions of antipathy to a gift which arise in order to avoid obligation of gratitude and expectation to provide a favour in return. The nineteenth-century American essayist and thinker, Ralph Waldo Emerson (1950: 404) holds that his 'independence is invaded' if he accepts a gift because a gift brings with it 'the expectation of gratitude' and the recipient of a gift is thereby an 'obliged person'. Indeed, because a gift—and the obligation that ensues in accepting it—may be unwanted, it is therefore always possible that the uninvited provision of a favour will be resisted or refused (Bourdieu 1992: 98–106; Coleman 1990: 309–10; Hwang 1987: 963–7; King 1991: 75–9; Simmel 1950: 392–3).

An offer and also an acceptance—or refusal—of a gift are elements of interaction in which both parties, the provider and the (intended) recipient, have agentic capacities so that the outcome of such an interaction is always contingent on the resolution of intentions, perceptions of those intentions, and the situational interests of participants. If a gift is perceived to be a bribe, say, or simply excessive or otherwise judged to be inappropriate, then avoidance is likely so that the intended recipient prevents a possibly damaging commitment (Komter 2007: 99–100; Ruan 2017: 84, 107). It was shown in Chapter 1 that the confidentiality of negotiation between prospective *guanxi* participants is to avoid the embarrassment of awareness, beyond the interlocutors, of a refusal to accept a favour (Lin 2001: 158). If a gift is accepted, though, the recipient experiences a sense of obligation to the provider to return their favour at some future time. What is particular about *guanxi* as favour exchange is not the sense of obligation that is internal to its operation, but the particular qualities of *ganqing* and *renqing* that ensure the maintenance of the relationship and the quality of its operations, as explored in Chapter 1. The idea that these factors are inherited from Confucian ethical theory, though, has been dispelled in this chapter.

The present chapter and the previous one have considered the relevance of aspects of Confucian ethical and social thought, and its institutional expression in the structures of both the Chinese family and Chinese language, or at least some particular terms, in order to better understand *guanxi*. This has been necessary because of the prevalence of the idea that *guanxi* exists as an inheritor of cultural forces that go back to the formative heritage of early China's moral, intellectual, and ritual endowments. In appraising the social operations of *guanxi*, rather than its cultural representation, forage for an ideational and customary bequest risks concealing rather than elucidating the actual qualities of *guanxi*, its requirements of and consequences for participants. In the following chapter the origins of *guanxi* shall continue to be of concern. But rather than search for distant sources more recent historical developments will be identified as significant for an apprehension of *guanxi*. In this discussion it is necessary to distinguish between the concept of *guanxi*, which has a long history in China's economy and society, and the word *guanxi* which, although lexically not new, has been used as the term for referring to enduring relations of favour exchange only from the early 1980s, displacing a number of other terms that emerged in the period from the formation of the People's Republic in 1949. When consideration of the sources of *guanxi* are concluded, the remaining chapters of this book will examine aspects of the structure of *guanxi*. Considerations of Chinese culture and society are not thereby abandoned, however, as these themes will continue to inform the exposition and the understanding of *guanxi*.

4

Renqing as *Guanxi* and in *Guanxi*

Commentators agree that 关系 *guanxi* is a broad and relatively loose category that refers to sentimental bonds of favour exchange between persons who have enduring social connections or relationships. In this sense, then, *guanxi* may provide those who participate in it with benefits or advantages of various kinds, including the acquisition of social regard or esteem, privileged access to the associates of those with whom one shares *guanxi*, and material enhancement in employment, commerce, politics, or some other domain of social life. *Guanxi* relations are informal and therefore beyond administrative or legal regulation. Also, because *guanxi* refers to practices of favour exchange without regard to the participants' motivation, a clear distinction is difficult to draw within the category itself between social support on the one hand and bribery or corruption on the other. In addition to these factors another complicating element in consideration of *guanxi* is that the application of this particular term to the phenomena described here is relatively recent, even though the behaviour it refers to is arguably a continuing feature of Chinese culture and society. These latter issues in particular will be addressed in the present chapter. The purpose in doing so is to specify more clearly the nature of *guanxi* by indicating its precursors, and therefore distinguishing its different forms and variable characteristics which are salient in different historical and social contexts.

It was shown in the previous chapter that, while it is difficult to sustain those arguments designed to show that *guanxi* has a Confucian basis, it is nevertheless possible to indicate historical cases in which particularistic ties are mobilized in order to achieve instrumental purposes. These are typically described as practices of 人情 *renqing*, which are widely regarded as culturally specific to social relations in China. The term *renqing* is usually translated as 'human feelings', but in the context of favour giving and receiving *renqing* has a compelling or obligatory aspect derived from norm-based expectations that, if contravened, have consequences such as the sanctioning of transgressors and possibly retribution against them (Chang 2009: 461–2; Yang 1994: 68–9). While the notion of *renqing* is readily and frequently invoked in discussions of what can be called 'instrumental

The Theory of Guanxi *and Chinese Society.* Jack Barbalet, Oxford University Press (2021). © Jack Barbalet.
DOI: 10.1093/oso/9780198808732.003.0005

particularism', it should be seen in this regard as a type of general orientation rather than a unitary social form. This is because the actual manifestation of *renqing* varies with historical and social context and informs different particular types of relationship, as we shall see.

It would be difficult to find an account of *guanxi* which did not regard *renqing* as a constitutive part of it or at least as having an underlying influence on the practice of *guanxi*. At the same time, though, as noted above, the term *renqing* has itself historically functioned to indicate a practice of instrumental particularism. In this case *renqing* is not a part of *guanxi* but operationally equivalent to it. The term *guanxi*, then, is most appropriately reserved as a label for the form taken by instrumental particularism in the post-1980s period in China. The relevant institutional context here includes the market reforms developed by the Communist Party from 1978. It is appropriate, also, in paying attention to institutional context, to consider what are the conditions through which instrumental particularism in preceding historical periods was identified by the term *renqing*. This chapter will examine how the descriptors of instrumental particularism in China have varied over time, from the late imperial period to the present.

In the first part of the discussion, two previously unexplored accounts of *renqing* practice written in the middle of last century are considered. The value of these sources is the way in which they identify aspects of Chinese social behaviour and its presuppositions which operated in the late imperial and Republican periods of China's history. This material sets the scene for the following section, which begins with the *renqing* practice of a late Qing dynasty imperial administrator, Li Hongzhang (1823–1901). By considering aspects of Li's *renqing* conduct, previously unexplored aspects of instrumental particularism are identified. These are examined further by revealing how such aspects of *renqing* operate in the context of rural China, both prior to and after the foundation of the People's Republic. This treatment shows not only how a particular aspect of *renqing* operates, but also how changes in the political and social structure of rural China following the ascendance of Communist Party rule fundamentally affected the nature and practice of *renqing*, and instrumental particularism in general. The third section considers the development of favour exchange under communism, showing how a number of distinct terms for instrumental particularism were employed and also how the basis of instrumental particularism changed over a relatively short period of time, until *guanxi* became a dominant name for the practices that took hold under conditions of market reform.

Finally, *guanxi* is considered in terms of the extant quality of the personal relations between participants. This discussion returns to an issue first mentioned in Chapter 1, regarding the contribution to *guanxi* of shared identity, and also in Chapter 2, in which non-kin affection and affinity were considered in terms of 感情 *ganqing*, emotional feelings or sentiment. The argument here is that *guanxi* scholars have too frequently invoked a late-modern American understanding of friendship when considering the associative bonds of *guanxi*, without properly appreciating that the notion of friendship is everywhere culturally infused and therefore that Chinese notions of friendship have to be understood in their own terms, which inform the enactment and routines of *guanxi*. Whereas the previous two chapters are devoted to showing that *guanxi* does not have a Confucian heritage, it is appropriate that the present chapter closes with an affirmation that the legacy of Chinese cultural forms are nevertheless integral to *guanxi*, and to how they operate within it.

Renqing as Instrumental Particularism

The practices of favour exchange in which *renqing* is implicated have always been understood as purposeful if not instrumental. Before examining social practices of *renqing* that operated in imperial China, accounts of the organization of action written during the Republican period will be examined which draw on the notion of *renqing* and its cultural attributes, but without assuming a Confucian heritage. Two separate studies will be discussed which provide important background for understanding instrumental particularism in general and therefore contribute to the analysis of *guanxi* in particular. The first of these is a study based on over 180 interviews conducted during 1947–8 with Chinese individuals residing at the time in New York City, including 'students and professional-class Chinese living around Columbia University', 'Cantonese laundry and restaurant workers' from Chinatown, and 'a smaller Central Chinese group on the Lower East Side' (Weakland 1950: 361). The Chinese population of New York City at this time was approximately 16,000 individuals, predominantly male, approximately half of whom had migrated from China during the preceding decade, three-quarters of them aged between 25 and 59 years; members of the professional class in this population included 'stranded Chinese scholars' unable to return home because of civil war (Wong 1985: 233–5). Interviewees therefore were able to report on their experiences in Republican China, and some of them in late imperial China. On the basis of these data cultural anthropologist

John Weakland developed a model of what he describes as 'the organization of sequences of related activity in Chinese culture, [namely] the whole sphere of "purposive" behavior' (Weakland 1950: 361).

Weakland's (1950) study provides an empirically based account of instrumental particularism that was published prior to the social science interest in *guanxi*; indeed, before that term became current. He reports experiences of *renqing* practice before the foundation of the People's Republic in 1949. Through his interviews with Chinese respondents, and also on the basis of participant observation of his Chinese informants, with whom he socially interacted, Weakland (1950: 364) discovered that:

> Sequences of behavior directed toward aims involve a considerable differentiation of preparation and execution. The preparation is largely private or undisclosed, and it often seems incomplete or inadequate to the aim, in which case the execution or attempted execution must be followed by further activity instrumental to it. Overt active preparations toward the protagonist's end are largely made for him by others on whom he has some claim and who react to the immediate need he reveals to them. There is some indication that this whole system is very repetitive, with alternation of roles in time—a favor granted calls for one in return, and so on again—and is extended widely in interlocking circles of social relationships.

This 'strong division of activity in Chinese culture into preparation and execution' (Weakland 1950: 366) is identified as manifest not only in the 'purposive behaviour' of *renqing*, the primary focus of Weakland's study, but prefigured in a variety of other characteristic cultural activities. For example, in Chinese classical painting, according to Weakland (1950: 365), 'artists conceive a painting in detail, over a period of time... then execute the picture rapidly... Each brush stroke... correct and final in one attempt.' Similarly, the way in which Chinese children learn to read and write involves 'the child [being] taught to read the characters in the classics—to give their sound at sight—without being told the meaning until much later... [requiring] long repetitions of copying a model as preparation for the eventual execution of one's own work' (Weakland 1950: 367). Many other examples of Chinese cultural practices requiring a clear separation between preparation and execution are provided by Weakland (1950: 366–8).

The schema, in which preparation for an action involving *renqing* is 'private and undisclosed' while its execution draws upon the support of others, must include the means whereby such support is brought to the execution of the action in question. The 'reliance on the aid of others' which is 'of major importance to a protagonist in achieving his aims' is secured, according to Weakland (1950: 364), through a 'prior bestowal of a gift or some other favor, followed by the exhibition of urgent and immediate need' on the part of the protagonist. This practice of 'reciprocal aid', Weakland (1950: 364) says, 'is centered around the concept of *jen-ch'ing* [*renqing*] (human feelings)', a concept described in detail in an unpublished manuscript by Hsien Chin Hu (Hu Xianjin) who at the time was a colleague of Weakland's at Columbia University. Weakland (1950: 364) quotes from Hu's manuscript:

> Where there has been a certain amount of *chiao-ch'ing* [交情 *jiaoqing*] (social intercourse) between two people, one of them may *ch'iu jen-ch'ing* [求人情 *qiu renqing*] (beg *jen-ch'ing* of the other), that is, ask a favor of him. To beg for *jen-ch'ing* implies that the recipient is willing to requite the service at some future date. The object of such a request may be anything: a job, a loan, officiating at some public function. *Ch'iu jen-ch'ing* quite frequently is preceded by an invitation or a gift, this is to 'make *jen-ch'ing*'...A person intending to...ask for a favor will *sung jen-ch'ing* [送人情 *song renqing*] (give human feelings). Particularly when A is not on a familiar footing with B he will give him some present, or invite him to dinner, before asking for *jen-ch'ing*.

Weakland goes on to say that within *renqing* practices a gift is not conceived as a condition for a return favour. In these circumstances a person who provides a gift or performs a service is ostensibly doing so freely, even though a return favour from the recipient typically follows at some future time. The social representation of favour exchange in *renqing*, rather, is that two separate and distinct acts are related to each other only through the 'human feelings' that exist between the participants. In these terms there is not an exchange of things in the sense of a commercial transaction, but rather a persistence of a relationship between two persons, a bond of friendliness that endures as a result of the initial contact, as shown in Chapter 1.

Inherent in the requirement of support from others in order for a person to achieve their purposes is, Weakland (1950: 365) says, an implicit element of dependency: 'a general pattern of dependence on aid from others in which one favor apparently freely given entails a responsibility to respond to a subsequent display of dependence, a need for help; and the favor returned begins a new cycle at the same time it finishes the old'. Such dependence on support from others is not seen as a sign of inadequacy or weakness, however: 'For the young man, the asking of advice and assistance from his elders is necessary and proper; for the mature man, the ability to judge the reactions of others so well that he can count on certain help from them indicates strength and wisdom' (Hu quoted in Weakland 1950: 365). This pattern of reliance on others is exemplified, Weakland (1950: 364) says, in the 'importance of social relationships throughout Chinese culture in getting things done and also the extensive use of middlemen [or] go-betweens'. He writes: 'The use of a go-between... both increases one's chances to succeed and shields one from the direct impact of possible failure and rejection... communication takes place not face-to-face between the principals but by intermediacy of an agent' (Weakland 1950: 369).

The 'employment of intermediaries' is taken by Weakland to be an enduring feature of social relations in China. Indeed, this is an aspect of behaviour that has been regarded as fundamental in relations between Chinese persons. A long-term observer of late Qing society, the American missionary Arthur A. Smith (1890: 193–200), reported the significance of intermediaries in commerce, marital match-making, and familial peace-keeping. The importance of 'indirect connections' or third-party brokerage in the development of *guanxi* between two persons has been frequently referred to in the literature (Chen and Chen 2004: 311–12; Hamilton and Wang 1992: 23; King 1991: 74; Qi 2013: 316–17; Yang 1989: 40–1), in which 中间人 *zhongjianren*, a middle person or intermediary, who has obligatory feelings (*renqing*) to each of the other parties, thereby has an interest in the success of the emerging relations between them (Barbalet 2015: 1044–6). While not all relations of instrumental particularism necessarily require intermediaries, persons occupying such a role provide a basis of assurance and common identity between participants who may not otherwise have had previous contact, as we saw in Chapter 1. An additional function of reliance on others in social relations is the avoidance of 'direct rivalries', according to Weakland (1950: 368); in Chinese culture, in which there is emphasis on role compliance and harmony, 'there is fear of and an attempt to avoid conflict between the self and... other persons'.

While this account of *renqing* exchanges in 'the organization of action in Chinese culture' provides a clear model of *guanxi*-like practices and their bases, its major limitation is an assumption of an apparent timelessness, informed as it is by what Weakland regards as a more or less fixed and enduring 'Chinese culture'. A source that Weakland draws upon and quotes, the unpublished paper by Hu Xianjin, on the other hand, indicates changes over time in *renqing* practices. Weakland conducted and published his research as a member of the 'Chinese Group' of the Columbia University Research in Contemporary Cultures, a research collective which operated from 1947 to 1951 led by the anthropologists Ruth Benedict and Margaret Mead (see Metraux 1980). A young Chinese anthropologist, Hu Xianjin

(Hsien Chin Hu), best known for her widely cited article on Chinese face (Hu 1944), was also a member of this group. Born in China in 1910, Hu most likely arrived in the United States around 1937, the year in which she was listed as an intern at the Brooklyn Museum, and completed a Ph.D. at Columbia University in 1948 (Hu 1948). Little more than this is known about her. Apart from Weakland's use of it, Hu's unpublished manuscript has not previously been discussed.

Hu (1949: 14–15) emphasizes the instrumental value of *renqing* when she reports:

> Merchants and bureaucrats rely heavily on *jen-ch'ing* to serve their own advancement. Merchants and officials all have *chiao-ch'ing* with each other and so can charge each other with *jen-ch'ing*...Landlords try to build up good relations with officials in order to have their taxes forgiven...In recent decades, it has been virtually impossible to win a lawsuit unless some way could be found, directly or indirectly, to influence the judge's decision through *jen-ch'ing*.

Such obvious instances of instrumental and self-interested uses of *renqing* leads the term to have 'an unpleasant connotation in the minds of some members of the present-day generation', for whom *renqing* has become associated with 'an element of compulsion' (Hu 1949: 14). Hu (1949: 15) argues that the situation she describes has arisen in Republican China as a result of the subversion of traditional society through the commercialization brought by the 'impact of Western civilization'; this, in turn, she says, has 'increased the scope of *jen-ch'ing*'. Hu (1949: 15) goes on to report that 'Whereas in the old society *jen-ch'ing* meant a reciprocity of services and signs of good-will, today it has come increasingly to serve the ends of the more astute individual.' And yet the difference may not entirely be in the practice of *renqing* but in broader changes of the social environment, as she indicates.

While Hu writes that instrumental *renqing* arises with the growth of commercialization in China, she also acknowledges that:

> In rural areas, the 'strong man' of the locality receives a great number of presents at New Year. Everyone understands the necessity for building up *jen-ch'ing* with this personage. To incur his enmity might have dire consequences in a society in which personal relationships are far more important than the rule of law.
>
> (Hu 1949: 12)

Even more telling, in discussing 'the long history of the Chinese Empire' Hu (1949: 17) notes that 'officials who have administered public affairs without regard for *jen-ch'ing* constitute the exception rather than the rule. Such officials, she says, were regarded as having 'an iron face and no human feelings' and 'often proved inconvenient to their colleagues'; indeed, their behaviour was 'contrary to the pattern of their society'. It will be argued that a supposed shift, during the Republican period, to a more decidedly instrumental *renqing* arises not simply because *renqing* is more frequently used to achieve a personalized advantage but because those who are able to engage *renqing* in such a manner incrementally descend the social ladder, so that over historical time less privileged persons are able to employ *renqing* in satisfaction of their needs. There is another dimension of differentiation within *renqing* that Hu observes that also relates to some of the differences to which she draws attention.

Hu (1949: 18) says that *renqing* 'may differ qualitatively [in the sense that it] may be "thick" or "thin", according to the sincerity of the individual' expressing it:

> When one is interested only in the purely social aspects of *chiao-ch'ing* [*jiaoqing*, relationships between acquaintances], *jen-ch'ing* is 'thin'; when one is concerned chiefly with the friendship of the other person and is willing to make sacrifices for it, *jen-ch'ing* is 'thick'. The concepts of 'thickness' and 'thinness', as applied to *jen-ch'ing* have the same connotation as when applied to friendship.   (Hu 1949: 18)

'Thin' friendship is a friendship of convenience or a friendship that is closer to mere acquaintance than a friendship based on committed loyalty. 'Thick' friendship, on the other hand, is more or less without qualification, a relationship in which one person identifies with the other and is orientated to the other's needs at least as much as to their own purposes. Hu says here that *renqing* yields to a similar distinction; that thin *renqing* is more instrumental in serving the interests of one or possibly both participants, whereas thick *renqing* operates to consolidate and maintain the relationship itself between the participants. But even thick *renqing* has its extrinsic purposes and is always available to be mobilized in order to achieve an advantage for at least one of the participants, as we shall see in the final section of this chapter.

Towards the end of her discussion Hu (1949: 20) suggests that the costs and limitations of *renqing* are more apparent than they used to be: 'Young Chinese have become aware of the fact that *jen-ch'ing* is time and energy consuming, and that it is not entirely compatible with respect for the law, which is the foundation of the modern state.' But in order to dispel any idea that with the modernizing influence of the Republic the old ways of imperial

China have receded with regard to *renqing* practice, she immediately adds: 'Yet this does not mean that they have repudiated *jen-ch'ing.*' Hu (1949: 20–1) goes on to list thirteen different definitions of *renqing* that were provided by interviewees from 'North, South, and Central China', each respondent providing 'one or more of these definitions', with 'no single individual' indicating all of them:

1. *Jen-ch'ing* is requital for kindness. In the older fiction, one often finds references to the '*ch'ing* of hospitality', the '*ch'ing* of succor', etc.
2. *Jen-ch'ing* is a feeling existing between people standing to each other in a slightly friendly relationship.
3. It is a favour rendered to someone.
4. It means the presents, invitations to meals, etc., given in payment of or in anticipation of a favour or in propitiation.
5. It means 'face' (*mien-tzu* [面子 *mianzi*]).
6. It is a means for building up friendship.
7. It is the beginning of a friendship, a means for initiating friendship.
8. It is a feeling uniting two persons having an institutionalized relationship to each other.
9. It was originally an instinct for making others feel well-disposed toward one. In time, it has become a set of forms of behaviour.
10. It is behaviour which gives a warm tone to human relationships.
11. It means the understanding of human emotions in various circumstances. For example, *jen-ch'ing shih-ku* [人情世故 *renqing shigu*] means 'an understanding of the motivation of human behavior and the affairs of the world'.
12. It means proper behaviour in terms of prescribed cultural patterns and a 'normal' way of life. An eccentric person can be said to be 'not close to *jen-ch'ing*'.
13. It means an understanding of the rules of life.

The first eight of these definitions Hu (1949: 21) says 'are the most commonly used'; but, even then, there is 'considerable latitude in the concept of *jen-ch'ing*', that a person's social and educational background may 'affect one's conception of the term', and also that its use may be either an affirmation of a sense of moral uprightness or 'merely a means to a personal end'.

What Hu says here regarding *renqing* does not meaningfully depart from more recent and current accounts of *renqing* and its relevance to *guanxi*. Indeed, the value of Hu's discussion is in the way it indicates the continuing salience of *renqing* in its support of instrumental particularism over the period of the twentieth century and earlier, and also today. Her account of the way in which 'merchants' and 'officials' use *renqing*, and the influence of *renqing* on 'the judge's decision' have a remarkably present currency. For instance, empirical studies of judicial decision-making in present-day China demonstrate that the informal *guanxi* relations between the judge and his or her family members or supervisors, on the one hand, and the plaintiff and his or her family members, on the other, on balance, frequently determine the outcome of proceedings in China's law courts (He and Ng 2017; Zhao 2019).

Weakland's account of the distinction between a social actor's preparation of their action and its ultimate execution, for which there is dependence on another person who is invariably recruited through *renqing*, especially the prior provision of a favour, can similarly be read as an anticipation of current treatments of *guanxi*, which nevertheless draws on evidence from an historical period earlier than one in which a *guanxi* discourse operates. The model of the organization of action presented by Weakland characterizes instrumental particularism in terms of cultural conventions that are distinctive. Indeed, the proximate similarity between characterizations of *guanxi* since the 1980s and the treatments here, by Hu (1949) and Weakland (1950) respectively, of *renqing*, suggest parallel if not operationally equivalent forms of instrumental particularism. In the following section a case of the use of *renqing* in late imperial China will be introduced in order to expand our appreciation of the scope of gift-giving and its social implications, and also to demonstrate the way in which changes in the social context have changed the nature of *renqing* practices.

Renqing from the Late Qing

In any consideration of social relationships and social organization it is important to take note of differences in the capacities and resources of those involved. This is because such differences relate to both outlook and performance, including those associated with gift-giving and *renqing*. In pre-Communist China privilege attached to official rank and academic title, factors underlying a distinct social category known as 绅 *shen*, the gentry (Fei 1953; Freedman 1979: 348–9). Agrarian producers, 農民 *nongmin*, the peasantry, on the other hand, existed quite outside of the realm of privilege (Eastman 1988: 80–99; Stover 1974: 89–100). In considering *renqing* practices during different periods of China's recent history, from the middle of the nineteenth century to the middle of the twentieth, such differences between protagonists are obvious and significant, as we shall see. Relatedly, it is important to distinguish the forms that *renqing* practices take in different historical periods and also in the practice of distinct social groups. As we shall see, variation in the historical context as well as the social location of those involved affect the form and application of *renqing*. In this section of the chapter, then, the focus of discussion will move from gentry to peasantry and from one period of Chinese history to another in setting out the elements of *renqing* in the changing nature and expression of instrumental particularism leading up to *guanxi* from the 1980s. A constant concern is the nature of *renqing* relations, how they change, what unifies them, and how different social groups employ them and how such employment changes over time.

The most accomplished and frequent practitioners of *renqing*, given their high cultural competency and their access to resources, were office holders in the imperial bureaucracy. These officials were occupied with gift-giving and favour exchange that not only facilitated the normal operations of their bureaucratic duties but also ensured that they continued to hold their official position and the privileges that went with it. In his discussion of administrative practices and forms during the late Qing dynasty the historian Kenneth Folsom (1968: 107) observes that:

> Money was a necessary adjunct to high position and power. It opened doors, provided protection, welded alliances and was the lubricant of human intercourse. Any high provincial official who did not fortify his position in the capital through sizable gifts of money would soon lose his backing and position.

Folsom goes on to describe the situation in this regard of Li Hongzhang, a leading scholar-administrator and a principal figure in 自强运动 *Ziqiang yundong*, China's defensive 'self-strengthening' movement of the second half of the nineteenth century:

> when Li was deprived of his Governor-Generalship and ordered to Peking in 1895, he was forced to distribute among the court officials and others a sum of eight million taels—equivalent to about eight and one-half million dollars—to protect himself from his political enemies. It is highly possible that one of the reasons why Li was able to maintain his position...for twenty-five years was because he regularly sent generous gifts to the Empress Dowager and other members of the court. The phenomenon of giving gifts was so common and such an accepted part of the course of official business that it was seldom, if ever, mentioned in the official records. (Folsom 1968: 107)

There are a number of important elements in this statement that can be explicitly indicated here, and one in particular that requires extended discussion.

The thing that stands out most obviously in the quotation is reference to the role of money in Li's relations with the court and its officials, which may seem an inappropriate instrument of *renqing*, being more suitable for bribery, or commerce. Indeed, the impersonality of money is arguably antithetical to the etiquette of *renqing* practices (Yang 1994: 202). In fact, of the distinctive types of resource available for social exchange, which can be differentiated on the two axes of symbolism versus concreteness and particularism versus universalism, money alone occupies the polar extremes of concreteness and universalism; this is in stark contrast with affection and esteem which are the most infused with symbolism and particularism (Foa and Foa 2012: 17–18). It goes without saying, then, that on these criteria the resources most appropriate to *renqing* are affection and esteem while money is the least appropriate. Nevertheless, there is much ambivalence concerning the place of money in *renqing*, and in *guanxi*. While Yang (1994: 163) says that monetary transactions 'do not involve *renqing* and its offshoots', she acknowledges that money 'may be given instead of gifts to fulfill *renqing* obligations'. The point is made explicit by Ruan (2017: 84–8) that within an existing *guanxi* relationship money may be provided to satisfy the requirements of *renqing* exchange, although an attempt by a 'stranger' to offer a money gift would be seen as a contravention of the rules of *renqing*. When money is given by a person who has an existing *renqing* with the recipient, then, it does not necessarily undermine the decorum, the symbolism, and the particularism of *renqing*, just as wrapping money in 红包 *hongbao*, a red envelope, gives it an acceptable form (Ruan 2017: 125–7). Actually, in rural society 礼金 *lijin*, a monetary gift, has long been an acceptable offering at major rituals, including weddings, funerals, and birthday celebrations (see Yan 1996: 50, 56, 82–3). The relevance of this will become clear shortly.

Two other things are implicit in Li's distribution of money to members of the court. One, that the distinction between a gift and a bribe in the context of social exchange practices is neither case neutral nor easy to define (Barbalet 2018; Li 2018; Smart 1993). Second, gifts (and favours) may be considered 'social investments' because when sending a gift one can be 'expected in return', and if such reciprocity does not occur then the defaulting person is regarded as 'lacking in human feelings (*jen-ch'ing*)' (Folsom 1968: 21), and thereby loses face and opportunities for future *renqing*. These two things are widely acknowledged and understood. A third thing is apparent in

Li's case described above, which unlike the first two mentioned here is seldom stated and may not always be fully understood; namely, that a gift may be given not on the basis of an expectation of a returned gift or favour, but is given simply in order to be let alone, as a purchase of protection:

> Aside from the aesthetic, emotional, and economic aspects of friendships, there was one other that seems to have been overlooked in most discussions of this phenomenon, and that is 'protection'... Because of a lack of faith in the law, and a training which emphasized human relations, each family or individual... built up a network of alliances of families and friends as a form of insurance against the depredations of the officials, their enemies, the ravages of nature, and the government itself.   (Folsom 1968: 24–5)

This passage refers to friendship but the element of protection it refers to is also a possibility in *renqing*, as where it was reported that Li gave gifts of 'eight million taels... to protect himself from his political enemies'. A third aspect of *renqing*, then, which is typically overlooked, is the provision of a gift as a consummatory act in itself rather than as an element of reciprocal exchange. Gift-giving is almost always understood to operate in terms of reciprocity or gift exchange. But not all gift-giving involves exchange; there is also sacrifice and protection. While Folsom indicates the relevance to officials of gift-giving, in order to have protection or to be let alone, it is also significant in this regard in rural society.

In shifting our focus to rural society, in order to better understand the distinction between 'social investment' and 'protection', between favour exchange and consummatory gifts as distinct forms within *renqing*, it is necessary to distinguish between village life in China during the late Qing and early Republican period, on the one hand, and after 1949, on the other. There is now an extensive discussion of *guanxi* and *renqing* in rural China (Chang 2009; Kipnis 1997; Ku 2003; Ruf 1998; Yan 1996). Kipnis (1997: 7), for instance, warns that there is no timeless cultural logic underlying village *guanxi*; rather, 'practices of *guanxi* production in modern rural China must be understood in the context of more than forty years of Chinese Communist Party policy'. As we shall see, the changes experienced in rural China since the 1950s means that these relatively recent studies of village *guanxi* are unhelpful in understanding rural China prior to 1949. Rural social relationships, including those in which gifts and favours are implicated, result from practices animated by the purposes of the actors involved which are themselves shaped by expectations, resources, and opportunities that are provided by given circumstances, and quite unlike those available under different historical circumstances. First, rural China in the late Qing and Republican periods will be described and then in the communist period, in order to highlight how *renqing* operated largely as protection and then came to serve the needs of social investment, how it changed from gift-giving to gift exchange.

The commonly formed image of any society, including traditional Chinese society, is based on available evidence, and that evidence is typically in the written record provided by literate observers or participants. In the case of traditional China that literate group was the gentry, which comprised a tiny portion of the population and which had interests and experiences that were quite unlike the rest of the population. The vast majority of people in late imperial and Republican China were agrarians, illiterate, wholly occupied with physical labour and, in varying degrees, capable of generating at best modest surpluses. The circumstances and dispositions of the gentry and the peasantry could not have been more dissimilar. An endeavour to capture the world of the Chinese peasant prior to 1949, as well as that of the gentry, is presented in a neglected overview by an historical anthropologist, Leon Stover (1974). Some controversy attaches to this book, which a contemporary review complained presents a 'hypostetization of a theoretical type [through which] all of the subtleties of coalition, cooperation, creativity and internecine exploitation among villagers responding to particular situations through complex idioms, are simply stripped away' (Tobias 1976: 412; but see also Cornell 1976; Fairbank 1976; Farmer 1974). On the other hand, however, there is the idea that, in attempting a 'depiction of interpersonal relations at an aggregative society-wide level…Stover's idiosyncratic book' avoids descriptive particularities and 'actually comes closer to the mark' than other notable endeavours (Gold 1985: 658–9). Stover's insights regarding gift-giving are particularly useful for the purposes of the present discussion.

A prevalent ethos of traditional Chinese society is that there is a more or less fixed supply of resources, including land, wealth, and privilege, and therefore that one person's or family's gain will necessarily be at the expense of another: 'The Chinese attitude towards business was that the total volume was constant and any increase on the part of one businessman must be offset by a corresponding loss on the part of the others' (Folsom 1968: 28). This mercantilist notion, that one party's economic gain must be at another party's expense, corresponds with the gentry's Confucian attitudes to profit making (Brook 1997). It also reflects the material consequences for peasant families of household division resulting from the death of the senior male, in which the property of the family is distributed to his sons (Barbalet 2017a: 113–15), as well as the consequences of commercial land acquisition. The peasant out-look, Stover (1974: 105) says, is that:

Beyond the fields of one village lie those of another. The agricultural landscape is filled in. Landed wealth cannot be expanded. It can only be divided, redistributed, exchanged, bought, and sold. Villagers are acutely aware that any gain in property by one family is another's loss.

The consequence of zero-sum property prospects for peasant families is a sense of social isolation in which each family is a source of security that stands against all other families. For the gentry this situation promotes the extended family, for the peasant family which is limited in size by the modesty of its assets, it leads to suspicion and rivalry: 'The disadvantages of peasant life do not induce a communal spirit of sharing...[but] rather a sense of rivalry...envy and distrust, based on a realistic appreciation of liability to loss' (Stover 1974: 106; see also 129). An obvious defence against the mutual suspicion, gossip, and envy that affects village relationships includes 'habits of underconsumption, together with a concealment of material gain' (Stover 1974: 106), so that frugality and thriftiness are features of peasant lifestyle (Stover 1974: 106, 134), a frequently noted aspect of Chinese non-Confucian culture (see, for example, Weber 1964: 158, 188, 242).

Thrift is an obvious means of controlling consumption: 'Wealthy children can overeat, but poor children must often tighten their belts' (Hsu 1948: 273). Fei (1939: 119) puts the proposition in an ecological rather than a social context when he says that in a 'rural community where production may be threatened by natural disasters, content[ment] and thrift have practical value'. He does notice an exception, however, in that the 'idea of thrift is absent on ceremonial occasions' (Fei 1939: 120), that is, at village weddings, for instance, generous gifts are expected and given. It is because thrift 'becomes meaningless when one is not able to reach the accepted standard of proper living' that the difference between thrift and generosity in ceremonial giving is explained; thrift sets an 'upper limit for the variation of livelihood' whereas 'generosity and kinship obligation in helping relatives...keeps individuals from sinking too much below the standard' (Fei 1939: 120). The problem here is that two contradictory principles are used to explain a livelihood outcome in which each principle renders the other unlikely if not unnecessary. A more consistent and sociologically meaningful argument is presented by Stover. For Stover, as we have seen, thrift derives not simply from material deprivation but is a response to social envy and mutual suspicion. In this context 'self-sacrificing cooperation...is a means...[of defence] in a hostile social environment riven with mutual jealousy' (Stover 1974: 139).

The ceremonial extravagance of gift-giving at weddings and funerals is on this basis best understood as a 'defence against mutual suspicion' insofar as ceremonial gift-giving is a discharge of social obligation in which a surplus is deployed not for personal consumption but to visibly achieve social merit, to gain face (Stover 1974: 131). These gift-giving ceremonies are not an affirmation of community life so much as a means to 'reduce the tensions of mutual suspicion by allowing economic surplus to be spent on a display of merit' (Stover 1974: 128, 130). In contrast to Fei's idea that ceremonial gift-giving and kinship benevolence converge, Stover (1974: 139) argues that:

> the institution of kinship is an expensive one for the peasant to maintain, costing him heavily at weddings and funerals without bringing in any revenue as do the ancestral temples of the gentry, those symbols of powerful joint-family corporations…For the peasant to justify his own property rights in the name of kinship can be nothing but platitudinous, witness the fact that in the same name he spends with ritual extravagance in order to be rid of the suspicion that he is accumulating wealth and hiding it.

This account provides an important dimension to the idea that gift-giving as *renqing* is a means of achieving 'social protection' rather than a form of 'social investment', to return to the categories introduced by Folsom. In this latter case gift-giving is a unilateral or consummatory act in the sense that giving a gift is terminal and does not require a return gift and recompense, whereas in the case of 'social investment' gift-giving is necessarily part of a reciprocal exchange.

An axiom of social exchange theory, with which this chapter began, is that gift-giving in dyadic relations typically gives rise to social obligation in the form of an expectation of a return gift or favour. In this case, *renqing* is social investment. When gift-giving is a consummatory act, on the other hand, then it is more appropriate to regard the provision not simply as a gift but as a sacrifice, in the sense of providing appeasement, which can be taken to be Stover's meaning in this discussion. The treatment in the literature of *renqing* and *guanxi* generally assumes reciprocal dyadic exchanges; but if the recipient is a generalized other, such as a village wedding or funeral, then the provision of a gift is more properly understood as an act of conciliation. In this case *renqing* is social protection. Indeed, much village gift-giving, not only during the imperial and republican periods, was not to generate reciprocal *renqing* but to avoid false accusations (Folsom 1968: 27; Stover 1974: 106, 120, 138). These practices are possibly parallel to 朝贡体制 *chaogong tizhi*, tributary provision, which operated between the Chinese imperial household and minor states (Zhang and Buzan 2012), in which the latter provided a suppliant, a tribute, to the former in an acknowledgement of their superiority. It has been observed that villagers maintain records of gifts, given and received (Wilson 2002: 169–70; Yan 1996: 49–60; 2009: 183–204). Such audits may facilitate appropriate exchange, but they also guide the extent to which sacrifice is required.

While Stover was writing of China prior to 1949 a recent report shows that the practices of consummatory gift-giving in Chinese villages continues today. Qi (2017a: 12–13) reports a number of cases in which large amounts of money are spent by rural-to-urban migrant workers in their home village in what Qi describes as 'face-oriented etiquette'. One respondent reported 'that over 80% of her husband's remittance was spent on village banquets and gifts', leaving insufficient to satisfy her family's daily needs. Another similarly remarked that it was 'not unusual for her family to not be able to afford meat, but at the same time it was unthinkable to avoid gift-giving in the village'. Another migrant worker said that when she returned to her home village during the Chinese New Year, she needed to distribute approximately ¥7,000 (equivalent to $1,000) in gifts. These respondents spent 'very little money on themselves'. Another respondent reported that she spent more than ¥60,000 on her mother-in-law's funeral, incurring a debt of ¥20,000. In addition to the banquets which went on for four days and three nights, payments were made for cigarettes, Daoist rituals, and also 腰鼓 *yaogu*, waist drum, and 舞狮 *wu shi*, lion dance, performances. Relatives and 'all the people from the *dui* (brigade or squadron)' attended. In response to the questions 'why was so much hard-earned money spent in this way, and why was so much more money borrowed' the respondent replied that it was the local custom to have extravagant funerals and 'if the custom was not followed her family would be laughed at and lose face'. These social obligations were discharged through gift-giving as sacrifice.

It was shown in Chapter 2 that the traditional Chinese village was not a closed association but rather an 'aggregate of households in a compact residential area' (Fei 1939: 106) and that these households related to members of other households in a more extensive standard marketing community (Fei 1939: 129, 141, 257–9; see also Skinner 1964). How 'compact' the residential area of the village in fact was varied regionally. Villages in Sichuan, in west China, for instance, unlike the village in east China studied by Fei, 'consisted of individual family homes dispersed throughout the countryside, rather than clustered together in a single, nucleated settlement' (Ruf 1998: p. xiv). Fei (1939: 8) says that the village 'is a *de facto* social unit recognized by the people themselves'. The residents of the village studied by

Ruf (1998: p. xiv), on the other hand, 'had come to share a sense of common identity only since the Communist revolution'. Not only did the traditional village lack legal status, as Fei (1939: 109) says, it was neither an administrative nor a fiscal unit in so far as only 'the names of the heads of households appear in the tax registers of local government' (Stover 1974: 89). This indecisive status of the village changed radically with the onset of communist collectivization from the mid-1950s. Collectivization, which led to the suppression of private markets and restrictions on the movements of villagers, resulted in an unavoidable withdrawal of villagers from participation in a standard marketing community and relegation to the insular confines of their village. This was achieved by an inhibition on extra-village contact and communication through the political suppression of extra-village market relations, the political organization of the members of villages through the activities of the Communist Party and its local cadres (Yang 1959: 254), and finally through enforcement of the 户口 *hukou*, household registration system, which effectively restricted rural residents to the village of their birth or marriage.

From the middle of the 1950s, then, collectivization and market controls in rural China led to a 'growing isolation of village communities', which in turn led those villages to experience 'extraordinary levels of stability' (Selden 1993: 153):

> With villagers prevented from buying and selling in the few remaining markets, with the closure of rural fairs and traditional cultural events after 1957, with the penetration of party-state networks deep into village life, and with attacks on old culture, customs, and ideas, including the purchase of brides, most people found their world restricted to the natural village.   (Selden 1993: 153)

The research focus of the study mentioned here is family strategies, including the 'pronounced tendency toward intra-village marriage [and] shrinking family size', but at the same time he notices that as 'extra-village social and economic ties were severed...the most valuable alliances for families struggling to survive shifted to within the village' (Selden 1993: 140, 153–4). These alliances or social support networks within the village were achieved and consolidated through gift and favour exchange, a mode of interaction that is the substance of *guanxi*, which is related in the village studies that have been published since the 1990s (Kipnis 1997; Yan 1996). Indeed, this is the context in which the development of extensive *guanxi* relations within village communities occurred from the 1950s but which were previously more-or-less absent. In the region of west China that was the location of research undertaken by Ruf, there 'were no "village communities" in the early-twentieth-century Baimapu countryside' and in the 1940s, to the 'extent that people associated themselves, and their fates, with a particular place or territory, those sentiments generally focused on ancestral halls, family property, earth god shrines, and the local market' (Ruf 1998: 29).

During the pre-communist period and throughout the Republican era, 'social and economic interaction was structured through communities of exchange based on relations of kinship, affinity, friendship...mediated through the township's periodic market' (Ruf 1998: 88). All of this changed with the communist revolution, which despite its national scale 'was profoundly local in character', beginning with Land Reform in 1950–1, which 'introduced new typologies of identity and created new forms of community organization' (Ruf 1998: 66). The transformation of the Chinese peasant and peasant society through these political changes and its gravity cannot be overstated, with traditionally privileged sectors of society disempowered and the previously disenfranchised peasantry provided with material and symbolic capacities previous unavailable to them (see Siu 1989). This was the ground from which *guanxi* developed within rural villages, as we shall see more fully shortly.

While the situation of isolation between villages and the intra-village focus indicated here were reversed during the 1980s through China's market reforms, the subsequent practices of *guanxi* between villagers persisted. The anthropological literature which treats village *guanxi* from the onset of the communist period, therefore, cannot be used to describe the practices and dispositions of village life in the earlier period of the late Qing and the Republic, in which sacrificial patterns of gift-giving operated to provide protection from vindictive jealousy and gossip, patterns which Qi (2017a) shows have not gone away. But at the same time, with the transformation of village society through communist collectivization, reciprocal gift-giving emerged and become widespread. Each form of *renqing*, as sacrifice and as social investment through exchange, is therefore commonplace in rural society, but variably dominant in respectively different historical periods.

Favour Exchange under Communism

A number of writers hold that the current practices now known as *guanxi* can be understood only in the context of China's communist revolution (Gold 1985; Kipnis 1997: 7; Yan 1996: 210; Yang 1994: 6–7). This is not to deny continuities with pre-communist practices of gift-giving and instrumental particularistic *renqing*, as indicated with regard to Li Hongzhang and in rural China during the late Qing, and in Republican China, as reported by Weakland (1950) and also Hu (1949). The 'old patterns [were] never eradicated', as Gold (1985: 674) put it, and at the 'micro-level...personal relations in China reveal the power of tradition'. But this acknowledgement is not to assert a direct lineal or historical continuity. On the contrary, communism in China brought with it two factors that were entirely new and which fundamentally modified the form and reach of personal relations based on *renqing* that justified a new name for such practices, *guanxi*, although it took approximately thirty years for this term to attain common usage after the practices it refers to began to be formed. The two factors in question are the wholesale reconfiguration of the structure of political and social power in China and the fundamental transformation of the peasantry, changed from an inert social category to a positively associated designation with newly ascribed economic and political entitlements.

The structures of administrative power in imperial and communist China could not have been more different. In the last decades of imperial China, a population of approximately 400,000,000 people was governed by 'not more than 40,000 officials' (Michael 1955: 420). At the local level, the district magistrate was typically responsible for administering an area with a population of between 200,000 and 300,000 persons, consisting of 200–500 villages (Yang 1959: 103). Officials at this time were appointed on the basis of their holding an academic degree conferred by success in an imperial examination. But not all degree holders were officials; by the end of the nineteenth century there were approximately one and a half million degree-holders in China, known collectively as the gentry; together with their families, this group—gentry and their family members—comprised up to seven and a half million individuals, no more than 2 per cent of the total population (Michael 1955: 422; Yang 1959: 255). As local notables, members of the gentry who did not hold office in the imperial administration nevertheless participated in local affairs, especially in supervising public works related to such vital concerns as flood prevention, through the building of dams, dikes, and canals, as well as the building of roads and bridges (Michael 1955: 422). They did this by directing village headmen to supply and organize villagers as conscripted labour. In this context it is understandable that 'the "strong man" of the locality', as we saw Hu (1949: 12) say, received 'a great number of presents at New Year'.

With the victory of the Communist Party the structure, locus, and reach of political administration at all levels was transformed and enlarged. At the local level the power structure was unified, with the same party apparatus that formed the central administration now governing the political order of the village. Local interest groups were no longer coordinated by local notables, the gentry, but by 干部 *ganbu*, cadres, orientated to a transformation of the countryside in concert with national policies, removing existing privilege and redefining the structure of land ownership and the basis on which status was conferred. The distinction of the previous era, between the magistrate and the gentry, one administering law, the other public works, no longer operated. By the mid-1950s the new administration included one and a half million government officials supported by thirty-five million Communist Party and Youth League members (Yang 1959: 254–6). Given the new structure of power, and the role of the party official and cadre in the management of production and distribution—including the allocation of work and determination of remuneration—opportunities for begging *renqing* or favour seeking at all levels, in all areas, urban as well as rural, was now much more widely located and practised than previously possible (see Oi 1985; Walder 1986).

In the pre-communist countryside, clan membership and lineage organization preserved the dependence of peasants on landlords and encouraged peasant passivity in the face of unequal social and economic conditions. Communist Party strategy redefined the agrarian population in class terms, disrupting the clan structure in which landlord and peasant were likely to share a surname and therefore a sense of 'family' unity. Under the newly prescribed communist terminology the tenant belonged to a class exploited by a class enemy, the landlord; and the general category of agrarians was stratified into class designations with corresponding political significance, namely, rich peasant, middle peasant, and poor peasant. This terminology and its political significance is developed as early as 1927 in Mao Zedong's 'Report on an Investigation of the Peasant Movement in Hunan' (Mao 1967a: 23–59) and succinctly clarified in 1933 in a Party document, 'How to Differentiate the Classes in the Rural Areas' (Mao 1967b: 137–9).

Poor and middle peasants were mobilized by rural cadres during the early period of communist rule as a land reform movement that lasted from 1949 to 1952 (Ruf 1998: 62–89; Yang 1959: 146–52). During this time, land owned by landlords, as well as temple land, land held by lineage associations, and land rented out by rich peasants, was confiscated by peasants' associations formed by rural cadres, and redistributed to landless labourers as well as to small and middle peasants. The small-scale family farms created by these developments were themselves replaced by collective farming by 1956. But the results of this initial transformation of the countryside continued;

peasant passivity and isolation gave way to new initiatives, including participation in *renqing* practices. As Yan (1996: 235) put it:

> Prior to the 1949 Revolution...only well-to-do families could afford to...offer a large, costly banquet...After land reform even the poorest villagers wanted to perform social ceremonies, and the social scope of gift exchange soon expanded to a much larger group.   (See also Kipnis 1997: 136.)

Gift exchange, and its expansion under communism, has not been uniformly appreciated, however, either by participants or by the Communist Party.

Discussion in the communist period of *renqing*, favour, or gift exchange, and instrumental particularism in general, was occupied with a number of connected themes, including corruption. Certainly, the role of cadres in political life and the attendant opportunities they had to engage in various forms of clientelist relations if not corrupt practices reinforced a perception that *guanxi*-like behaviour was more rather than less inclined towards extortion and possibly bribery. Discussing the situation among factory workers and officials during the 1970s Walder (1986: 179) observes that *guanxi* 'is not a sociologically precise term: in common usage, it refers to instrumental personal ties that range from strong personal loyalties to ceremonialized bribery'. The Cultural Revolution that lasted from 1966 to 1976 is often seen as a watershed period in the growth of corruption in China, a perception supported by a number of factors. A feature of this period, through which many of the elements of the association of *guanxi* with cadre corruption become clear, is 上山下乡运动 *shangshan xia xiang yundong*, the Up to the Mountains and Down to the Countryside Movement, in which its subjects, 下放 知青 *xiafang zhiqing*, 'sent-down educated youth', usually abbreviated to 知青 *zhiqing*, 'educated youth', or their parents, engaged in possibly corrupt *guanxi* with cadres and also with medical personnel.

For twelve years, from the end of 1968, as part of a campaign to maintain the focus of the Maoist revolution, millions of educated urban youth were relocated by the Party to rural villages and frontier settlements in order to 'learn' from poor and middle peasants, with whom they lived. In these circumstances many parents, especially those with social 'connections', engaged in 拉弦 *la xian*, 'string pulling', in order to ensure that, rather than suffer rustication, a son or daughter was instead provided with university entrance or military enlistment. Those involved were often high-ranking cadres with influence or the means to purchase it (Bonnin 2013: 85–7, 281) and also medical doctors who, through contacts or persuasive consideration, could be encouraged to provide certificates allowing rusticated youths to return to their urban homes (Bonnin 2013: 140, 313). The situation created by the Down to the Countryside Movement encouraged 'bargaining at all levels and encouraged the *zhiqing* to become experts in "relationship networking" (*guanxixue* 關係學 [关系学]), seeking out and maintaining the best possible contacts, rather than studying academic subjects or working in the fields' (Bonnin 2013: 315). During the mid-1970s a press campaign exposed the prevalence of 'string pulling' and 走后门 *zou houmen*, 'going through the back door', to use the terms of the day, but as official opposition to these practices grew in intensity Mao 'sabotaged' the Party's struggle against 'back-door' practices (Bonnin 2013: 105–7, see also 87). Such ambivalence by the Party to particularistic connections and their self-interested mobilization is not confined to this episode.

Liu Shaoqi, a leading theoretician of the Chinese revolution, in reporting on revisions in the Party Constitution of 1945, discussed among other things, 'The Problem of Cadres' (Liu 1950: 101–22). According to Liu (1950: 102) cadres are 'the nucleus of leadership among the masses' and therefore their significance lies in 'the intimacy of their connections with the masses'. It follows, then, that 'the solidarity of the cadres… [cannot be] founded on the interests or feelings of personal life' (Liu 1950: 105). The problem with these latter for cadres is that the 'interests or feelings of personal life' prevent connections with the masses: 'In their own company they talk and joke, and get along together perfectly, *looking after each other* and conversing without reservation. But they are *inaccessible, distant, indifferent and inconsiderate to others not of their group*' (Liu 1950: 108; emphasis added). Instrumental particularism is not simply a problem for the revolution but is itself a consequence of the revolution, especially during the Civil War period: 'The prolonged segmentation of the different sections of the party under conditions of rural guerrilla warfare, result[ed] in unique histories, *particular connections* and particular styles of work, which are different from each other' (Liu 1950: 107; emphasis added). This situation is described in the party literature as 山头主义 *shantou zhuyi*, 'mountain-top-ism', reflecting the fact that revolutionary bases from the mid-1930s were established in mountainous areas, most notably in Yan'an (for an overview see Saich 1994). While the coherence of Party practices required a suppression of particularistic connections in order to be accessible to the masses, the reality of Party factionalism—of politics within the Party—meant that even the most senior Party leaders relied on particularistic connections, including those forged in the mountains (Guo 2001). In various ways, then, while the Party opposed instrumental particularism, its practices and policies in effect encouraged it (Kipnis 1997:157–64; Walder 1986: 7).

As we have seen, Communist Party recognition of the possible impact of instrumental particularistic relations goes back to at least 1945, with Liu's reflections on the limitations of the responsibilities of cadres with 'mountain-top-ism', and during the Cultural Revolution the concerns with 'string pulling' and 'going through the back door'. It is not clear when the term *guanxi* was first used to refer to what is indicated by these more metaphorical expressions for instrumental particularistic relationships. Jacobs (1979: 237) quotes Mao as referring, in a speech given in 1967, to the fact that 'Personal acquaintances (*ssu-jen* [*shuren* 熟人]) are employed...and there are feudal relationships (*kuan-hsi* [*guanxi*])'. This is not a convincing example of the use of *guanxi* in the now current sense of instrumental particularistic relationship, however, as the emphasis here is more on 'feudal' than on 'relationship'. It is of interest that, in a discussion of the effects of 'communist terminology' on 'speech patterns' in China in an article in 1975, *guanxi* is referred to but in a quite different context of meaning for 'relationship' than might be expected on the basis of the discussion so far, suggesting that the current denotation of the term *guanxi* had not yet formed:

> The overwhelming number of expressions built with the term guānxi (关系) 'rela-tions' in philosophical and political discussions seem to have an interesting effect on the speech of daily life. The formal term for a young couple in love is kěndìng guānxi (肯定关系) 'to confirm the relationship', which is functionally equivalent to the old term liànài (恋爱) 'to fall in love'. The expression luàn gǎo nánnü guānxi (乱搞男女关系) 'to unorderly make relations between man and woman' is used to refer to love affairs of married people.   (Tai 1975: 236)

Gold (1985: 660 n. 17) cites references to *guanxi*, as the term is now com-monly understood, in Party publications in 1981 but he does not claim that these are necessarily originating appearances. It is additionally reported that quite different sources in the Chinese press, also dated from 1981, make use of the term *guanxi* (Chan and Unger 1982: 466 n. 26). Following a random survey of the *People's Daily* for the period 1957 to 1987 it is reported that 'discussions of *guanxixue* [*guanxi*-ology, art of *guanxi*] first appeared in the newspaper around 1978, when *guanxi* practices were condemned as harmful to the country' (Yang 1994: 147). Readers assume that this is a report of the first appearance of the term '*guanxi*' (for instance, Fan 2002: 545–6), but that is not what is being reported here; Yang refers to the concept and not the term in order to make a point about the novelty of *guanxi* practices. At best it can be concluded that a number of practices developed during the commun-ist period that are now called *guanxi*, a term whose appearance cannot be precisely dated but which emerged to displace related terms, including *la xian*, string pulling, and *zou houmen*, going through the back door, around the early 1980s.

Guanxi as Friendship, Chinese-Friendship

Most writers agree that *guanxi* is not a precise term, but it in fact has an agreed meaning when associated with *renqing* exchange and decorum, in spite of the absence of a resolute consensus regarding lexical finality. Some distinctions are readily identified. Walder (1986), for instance, insists that *guanxi* and clientelism are not identical. He writes of an 'informal "natural economy" of personal connections through which [individuals] pursue their interests... popularly referred to in China by the term *guanxi*...[which] refers to an exchange relationship that mingles instrumental intentions with personal feelings' (Walder 1986: 179). While *guanxi* may range from 'particularism', namely 'showing favoritism toward people with whom one has a preexisting personal tie', to 'ceremonialized bribery...[which] involves a straightforward exchange of favors for material gain or a compensatory favor' (Walder 1986: 179–80), these instrumental-personal ties are analytically distinct from patron–client relations between officials and their subordinates:

> Whereas patron-client ties represent the mingling of the public and the private, orthodox and personal, *guanxi* is a purely private and personal relationship... Instrumental-personal ties are less stable than the patron-client variety...[and] can arise between individuals who are not in a superior-subordinate relationship and indeed may arise between people who are barely acquainted.
>
> (Walder 1986: 181)

The distinction here is on the basis of whether the relationship operates on a horizontal axis, as with *guanxi*, or a vertical axis, as with clientelism.

Gold (1985), like Walder (1986), agrees that patron–client and *guanxi* relations must be distinguished, but he sees patron–client relations as an 'example' of *guanxi*. This is because while patron–client relations are only vertical, 'a *guanxiwang* [*guanxi* network] is composed of both vertical and horizontal connections' (Gold 1985: 660). The vertical aspect of *guanxi* relations, according to Gold (1985: 660), is that *guanxi* 'is a power relationship as one's control over a valued good or access to it gives power over others'. The problem with this proposition is that the first part is a truism, if one is to give something to another then one must have control of the thing that is given. It could be said that in such circumstances, of being able to give something to another, one has 'power' over that thing. But it is an entirely different matter to say that on this basis the giver has power over the recipient. 'Power over' is typically understood as a zero-sum situation: if A has power over B then B is subordinate to A and therefore cannot have power over A. But as Gold (1985: 659–60) in fact shows: '*Guanxi* is based on reciprocity...one does favours for others as "social investments", clearly expecting something in return'. If A has power over B by virtue of A providing a valued good or service to B, and then B has power over A by virtue of B providing a valued good or service to A, then the relationship cannot be conceived as vertical. It is a horizontal relationship of exchange. This is not to deny that *guanxi* relations may lead to the exploitation or even the oppression of one participant by another (see Zhang 2011). But this is not a function of the *guanxi* relationship itself but results from prior capacities and resources of the participants. Any power that operates in a *guanxi* relationship cannot be a consequence of *guanxi* exchanges themselves, but is a contingent factor which has a source necessarily external to the exchange.

A feature of *guanxi* widely recognized in the early discussion of the phenomenon is its basis in or similarity with friendship. While Jacobs (1979: 255–6), for instance, recognizes the importance of friendship in Chinese society in general, he writes that in the Taiwanese case which he examines *p'eng-yu* (*pengyou*) or friendship 'is not a true *kuan-hsi* [*guanxi*] base', that political 'alliances are based on close *kuan-hsi*, not on close friendships', even though 'friendship can make a *kuan-hsi* closer'. Indeed, the relationship, he says, runs in the other direction: 'a *kuan-hsi* base such as classmate, co-worker or fellow-villager seems a prerequisite to the establishment of friendship' (Jacobs 1979: 256). In this manner Jacobs postulates that, while friendship is not required for *guanxi*, if there is *guanxi* then it may be strengthened by friendship, and also that a *guanxi* base, 'such as classmate, co-worker or fellow-villager', is itself necessary for friendship. The problem here is that the presentation of 'friendship' is culturally insular, predicated on an American, say, rather than a Chinese sense of friendship, with the former emphasizing mutual empathy or sentiment while the latter is multidimensional and more thoroughly complex.

The connotation of 朋友 *pengyou*, the term used by Jacobs to indicate friendship, includes sentiment, as in 女朋友 *nu pengyou*, girlfriend, or 男朋友 *nan pengyou*, boyfriend; but classmate, co-worker, and fellow-villager, which Jacobs says may lead to friendship, are instances of what in Chinese culture and language are regarded as 同 *tong*, same-situation or shared connections that are a particular category of friendship according to Chinese cultural assumptions. As indicated in Chapter 1, 同学 *tongxue*, classmate, can always be called on for support, long after graduation; similarly, a 同事 *tongshi*, co-worker, is more than someone with the same employer; someone from the same town or village, generically, 同乡 *tongxiang*, native place, is particularly important in the formation of an especially reliable friendship, as testified by earlier generations of sojourning Chinese merchants in South East Asia and today by rural-to-urban migrant workers in China, each of whom relies on *tongxiang* when among strangers.

Recognition of the relevance of friendship for *guanxi* and, at the same time, a culturally insular view of friendship, is common in the relevant litera-ture. Without directly referring to *guanxi*, in a discussion of the transform-ations friendship has been subject to in China as a result of communist rule, Vogel (1965: 54) distinguishes between friendship as a 'relationship of mutual trust and privacy' and as 'a "feudalistic" relationship between benefactor and recipient'. Similarly, Gold (1985: 665) distinguishes between friendship as an intimate private and sentimental or affective relationship on the one hand, and friendship that is 'tinged with instrumental considerations' on the other (Gold 1985: 665). Such bifurcations of friendship are not confined to these sources (see Kipnis 1997: 148–9; Yan 1996: 237; Yang 1994: 111–18). The dis-tinctions characterized by these writers are internal to the English-language term 'friendship', which are by no means universal (Wierzbicka 1997: 32–55).

Chinese understandings of 'friendship' are complex and do not necessarily partake of the dichotomies suggested by the English-language term. For instance, the public–private distinction does not operate in a direct and clear-cut way with regard to Chinese friendship. The most intimate type of friendship formed freely between two persons is consummated in a formal ceremony, so that 把兄弟 *baxiongdi*, sworn brothers, have great personal intimacy that is necessarily publicly generated and not simply publicly recognized and acknowledged. Similarly, 义 *yi*, righteous friendship, means selfless intimacy based on public morality. In each of these cases there is an assumption of unfailing support, not only emotional but material, that is given freely without expectation of repayment but with a strong sense of reciprocity. In contradistinction to these intense direct forms of friendship, the indirect forms of friendship, the *tong* connections, assume not only an affinity between persons and a loyalty to the relationship, but also that the participants in *tong* connections of friendship are available for assistance and support through *renqing*, with an associated expectation of returned favours. Thus, the distinction between affective or expressive friendship, on the one hand, and instrumental friendship, on the other, cannot be located in Chinese understandings of friendship: Chinese friendship is both expressive and instrumental, private and public (Folsom 1968: 18–25; Smart 1999).

Guanxi, like the friendship forms, involves both affectual and expressive elements, on the one hand, and instrumental elements on the other. It has been shown elsewhere (Barbalet 2015: 1039–40) that expressivity and instrumentality in *guanxi* are second-order qualities that together serve a first-order characteristic of *guanxi*, namely enhancement of public standing, 面子 *mianzi*, or face. The provider of a *guanxi* favour is seen as a person of material means and moral capacities, through which the person in question will gain face in the assessment of their peers, by virtue of their association. The recipient of a *guanxi* favour is regarded as worthy to receive resources controlled by another and is held to be sufficiently reliable to fulfil future repayment obligations, through which that person will similarly gain face. If public reputation is a symbolic resource at the centre of *guanxi* exchanges, then their expressive and instrumental aspects are not in tension, rather, they together serve reputational enhancement. Underlying *guanxi*, then, are the various elements of friendship that in the Chinese context incorporate both human feelings as *renqing* and sentiments of attachment or affection as with *ganqing* (Barbalet 2018: 940–2) as well as instrumental support. Indeed, that there are 'no sharp and uncontested boundaries between friendship and *guanxi*' (Smart 1999: 132) arises from the morphological similarity between the two. Friendship and *guanxi* are not identical, but any difference between them will arise through contextual variation. As Smart (1999: 132) says: '*Guanxi* occupies some of the same conceptual ground as friendship'.

Conclusion

In seeking to discover *guanxi*, by examining *renqing* practices in a number of different historical and social contexts, this chapter has not only considered some of the traditional elements that underpin instrumental particularism, therefore continuing the discussion of Chapters 2 and 3, but also uncovered aspects of *renqing*, as well as its associated conventions and behaviours, not usually acknowledged in the literature. The discussion of Chapter 3 concluded with a brief account of *renqing*, which has been expanded in the first section of this chapter through reports of its nature and relevance in two papers written in the late 1940s. The article by Weakland (1950) and the unpublished manuscript by Hu (1949) provide concise statements of *renqing* practice in Republican China which not only complement more recent accounts of *guanxi* in present-day China, but do so in a manner that acknowledges both distinctive social processes of favour exchange as well as their cultural context and meaning.

Through a brief description of the *renqing* practice of a late imperial administrator, Li Hongzhang, a neglected aspect of gift-giving—as a consummatory act rather than as an element of reciprocal exchange—was identified and explored. We saw that gift-giving as sacrifice, or as a means of acquiring protection, was not only engaged by members of the gentry but also practised in the rural population when attempting to avoid the envy and suspicion of neighbours and kin. Similar actions continue today, engaged in by rural-to-urban migrant workers who are obliged to present handsome gifts to fellow villagers when they return home for Chinese New Year or on other ceremonial occasions, for a wedding or funeral, in order to preserve face and avoid being shamed. But this continuity cannot hide the enormous changes that have occurred in rural China as a result of the political rule of the Communist Party since 1949, in which the expansion of political authority and its administrative apparatus, and the ways in which they have transformed the peasantry, generated possibilities for favour exchange and instrumental particularism in general that were previously not possible for large sections of the population.

By enormously increasing the numbers of officials, in the form of cadres, and by facilitating for the first time the reach of officials into the intimate patterns of village life, communist administration encouraged possibilities for *renqing*, as social support through social exchange, to emerge where they had previously been absent. As a result of communist collectivization, China's villages now operated as administrative units that formed associated social structures, leading them to became integral and, in a sense, self-contained so that intra-village *renqing* occupied families in an entirely new manner. In urban areas as well, favour exchange became extensive as a means of securing benefits, and a new vocabulary emerged to describe the associated practices, namely *la xian*, string pulling, *zou houmen*, going through the back door, and, by the early 1980s, *guanxi*, connection or relationship. The informality of these various *renqing* practices, practices of instrumental particularism, is indicated in the frequency with which they are associated with or referred to in the context of friendship. We saw Hu (1949: 18) implicate friendship in *renqing*, as did Folsom (1968: 24–5) in his discussion of Li. Indeed, the connection between friendship and *guanxi* is unavoidable, as we shall see again in Chapter 6, and as a number of writers have shown (Gold 1985; Kipnis 1997; Smart 1999; Yan 1996; Yang 1994). It is appropriate that this chapter closes with an argument concerning the fact that 'friendship' is a notion that carries significant cultural meaning, and that the characteristically Chinese sense of friendship must be appreciated in understanding its relation with *renqing* and *guanxi*.

5
Trust in *Guanxi*

The relevance of trust to 关系 *guanxi* is unavoidable. In his 'Introduction' to a recent collection of essays by trust researchers, the Japanese sociologist Masamichi Sasaki (2019: 1) reminds us that trust 'is extraordinarily important because of its influence on interpersonal and group relationships' and that it has 'profound implications for interpersonal and social cooperation'. He goes on to say that trust 'in interpersonal and social cooperation implies commitment, which is intimately tied to obligation'. Here are all the operational elements of *guanxi*. The commitment to provide a favour to a *guanxi* partner, and the obligation to satisfy the needs for social support of someone with whom *guanxi* is shared, are elemental properties of *guanxi*, as we have seen. Given the informality of *guanxi*, and therefore the absence in it of formal structures and regulation, it is reasonable to expect that trust has an important role in assuring participants of the reliability of those whose cooperation is relied on. Indeed, in a recent treatment of *guanxi*, 'high trust' is designated as a relational manifestation or characteristic of a *guanxi* tie, through which the people involved are 'accountable to each other' (Bian 2019: 9).

One question concerning the relation between *guanxi* and trust is: which comes first? Is trust a requirement of *guanxi* or does trust arise from *guanxi*? If trust is a consequence of *guanxi* relations, then it need not be part of the definition of *guanxi*. We are told that, at 'its basic level', *guanxi* is 'a dyadic, particular, and sentimental tie that has the potential for facilitating the exchange of favours between the two parties connected by the tie' (Bian 2019: 6). The place of trust in *guanxi* is unstated here, possibly because it is a consequence of the development of *guanxi* rather than a founding element. This is arguably the situation regarding social exchange in general. In his classic statement of social exchange theory Peter Blau (1964: 94) writes: 'Since there is no way to assure an appropriate return for a favor, social exchange requires trusting others to discharge their obligations... [and while social exchange] may originate in pure self-interest [it generates] trust in social relations through their recurrent and gradually expanding character.' The scenario set out here indicates that a favour receiver demonstrates her

The Theory of Guanxi *and Chinese Society.* Jack Barbalet, Oxford University Press (2021). © Jack Barbalet.
DOI: 10.1093/oso/9780198808732.003.0006

trustworthiness by reciprocating a favour in response to the one that she has received. In this way, the favour provider comes to have trust in the recipient of a favour, and as this is a two-way relationship in which the provider becomes a recipient and the recipient a provider, the trust generated becomes generalized between participants. In this way, repeated cycles of favour exchange build trust between those involved. The idea that trust is both 'required for and promoted by' exchange, as Blau (1964: 8) says, relates to what is often regarded as an elemental property of trust, that trustworthiness has a propensity for self-enforcement (Blau 1964: 98–9; see also Coleman 1990: 306–7).

The topic of trust is now of considerable interest to social science, which has led to a large, diverse, and growing literature (Barbalet 2009, 2019). While trust is frequently referred to in discussions of *guanxi*, if the trustworthiness of participants emerges from social exchange, then a reference to it is not required in a definition of *guanxi* itself. It is of interest, therefore, that a recent contribution to the analysis of business *guanxi* has placed trust in the core of the *guanxi* relation, amounting to a new definition of it (Bian 2019: 125). In an empirical study of approximately 700 entrepreneurs in three provinces surrounding China's Yangtze River Delta a distinctive image of *guanxi* relations is presented that involves 'three qualities: (1) familiarity, intimacy, (2) trust, and (3) mutual obligation' (Burt and Burzynska 2017: 239). The three qualities of *guanxi* mentioned here are each important and familiar. The first, 'familiarity, intimacy', may be taken as more or less equivalent to what is usually referred to as 'sentiment' in conventional approaches to *guanxi*, given that the sentiment in question, 感情 *ganqing*, indicates focused emotional connections between two people. Similarly, 'mutual obligation' can be regarded as the responsibilities that 人情 *renqing* partners experience through their commitment to reciprocation in favour exchange. The novelty claimed by Burt and Burzynska (2017) is in the idea that trust is necessary in the formation, structure, and practice of *guanxi*.

In the study, respondents were asked on a five-point scale the extent to which they trusted the people they listed as contacts (Burt and Burzynska 2017: 254). It was revealed that, among those with 'event contacts', entrepreneurs reported significant levels of high trust. An event contact is a contact that has 'provided significant help in the history of a long-standing relation' (Burt *et al.* 2018: 13), which arguably satisfies one side of the 'mutual obligation' component of *guanxi*. Such levels of trust were not similarly reported for non-event contacts, and where there were notable levels of trust in such cases it was held to reflect the numbers of third parties that stood between the entrepreneur and their non-event contacts, suggesting that the trust in question arose indirectly as a 'conferred' or 'bestowed' trust. Trust associated with event contacts, in this account, is taken to signify a *guanxi* tie, whereas non-event contacts are not implicated in the generation of *guanxi*. Distinctive in this account is the contrast between *guanxi* ties and non-*guanxi* ties in terms of a high level of unmediated trust in the former and its relative absence in the latter. *Guanxi*, accordingly, is seen to be based on the respondent's trust of their contact associated with an event that consolidated the relationship between the two of them.

While the original article by Burt and Burzynska (2017) does not specify which Chinese term is used for 'trust' in the questionnaire given to the entrepreneurs in their sample, a subsequent and related article indicates that the word 信任 *xinren* was used, 'a word as ambiguous in Chinese as "trust" is in English' (Burt *et al.* 2018: 14). The authors feel, though, that such ambiguity is irrelevant to their findings because, by using 'a measure of trust open to respondent interpretation [it] is likely to generate trust ratings of cited contacts that co-vary with trust-related respondent differences, and our goal in this paper is to inventory those differences' (Burt *et al.* 2018: 14–15). Regarding the comment concerning the linguistic ambiguity of the Chinese term *xinren*, it is relevant to note that *xinren* is actually less ambiguous than the English-language term 'trust'.

In English, 'trust' includes both the notion of an act of trusting or the giving of trust, on the one hand, and also the quality of trustworthiness, of demonstrating that one can be trusted, on the other (Hardin 1993: 512–13; Hardin 1996: 28–9; Tullberg 2008: 2060–1; Yamagishi and Yamagishi 1994: 139–40). The difference between trusting another, of being trustful, and being worthy of that trust, or trustworthiness, in the context of understanding *guanxi* will be developed in this chapter. At this point the concern is only with the distinction itself and therefore ambiguity in the notion of 'trust'. In Chinese, *xinren* is typically taken to mean to 'give trust', to be 'trustful', or to refer to the quality of 'trustfulness'. Another word, 信用 *xinyong*, 'literally means the use or usefulness of trust' and at a general level 'refers to the integrity, credibility, trustworthiness, or the reputation and character of a person' (Tong and Yong 1998: 85). The importance of trustworthiness to *guanxi* is noted by Chen and Chen (2004: 313–14), but in this case they translate trust as *xing*, presumably meaning to refer to 信 *xin*. *Xin* is a root term for trust-related states, as shown with regard to *xinren*, trustful, and *xinyong*, trustworthy; similar examples of two-character trust terms include, for instance, 忠信 *zhong xin*, meaning loyal and sincere, or trustworthy, 失信 *shi xin*, to break trust, and 轻信 *qing xin*, to easily trust, to be gullible. The character 信 *xin* is composed of two distinct characters, namely 人 *ren*, meaning 'person', and 言 (also) *xin*, meaning 'words' or 'speech'. Thus, 信 *xin* can be taken to imply that a person does what she says she will do, that a person is trustworthy. We shall see that in the context of Chinese-language usage, the default for the Chinese-language equivalent of 'trust' is 'trustworthy', whereas the English-language default is 'trustful' or 'trusting'. While the Burt study indicates use of the term *xinren*, giving trust or being trustful, the relevant question in the research questionnaire in fact asks about *xinyong*, the trustworthiness of the respondent's contact: 'if the person was asking for a loan would they fully inform you about the risks of them being able to repay the loan?' (Burt and Burzynska 2017: 254).

In addition to ambiguity in the term 'trust', noted by Burt and his associates, there is also a question regarding the nature of the link between trust in the event contact, on the one hand, and *guanxi*, on the other. The trust measure of a *guanxi* tie identified by Burt and Burzynska (2017) is limited in so far as a causal link between the *guanxi* tie and the trust measure cannot be discerned from the network properties indicated in the study (Lin 2017: 272). The trust in question may be responsible for the *guanxi* connection; it may be its cause, or alternatively, the trust may be an outcome of the prior connection, in this case the trust in question may be caused by the *guanxi*. The design of the study does not make it possible to know which came first, the trust or the *guanxi*, only that they co-vary. In simple terms, a *guanxi* connection may be responsible for the sense of trustworthiness of the contact rather than the sense of the contact's trustworthiness giving rise to the *guanxi*. In fact, as we shall see, the trustworthiness of a *guanxi* partner is best understood as a construct of the *guanxi* relationship itself and not principally its cause.

The importance of the study conducted by Burt and his associates is not in its introduction of the notion of trust to consideration of *guanxi* because, as we shall see, many researchers have dwelt on trust in *guanxi*. Rather, the contribution of this particular study is its introduction of the notion of an 'event contact', and the opportunities that this latter concept provides to social network analysis for identifying and characterizing particular tie formations which are constructive in network formation and the associated dissemination of network relevant information to network members. The idea that trust is implicit in networks is not in itself original to the study in question but rather is an established feature of the relevant literature, as these authors acknowledge (Burt and Burzynska 2017: 233; Burt *et al.* 2018: 12).

Attention has been drawn to this particular study of trust and *guanxi* because it raises a number of important issues concerning the structure of *guanxi* relations, the cultural meaning of salient components of those relations, especially trust, and the nature of social solidarity in *guanxi*, a solidarity assumed to be explicable in terms of trust but which actually may involve additional or, indeed, quite different factors. Before examining more fully the relevance of trust for understanding *guanxi*, and therefore its cultural meaning in the context of Chinese society, it will be useful to begin by considering the connection between trust and social networks in general. The nature of assurance more broadly, not simply trust, in *guanxi* relations will also be treated in this chapter. Finally, the solidarity of network membership through *guanxi* ties is shown to be cultivated by participants and takes a compulsive form, possibly analogous to but nevertheless distinct from trust. By focusing on trust in *guanxi* this chapter gives attention to a factor commonly mentioned and widely discussed in the literature. But by acknowledging the need to respect variation in specific meanings of a general concept, between different cultural settings, as we saw at the end of the previous chapter with regard to friendship, an entirely new perspective on the relation between trust and *guanxi* is achieved.

Trust in Networks

Research concerned with resource distribution necessarily distinguishes between markets and networks. This is relevant to the discussion here because, while markets are seen to be based on property rights, networks are understood to be based on trust. Market transactions, it is held, occur between property rights holders who engage in contractual relations. Contractual relations between persons who have rights in the property they control are subject to the possibility of third-party enforcement through regulatory sanctions or similar legal instruments. In markets, then, legal enforcement operates to protect the property rights of participants. In this case, trust is more or less redundant; in the vocabulary of Japanese social psychologists Toshio Yamagishi and Midori Yamagishi (1994: 158–60) legal assurance operates in the place of trust (see also Hardin 1996: 34–5). Trust may 'lubricate' social systems (Arrow 1974: 23) but it is not necessary in market exchanges (Williamson 1993).

Market situations diverge from networked arrangements because the latter do not rely on third-party (legal) enforcement but on trust, on a sense of confidence shared between two parties that dependence on the other will not lead to failure to achieve a joint purpose. In an analysis of the historical evolution of institutions in medieval trade the economic historian Avner Greif (2006) contrasts developments among traders from the Republic of

Genoa, on the north-western Italian coast, with those that emerged among the Maghribi traders, who engaged in commerce in Tunisia and other Arab regions of north Africa. Greif shows that the bilateral trading relations of the Genoese generated legally tempered property rights which prefigured modern Western market institutions, whereas the practices of the Maghribi traders evolved into an alternative pattern, in which 'agency relations were characterized by trust... [and] not based on legal contracts' (Greif 2006: 63; see also 86–7). Trust, then, can preliminarily be understood in terms of an absence of third-party assurance mechanisms. This fits with the definition already noted of *guanxi* as a 'dyadic, particular, and sentimental tie'.

China developed a monetized economy with extensive marketization in the early imperial period (Elvin 1973: 164–78), and while a legal system similarly emerged in early imperial China, it was primarily focused on criminal rather than civil law. This does not mean that commercial contracts did not exist in early China (Hansen 1995), but they were not primarily legal documents as they were adjudicated by guilds, and business disputes were typically resolved outside a court of law (Elvin 1973: 172–3, 292–3). Property rights in particular were at best ambiguous in China. While property law did exist, it was not effective as land especially could be confiscated and redistributed by imperial fiat (Alsen 1996: 4–5) and in early China property did not attach to individuals but to joint families (Schurmann 1956) or corporate entities (Zelin 2009). Elvin (1973: 295) says that, although 'commercial contracts *could* be enforced in the lawcourts, at least up to a point', the general picture is accurate which holds that 'there was no commercial law worthy of the name, except that sometimes imposed by powerful guilds'. While the Chinese case does not correspond to a strictly 'Maghribi' situation, then, nor does it prefigure a 'Genoese' situation; rather, 'Chinese merchants relied on trust, guarantors and a web of interlocking obligations' (Alsen 1996: 5). When legal protection of private property rights was guaranteed for the first time in China's history, with the Property Law of 2007 (Zhang 2008), it existed alongside *guanxi* and did not replace it.

The different historical trajectories indicated by Greif point to a widely accepted institutional distinction between markets and networks, respectively grounded in legally enforced property rights and trust relations. A representative statement succinctly summarizes the convention: 'In market transactions the benefits to be exchanged are clearly specified, no trust is required, and agreements are bolstered by the power of legal sanction. Network forms of exchange, however, entail indefinite, sequential transactions within the context of a general pattern of interaction. Sanctions are typically normative rather than legal' (Powell 1990: 301). The normative sanctions indicated here are predominantly regarded to be those of trust. Indeed, it is widely accepted that there is a likelihood of network patterns emerging when exchanges are based on long-term and continuous reciprocity in which reputational profiles are evident and a commonality of the background of participants—ethnic, geographic, ideological, or professional—is established (Powell 1990: 326). This last point, which incidentally indicates factors parallel to what has in previous chapters been referred to as '*guanxi* bases', seems to reinforce the other two points Powell mentions in the quotation because, as he goes on to say, the 'more homogenous the group, the greater the trust, hence the easier it is to sustain network like arrangements' (Powell 1990: 326; see also Molm *et al.* 2000; Wellman and Wortley 1990).

The absence of any requirement of trust in markets, which are instead governed by property rights enforced by law, does not imply that trust is necessarily absent from markets. This is a position at some distance from Durkheim's (2014: 158–68) well-known argument, however, concerning the non-contractual basis of contract in trust. It is worth noticing, though, that for Durkheim trust is a quality of organic solidarity and exists in the form of 'purely moral rules' that operate as a 'network of obligation' (Durkheim 2014: 177–8) which is quite unlike the trust that an individual voluntarily accords to another. The primary significance of trust for the operation of networks, rather than markets, is not a claim about the contingent usefulness of trust to networks but its necessity, a claim that is reflected in the conventional conceptualization of social capital in terms of trust and the correlative assumption that networks are expressions of or a mechanism in the formation of social capital (Coleman 1990; Fukuyama 1995; Putnam 1993). The assumption that trust is the basis of networks and of social capital is central in much of the discussion of *guanxi*. The dyadic connections constitutive of *guanxi* can serially iterate or concatenate to form *guanxi* networks, which like networks in general are presumed to function as a form of social capital (Bian 2001; Qi 2013; Wang *et al.* 2016).

The contrast, between *guanxi* as trust-based and market relations that are based on legal contract, is frequently mentioned in discussions regarding the advantages of *guanxi* over strictly market exchanges (Boisot and Child 1996: 612–13, 617, 619, 625; Lee and Dawes 2005: 48–52; Lovett *et al.* 1999: 243; Tong and Yong 1998: 84; Tsang 1998: 66; Whyte 1996: 12; Yeung and Tung 1996: 63). A point often made in this context is that, as networks based on trust, *guanxi* networks provide transaction-cost benefits denied to market participants who instead incur contract-related costs including expensive legal support (but see Barbalet 2017b: 343–4). Not only is there an almost universal assumption, then, that *guanxi* is based on trust, but also an acceptance that trust is generated in *guanxi* exchanges (Smart 1993: 400, 403; Lee and Dawes 2005). Indeed, it is an ironic feature of the discussion of *guanxi* that, while it is frequently regarded as an indigenous Chinese cultural form, it is at the same time explicated, as indicated here, in terms of trust. Trust is an indigenous European concept associated with the liberal political tradition (Silver 1985), a tradition whose institutional expression is remote from China's historical experience and which has been given ideological representation in China only since the early twentieth century (Fung 2010: 128–58), and then as a departure from rather than in support of established cultural and political practices.

Trust in its Cultural Setting

It has been indicated that the notion of trust in networks, and also provisionally in *guanxi*, can be taken to refer to a sense of confidence shared between two parties that dependence on the other will not lead to failure to achieve a joint purpose, that is, the act of trust entails a 'willingness to be vulnerable under conditions of risk and interdependence' (Rousseau *et al.* 1998: 395; see also Luhmann 1979: 15). This understanding of trust, while accepted in much of the literature, arguably covers only a small portion of what is usually referred by the term 'trust' and, in addition, neglects a number of discernments concerning trust including the distinction, mentioned above, between trusting in another and being trustworthy. Before considering what trust might entail in *guanxi* it is necessary first to expand briefly on what the notion of 'trust' can be taken to mean.

There is a widely accepted distinction between trust in those with whom a person has everyday interactions, on the one hand, and trust in strangers on the other, typically understood respectively as 'particularistic trust' and 'generalized trust' (Freitag and Traunmüller 2009). As each of these relate to the trusting of persons, either familiar or remote, they are described as distinct forms of interpersonal trust. There is also trust in institutions, treated in some contexts as 'trust in abstract systems' (Giddens 1990: 83–8) or, rather confusingly, as either 'political trust' or 'social trust' (Zmerli and Newton 2008). One way of clearly distinguishing these quite different referents of 'trust' is to regard particularistic and generalized trust as operating as polar opposites on a horizontal axis, and trust in institutions, abstract, political, or social trust, as being vertically related to the trustor (see Tullberg 2008: 2066–7). In consideration of *guanxi*, particularistic trust is the most relevant form.

If the provision and reciprocation of trust, and its object, are restricted to individual persons who are known to each other, then for someone to trust another it is necessary that the trust-giver expects that the person they trust can be relied on to satisfy their needs or serve their interests. This is more than an expectation of benign intent and typically includes a sense that dependence on the other's capacities or actions, by trusting them, will yield some benefit. Internal to this proposition is a second attribute of interpersonal particularistic trust, namely the idea that trust is a belief or a feeling. The point here is not to arbitrate on these alternatives regarding the subjective composition of trust, but to appreciate that trust is always based on something other than knowledge or certainty. This connects with a third characteristic of particularistic trust, namely that it is always future-orientated. Trust is not simply a belief or feeling about another person but especially about what that person is likely to do in the future. Thus, trust facilitates relations between persons by providing a sense of assured expectation that one will not be subject to incompetent support or betrayal after the commitment to trust has been given (see Barbalet 2009).

While it is not possible to predict the future behaviour of others, an obvious indicator of their reliability in the context of trust is their honesty, so that in trust relations a premium is placed on strict truthfulness, the absence of which can be readily taken as evidence of untrustworthiness (Offe 1999: 73–4). Another essential element of trust, associated with the risk and vulnerability a person enters into by relying on another through trust, is that trust is given by one person to another as a matter of individual choice and that compulsion can have no role in trusting another (Baier 1986: 244–5, 247; Luhmann 1979: 45); it is therefore 'not possible to demand the trust of others' (Luhmann 1979: 47).

It has been shown that the root term for trust-related concepts in China is *xin*, denoting a person doing what she says she will do, and the term *xin* is therefore translated as 'truthful', along with related notions, including 'to believe', 'trust', and 'confidence'. In Chinese culture the notion of truthfulness or honesty operates not in the context of literal veracity but in the context of good intentions related to safeguarding relationships. In Chinese culture malfeasance tends to be dealt with by attempting to return disrupted relations between persons to harmony, not by necessarily correcting wrongs with rights but through compromise and preservation of face, including for the wrongdoer, and always with regard to status and status differences. In these circumstances, courtesy is more important than verisimilitude, and not telling the truth is not necessarily regarded as lying (Blum 2007). As Choi and Han (2008: 95) put it in their discussion of truthfulness in Korea, telling an untruth in the context of interpersonal relations is not necessarily problematic, as it would be in a relationship between Americans or Australians, say, if it is 'in the service of preserving smooth interpersonal relationships'.

An untruth of this sort is described in Korean as 의례성 *uilyeseong*, literally courtesy, and in this context a semi-ritual benign deception. As Choi and Han (2008: 96) go on to claim:

> target persons of *uiryesung* [*uilyeseong*] behavior do not experience any unpleasant feelings and even feel satisfaction or gratitude. The motive behind *uiryesung* is not selfish, indeed it intends to benefit the recipient, and thus being the target of such behavior is a positive experience. Like this, *uiryesung* centers around the other-serving motivations hidden behind external expressions of words.

Failing to tell the truth in Korea, and similarly in China, is therefore not necessarily something that could undermine trust, but rather may even be an element in the generation of trust (Choi and Han 2008: 96). This apparently contradictory situation can be explained in terms of a significant difference between Chinese (and Korean) culture on the one hand and West European and American cultures on the other, responsible for the different understandings and evaluations of strict truthfulness.

A key element in the differences mentioned include the hierarchical nature of social relations in East Asia and the determination of social obligation through role requirements, on the one hand, and the cultural significance of horizontal equivalence between persons in Europe and America, on the other. It is out of this difference that arise the dissimilar assessments of what threatens trust, and of what lying (in the sense of not conveying what is strictly true), and also trust, consists. Between horizontally equivalent persons a mistruth is a deception that challenges a perceived sense of reality, and between putative equals is therefore a betrayal of trust because it can be taken to be associated with a manipulation or distortion of reality-perception that is seen to necessarily disadvantage the deceived. In a hierarchical relationship, as Choi and Han suggest, on the other hand, mistruth is possibly a cushion or comfort that protects the deceived from a harsh or inconvenient reality, as a 'white lie' in the West might do between confidants. But the notion of a 'white lie' does not completely absorb mistruth as it is experienced in East Asia.

Deception may be benevolent, as Choi and Han (2008) suggest, and it may be polite, especially in saving the face of another, as with a white lie. But deception may also be performed to serve the convenience or interests of the teller of an untruth; but in the context of relations between Chinese persons, this may not in itself be a challenge to trust, as it is practised between them. It has been reported, for instance, that pervasive book-keeping practices among Chinese entrepreneurs include the routine provision of inaccurate reporting of transactions to business partners (Kao 1996: 66; Wank 2001: 73 n. 4; Zhang 2014: 25, 97). In such cases, while the shared information may be untrue in itself, it is unlikely to disrupt the solidarity between business partners, especially if they share *guanxi*, and also such *guanxi* would typically be unaffected by such deception.

The most proximate reason why such deception is not experienced as betrayal is that the 'deceiver' and the 'deceived' are likely to be equally complicit in such behaviour and aware of its occurrence through their 聪明 *congming*, through their being 'clever' or 'smart'. In this context having *congming* means that the deceiver's motives are understood by the recipient of a falsehood, so that one's response to inaccurate reporting is proportionate and accommodating in order to achieve positive outcomes for both parties. Paradoxically, in these circumstances, the consequences of such 'grey lies' may not be to disadvantage the deceived but through the recipient's *congming* enhance the solidarity between them. The necessary context for this outcome relates to the second requirement of trust mentioned, namely the lack of compulsion within trust relations, a requirement that is contravened in the solidarity between *guanxi* participants.

The significance of role compliance in Chinese society relates to another aspect of trust and the significant cultural differences in how trust may be understood. The element of trust, that compulsion has no place in trust relations, is difficult to achieve in a society in which close personal monitoring, pervasive hierarchy-based dependence, and role obligation together mean that interpersonal trust, understood on the basis of the criterion that one must be free to choose whom one trusts, is not possible. Trust is this sense, which emphasizes trust giving, requires that trust is located in the choice that the trust giver makes. This is a choice to depend on another in spite of an absence of information concerning the outcome of that dependency: in this sense the trust giver is necessarily vulnerable, and risk is an unavoidable element of the choice to trust (Barbalet 2009: 373). The feature of 'trust' that operates in the context of *guanxi*, on the other hand, and a factor entirely congruent with role obligation and not disrupted by the need to finesse deception with *congming*, is in the demonstration of one's trustworthiness, of one's *xinyong*.

The distinction between *xinren*, trustfulness, and *xinyong*, trustworthiness, has already been indicated. The effective bond between persons in *guanxi* relationships is what can be described as 'sincerity', 'integrity', 'credibility', 'reputation', and of course, 'trustworthiness', all of which are cap-tured by the Chinese-language term *xinyong*. Indicators of reliability between *guanxi* partners are displayed through habituated behaviour which expresses the obligations inherent in the *renqing* role, through signals of probity; these are achieved through repeated and close contact and other bases of familiar-ity designed to reassure the other of the dependability of the person entering a *guanxi* exchange or continuing a *guanxi* relationship. Trustworthiness in this sense is premised on a social perception of reliability as expressed in reputation or face. Indeed, 面子 *mianzi*, face or reputation, stands as a proxy for reliability or 'trustworthiness' in *guanxi* relations. The emphasis here, on an institutionalization of demonstrations of reliability, through familiarity and face, reduces the element of risk—characteristic of trust as portrayed in the sociological literature—and, as we shall see, providing assurance through third-party involvement, although quite unlike legal enforcement of contract.

The trustworthiness of participants in *guanxi* relationships does not correspond with the self-willed freedom to choose, which is associated with the concept of trust as it is typically understood in the specialist literature on the subject, and in vernacular usage in English-language communication. It is associated, rather, with the habituated behaviour expressive of *renqing* obligation in which signals of sincerity or estimableness are conveyed through the reassurance of familiarity generated in repeated and close contact and interpersonal monitoring. The conflation of 'trust' and 'trustworthiness' that pervades the discussion of *guanxi* in the specialist literature is implicitly cor-rected in the analysis of 'trust' presented by Cheng-shu Kao (1996), in which the nature of trustworthiness as it relates to *guanxi* is indicated in his depic-tion of the basic characteristics of 'personal trust' in Taiwan: 'This type of "trust" is certainly particularistic, but it is not based upon ascribed relation-ships alone . . . It depends upon [a person's] achievements, upon demonstrat-ing that they can be trusted. Therefore, in Chinese society "trust" is inseparable from "personal intimacy"' (Kao 1996: 63). If a person is 'able to demonstrate his loyalty, then he becomes "trustworthy"' (Kao 1996: 62); trustworthiness derives from being 'familiar' with 'somebody you already know' (Kao 1996: 67) and relations of dependence and obligation are there-fore, on the basis of this account, the structural prerequisites of trustworthi-ness in *guanxi* relations.

The understanding of trust provided by Kao, which emphasizes its special meaning in Chinese society, is similar to others in this regard. It was mentioned that successful *guanxi* exchanges enhance the standing or reputation of the participants, that in their practice of *guanxi* participants gain face. Face and reputation stand as proxies of reliability or trustworthiness in *guanxi* relations. In a discussion which attempts to disconnect face from social standing in *guanxi*, in order to connect face with trust, social psychologist Olwen Bedford (2011: 153) notes that in the Chinese language there are 'two types of face: *mianzi* and *lian*...*mianzi* refers to status, prestige, and respect [while] *lian* refers to the moral aspects of face'. In making this distinction Bedford draws on the analysis set out in a classic paper by Hu (1944), mentioned in Chapter 4, although subsequent research (Ho 1976: 868; Qi 2014: 152–5) indicates that the two terms cannot be so easily separated in this way. Indeed, Hu acknowledges that in many situations the two terms can be used interchangeably because '*lien* [*lian*] and *mien-tzu* [*mianzi*] are not two entirely independent concepts' (Hu 1944: 62). The purpose of the distinction claimed by Bedford, however, is to foreground trust; but not trust as it is normally understood: 'During the *guanxi* development process, trust related to the character of the target person is key; trust therefore refers to trust in the other person's *lian*, which is not the same as the general Western conception of trust...Trust in *lian* is established through observation of social norms' (Bedford 2011: 155). The 'observation of social norms' can be understood in two senses, first, the subject's conforming with social norms, and also the visibility to others of their doing so. Here, then, *guanxi* operates through the surveillance of the other in order to establish their satisfying the requirement of observing social norms, to establish their reliability or trustworthiness.

An inclination to discover a special Chinese form of 'trust', which can readily be understood as trustworthiness, is not uncommon in the discussion of *guanxi*. For instance, one researcher refers to a 'norm of mutual commitment between group members that promotes trustworthy and cooperative behaviour' as indicative of what he calls 'enforceable trust' (Peng 2004: 1052 n. 5). In a parallel manner, Luo (2005: 439) holds that 'an indigenous Chinese concept called *pao* [报 *bao*], (translated as the norm of reciprocity in English), is a highly appreciated basis of morality in China' and that 'the principle of *pao* in long-term favor-exchanging processes enhances the probability that all parties of the *guanxi* will come to trust each other'. This is to say that the 'normative structure of *pao* implies...particularistic trust' (Luo 2005: 455). In this case 回报 *hui bao* indicates not simply reciprocity, the behaviour of paying back, but more completely the disposition of showing appreciation through payback, as we saw in Chapter 3. The particularly Chinese mode of trust is made even more explicit in a discussion of the fact that 'in rural society', by which Fei (1992: 43) means traditional Chinese society, 'trust derives from familiarity'. He goes on to write: 'This kind of trust has very solid foundations, for it is rooted in customary norms...Trust in rural society is based...on the dependability of people, people who are so enmeshed in customary norms that they cannot behave in any other way.' Although he does not entertain the face dimension of 'familiarity' and 'dependability' Fei (1992: 43) acknowledges that the 'distinctive characteristic' of this 'sort of familiarity' is that 'people...come to know everybody's life'.

A common feature of these accounts of what might be called 'indigenous' Chinese understandings of 'trust' is the reliance, for an assessment of trustworthiness, on knowledge of the other carried by close familiarity through observation of their behaviour. In this sense, then, trustworthiness derives from reputation based on publicly visible behaviour. In his discussion of relations within a Taiwanese business community, anthropologist Ronald DeGlopper (1995: 205–6) indicates that the 'firm's most valuable asset is *hsin-yung* [*xinyong*]...a reputation for meeting one's obligations'. The achievement of this reputational trustworthiness, he goes on to say, is in the fact that 'All transactions take place before an audience or chorus of *nei-hang-ren* [fellow businessmen], who continually observe and comment on each other's doings' (DeGlopper 1995: 206). This raises again the relevance of face in understanding the *xinyong* between *guanxi* participants. The observation by Ho (1976: 872) is relevant here: 'the social dynamics involved in losing face are more deserving of our attention than those involved in gaining face...everyone who cares for maintaining a minimum level of effective social functioning must see to it that his face is protected from being lost'. A person's concern for preservation of their 'face' cannot be conceived as merely an individual or personal matter because 'the concern for face exerts a mutually restrictive, even coercive, power upon each member of the social network...the individual's actions, far from being directed by [their] own wishes, are in effect dictated by the necessity of meeting the expectation of others' (Ho 1976: 873). Failure to meet such expectations will lead to a loss of face which will impose limits on the person's ability to engage in future *guanxi* exchanges. In this sense, then, face is a social resource which exists through a complex interaction of performance, self-evaluation, public visibility, and the approbation of others. Withdrawal of the last of these nullifies the value of the first two and intensifies the third, which now has negative consequences for the one who has 'lost face'.

A necessary feature of trust relations is their dyadic structure, trust is a relation between the trustor and the trusted. When the reputational element of 'trustworthiness' is primary, however, especially through the regulatory mechanism of face, the relation in question is no longer dyadic but triadic because in this case 'trustworthiness' is a function of the public visibility or third-party judgements of performance of expectations regarding *guanxi* decorum and adherence to *guanxi* norms. That *guanxi* exchanges necessarily involve third-party observation, through which the currency of reputation is maintained and sanctions against possible defection from agreements are executed, indicates a triadic form distinct from and unlike the dyadic structure of trust relations. The assurance shared by participants in *guanxi*, then, derives not from interpersonal trust but from public or third-party scrutiny in which successful adherence to the norms and expectations of participation, often described as *renqing*, leads to enhancement of social reputation or the gaining of face, and defection or incompetence in maintaining the decorum or norms of *guanxi* leads to loss of reputation or loss of face, and therefore likely exclusion from future *guanxi* exchanges.

Knowledge concerning adherence to the *renqing* norms underpinning *guanxi* derives from mutual surveillance and close monitoring, which are irrelevant for trust because trust generates expectations about another's behaviour before it can be monitored (Gambetta 1990: 217). It will be shown in the following section that while the assurance mechanism of *guanxi* is triadic, in the initial formation of a *guanxi* relation two persons relate to each other dyadically, often disclosing personal information as evidence of their sincerity, as discussed in Chapter 1. It is possible that these practices of self-disclosure may be seen to be similar to those that are regarded by some writers as generative of what has been called 'swift trust' (Meyerson *et al.* 1996; Robert *et al.* 2009) or 'fast trust' (Blomqvist 2005; Perks and Halliday 2003). In the present case, however, the notion of trust—swift, fast, or otherwise—as a basis of *guanxi* cooperation is misplaced. This is because the intimate bonding practices of *guanxi*, while convivial, also possess an underlying coercive element that is the obverse of trust, as noted regarding false presentation of business data to partners. This latter factor is not pernicious, as in blackmail, say, but only because the covert potential threat is mutual rather than asymmetrical. These bonding practices are close to those engaged by 把兄弟 *baxiongdi*, sworn brothers, entailing not only secrecy but self-interest dressed as group loyalty. The basis of cooperation in these cases, then, is not conceivably based on trust as it is normally understood, but something that departs markedly from it.

Assurance and the Triadic Structure of *Guanxi*

In the preceding discussion of trust and the special characteristics of trustworthiness in *guanxi*, it was noted that the assurance mechanism of *guanxi* operates in terms of triadic relations, whereas trust relations are necessarily dyadic—between the person who trusts another and the other who is trusted. In this section of the chapter the structure of *guanxi* in terms of its initial or atomic formation, which is dyadic, will be contrasted with the triadic or molecular structure. In the first of these, trust is typically assumed to operate, although we shall see how such a view requires qualification, and, in the second, assurance rather than trust is shown to be located. The distinction between trust and assurance is preliminarily clarified in a frequently cited article by Yamagishi and Yamagishi (1994: 132):

> Trust is…an expectation of goodwill and benign intent. Assurance, on the other hand, is…an expectation of benign behavior for reasons other than goodwill of the partner. Trust is based on an inference of the interaction partner's personal traits and intentions, whereas *assurance is based on the knowledge of the incentive structure surrounding the relationship.*   (emphasis added)

Assurance, then, in contrast to trust, relates to an incentive structure external to the individuals who participate in exchange relations and goes beyond their personal expectations of others in the network of relations in which they are involved. Reference to assurance takes us only part of the way, however, in understanding the molecular structure of *guanxi*. Assurance as predicated on the existence of an incentive structure requires institutional grounding. There are at least two possible ways of grounding assurance practices: one is in legal institutions and another is through network participation. Law and networks as assurance structures share a common quality that is acknowledged for law but neglected in appreciating how *guanxi* networks operate, namely the mechanism of third-party enforcement. Recognition of this leads to clarity in conceptualization of the molecular structure of *guanxi* networks.

Networks are typically regarded as composed of a series of dyadic relations. Summarizing the conventional understanding of them, networks can be defined as 'several interwoven, dyadic (binary) ongoing interaction relations between actors (nodes) characterized by reciprocity' (Aspers 2011: 20). *Guanxi* can similarly be defined as having a dyadic form or structure, as an 'informal, particularistic personal connection between two individuals… bounded by…a long-term relationship, mutual commitment, loyalty, and obligation' (Chen and Chen 2004: 306). In order to understand the operation of assurance in networks, and especially *guanxi* networks, it is necessary to appreciate that, while binary relations constitute the most elemental aspect of networks, their atomic structure, such relations are not characteristic of the operational form of networks which have instead a molecular triadic structure. This is because the assurance of compliance within network exchanges, and especially *guanxi* exchanges, is achieved through the third-party enforcement of reputation, which can therefore occur only within triadic relations. This effect is indicated in a classic account of the embeddedness of trust in networks, but which in fact relates to third-party assurance, when Granovetter (1985: 487–93) proposes that through repeated exchanges participants acquire information about each other so that, should opportunistic behaviour occur, it would be exposed, generating in others prosocial conduct through a fear of acquiring a reputation for unreliability or untrustworthiness with consequent loss of future transaction opportunities.

Through a conceptual analysis of *guanxi* it is possible to distinguish two distinct phases of their formation, one based on the confidentially between participants, and in that sense private, and the other open to public awareness and therefore public scrutiny. The initial negotiation of a favour involves only the favour seeker and the one from whom the favour is sought, and is therefore dyadic in its structure. An 'operating principle' of this first phase of *guanxi* relations, to use Chen and Chen's term, which they say is 'essential for establishing *guanxi* bases', is personal or self-disclosure (Chen and Chen 2004: 310, 316). A characteristic and unique feature of dyadic relations is indeed the possibility of secrecy between the participants (Simmel 1950: 123). A key element of the first phase of a (potential) *guanxi* exchange is the need for both parties to maintain confidentiality (Lin 2001: 158). Because there are social costs in failing to acquire a favour and also in refusing to provide a favour to another, the interests of both parties are safeguarded by avoiding public knowledge of their negotiations, as we saw in Chapter 1. Any suggestion that trust is necessary in this confidential exchange (Chen and Chen 2004: 313–14) may be dispelled, for the negotiations will typically be conducted on the basis of a sense of obligation to preserve the face of both parties by avoiding visibility beyond the intimate dialogue, and with an orientation guided by calculability concerning creditworthiness, the accessibility and valorization of means to achieve joint purposes, and so on (Yan 2009: 192–202).

On the successful conclusion of the dyadic and confidential first phase, *guanxi* enters a second phase in which public propagation and recognition of the exchange is essential (Lin 2001: 159). Indeed, it is in the public second phase of *guanxi* where the payoffs for both parties engaged in the first phase negotiations are located:

> For the giver, being recognized in the social networks for one's ability to render favours increases one's standing or reputation in the community…[which is] the

payoff sought by favour givers in *guanxi*...For the favour seeker, obtaining a successful favour indicates his or her capability in vertical and upward access to valued resources in the society...[so] word-of-mouth diffusion of a successful *guanxi* enhances the reputation or social standing of the favour seeker as well.

(Lin 2001: 157)

In each instance, for both favour seeker and favour provider, the success of their transactions is registered in the public visibility of their exchange. This corresponds with the role in *guanxi* exchanges of third-party observation underpinning face, through which the currency of reputation is maintained and sanctions against possible defection from exchange decorum are executed. The molecular structure of *guanxi* networks in their triadic form entails an assurance of enforcement against defection through the mechanism of reputation subject not only to public recognition but more importantly to public scrutiny and sanction. Loss of reputation through defection leads to exclusion from future network exchanges; enhancement of reputation, through successful *guanxi*, leads to continuing access to future exchanges and the possibility of accessing increasingly beneficial favours and a widening arena of contacts. Without the public visibility internal to triadic forms such an assurance regime would not be available and reputation would be without meaning or purchase. It is in this context that the importance of trustworthiness is derived, and the characteristic form of trustworthiness in interactive familiarity based on interdependent relations of normative obligation associated with role expectations is established in *guanxi* relations.

Reference to the presence of a triadic form here does not imply that *guanxi* exchanges necessarily incorporate triangular relationships, although some do. Ambrose King (1991: 74) mentions that third-party brokerage may facilitate *guanxi* building when two parties wishing to establish *guanxi* with each other have no previous interaction, as we saw in Chapters 1 and 4. It is commonly assumed that a 中间人 *zhongjianren*, an intermediary, known to the two parties of an eventual *guanxi* exchange, may provide an element of assurance, in so far as each party to the exchange owes *renqing*, obligatory feelings, not only to the other party but especially to the intermediary, who by virtue of his or her role in bringing the participants of a (potential) *guanxi* exchange together has an interest in its success. In fact, the function of the intermediary is to establish a shared social identity by providing a common link with the participants (Hamilton and Wang 1992: 23; Yang 1989: 40–1). Triangular relations incorporating *zhongjianren* therefore primarily relate to the conditions of possibility of entering a *guanxi* relation in the first phase and are not necessary for the conditions of its realization, in the second phase, in which triadic relations provide the basis of assurance, as some authors have assumed (Lui 2001: 391; Qi 2013: 316–17). In any event, not all *guanxi* relations require intermediaries. Chen and Chen (2004: 311–12) indicate that the bases of *guanxi* relations are of three types, only one of which involves a triangular relationship, a common third party; the other two are binary relationships founded respectively on, first, common social identity of birthplace, educational institution, or workplace, and, secondly, what they call an 'anticipatory' base of future intention to form a *guanxi* relation, what more generally might be called being on a common trajectory.

The broad consensus that trust is implicated in *guanxi* relations is typically explained in terms of a common identity shared by participants, through which they are bonded by strong ties. This is indicated in a number of ways. Some writers argue that in China trust is more or less confined to family members (Liu 2008: 56–60; Wong 1996). In his discussion of 'Chinese Entrepreneurs and Business Trust' eminent Hong Kong sociologist Siu-Lun Wong (1996: 19–20), for instance, treats personal trust exclusively in terms of trust between family members. The obvious question, of whether personal trust among family members may create distrust outside the family, is answered by claiming that 'trust and distrust are not mutually exclusive [but relate] in graduation not dichotomy' (Wong 1996: 20). This view makes sense only in the context of the way in which deception and its tactful perspicacity through *congming* supports rather than inhibits solidarity. But, in fact, the evidence suggests that a prevalence of family involvement in business is likely to mean that non-family members tend to be regarded with suspicion (Ermisch and Gambetta 2010; Whyte 1996: 3–4).

The question of the relation between *guanxi* and family ties was critically assessed in Chapter 2, and will be discussed further in the next chapter. Certainly, there is a tendency in discussions of social relations in China to privilege family ties over other types of connection. Nevertheless, accounts of *guanxi* typically acknowledge that the shared background of participants underlying homogeneity, possibly generative of trust, usually described as *guanxi* bases, will include kinship but are not confined to it (Jacobs 1979; Tong and Yong 1998; Chen and Chen 2004). As shown in previous chapters, *guanxi* bases are selected by individuals to support the formation of relations facilitating their purposes so that the will to found *guanxi* arises independently of the *guanxi* bases themselves. *Guanxi* bases, then, are best regarded as resources that individuals draw upon in creating a sense of common identity with another for their mutual benefit. As we shall see, *guanxi* is cultivated in order to achieve the purpose of the cultivator in cooperation with a *guanxi* partner and is not in any direct sense an emergent outcome of latent structures in a pre-existing 'base' from which trust emanates.

Influence in *Guanxi* Ties

Earlier in this chapter, in consideration of trust in networks as opposed to contract in markets, it was shown that an assured feature of relations between network participants is taken to be the trust embedded in the ties between network members, based on their reciprocity and the sense of common purpose that flows from it. In this sense trust is latent in the networks in question. It will be shown here, on the other hand, that a primary feature of *guanxi* is that it is cultivated, that the ties constitutive of *guanxi* are intentionally formed rather than latent in such things as kinship, native-place, or other pre-existing potential identity marker. These latter may be selectively drawn on in *guanxi*, as shown elsewhere, but only in terms that suit the initiator of a *guanxi* exchange and the recipient of a *guanxi* favour. While there is acknowledgement of the cultivated nature of *guanxi* in much of the literature, such acknowledgement coexists with a supposition regarding a morphological similarity between *guanxi* and what might be called 'standard networks', including related assumptions concerning trust which I have shown to require fundamental revision in the context of Chinese cultural practices and *guanxi* networks in particular. Related to these considerations is a question of the suitability of the standard network notion of 'tie strength' applied to the bonds between *guanxi* participants.

In discussion of social networks, it is assumed that the higher the trust between network members the higher the strength of the network tie which binds them together. It is important to begin, then, with the concept of tie strength. The predictors of tie strength in standard network analysis are structured relations, relations that are prior to or independent of the will of the participants; in this case, 'kinship-based ties are stronger, while ties to neighbors or co-workers are weaker' (Marsden and Campbell 1984: 499). The tie-strength distinction between kin on the one hand and neighbours and co-workers on the other conceals something which they have in common, however, namely that a person does not typically choose who is their neighbour or co-worker any more than they choose their kin. These connections have in common the fact that they are 'found' rather than 'chosen'. In standard network analysis tie strength and its differential indicators in kinship and acquaintance are latent in the structural relationships in which people find themselves: 'tie strength is a unidimensional latent construct' (Marsden and Campbell 2012: 18).

The ties out of which relations form between individuals in networks are characterized as given in the interactions between persons, which they do not consciously create themselves. Network analysis is committed to explanations of the behaviour of network members or participants in terms of the structure of the interconnections between them. These interconnections are inherent in latent structures and independent of the social actor's intentions. This approach, however, has been criticized for its neglect of agency and culture (Emirbayer and Goodwin 1994; Pachucki and Breiger 2010). Granovetter's (1973: 1372) focus on 'weak' rather than 'strong' ties has been thought to bring agency to networks (Emirbayer and Goodwin 1994: 1419), possibly because of a supposition that a person chooses his or her friends and acquaintances. Granovetter (1973, 1368) distinguishes between the 'categories... "friend" and "acquaintance"... [which] correspond to "strong" and "weak" ties' but does not provide encouragement to the idea that such categories, friend and acquaintance, are inconsistent with the latent structure approach in the standard notion of network tie. This contrasts with *guanxi*, however, in that the ties constitutive of it are intentionally formed and therefore not latent in the sense found in network analysis. *Guanxi* relations are always self-consciously cultivated by the participants. Because of this, *guanxi* cannot be adequately characterized in terms of tie strength, as we shall see.

It is possible to find some acknowledgement, even if implicit, that conventionally defined tie strength is an inadequate predictor of the behaviour of persons within *guanxi*. The observation that the 'art of *guanxi* involves the strategic strengthening of weak into strong ties' may not only encourage the idea 'that weak and strong ties are not permanently distinct categories' in the context of understanding *guanxi*, as Smart (1998: 561) indicates and as we shall see in more detail in the next chapter; but, more pertinently, such an observation might lead to a questioning of why these categories are used at all in attempts to understand *guanxi*. Indeed, such a perspective could appropriately give rise to an acknowledgement of the need to ask instead how *guanxi* connections may be more adequately theorized. A predictor with greater reliability than tie strength for understanding the behaviour of persons in *guanxi* relations is the extent or degree of felt obligation between participants as a constructive element in their agency. Such a sense of obligation may be activated by shared attributions of kinship, place of origin, or other situational tie, or by some other self-willed construction, such as attracting feelings or shared purposes and intentions.

The point, though, is that in this context the notion of a *guanxi* tie is a proxy not of the strength of trust embedded in latent structures but of obligations strategically formed and generated by seeking alliances and other facilitating relationships with persons identified for their capacities to contribute to a common purpose, assessed through close interactions and surveillance.

If the ties that bind *guanxi* participants are not internal to latent structures—strong or weak—but obtain through evaluations concerning the generation and execution of obligations that arise in *renqing* favour exchange, then another assumption concerning standard networks, and its inappropriateness for understanding *guanxi*, can be highlighted. Granovetter's (1973) classic discussion of networks and labour markets is concerned with flows of information and influence. Neither of these terms, 'information' and 'influence', are defined by Granovetter. He is concerned with employment-relevant information shared between acquaintances who are outside the recipient's close-knit network, that is, job-information conveyed by weak ties. This information is shown to influence labour-market behaviour, so that Granovetter (1973: 1360) refers to the 'diffusion of influence and information' in a single breath, as well as implying that 'information or influence' (Granovetter 1973: 1364) are in this case interchangeable. The exception is when the information is from either mixed or institutional sources, in which case recipients 'receive information without influence' (Granovetter 1973: 1372).

In a now classic discussion of Chinese labour markets, which borrows from Granovetter (1973), Yanjie Bian (1997: 368, 371, 381) makes a firm distinction between 'information' and 'influence' in order to argue that the resource distributed in labour markets in China through *guanxi* networks is 'influence' rather than 'information'. Because of the managed nature of Chinese labour markets, information itself could not lead to the acquisition of a job because, 'even when they have information, job-seekers cannot apply for jobs; jobs are secretly assigned by officials as favors to those who are directly or indirectly connected to them' (Bian 1997: 367). This leads Bian to associate 'influence' with 'trust and obligation' because 'the strong ties of trust and obligation may be more advantageous in accessing influence' than the weak ties Granovetter has focused on (Bian 1997: 367). Indeed, 'influence' and 'obligation' tend to become coterminous if not conflated in Bian's account, as 'information' and 'influence' are in Granovetter's. For Bian (2002: 119) *guanxi* obligation is the means of influence in question: 'social networks were used by job seekers to influence job-assigning authorities through intimate and reciprocal relationships of trust and obligation—or *guanxi*—so jobs could be assigned as favours to someone who was strongly connected, either directly or indirectly, to the authorities'. There is an important difference, however, between 'influence' and 'obligation' that distinguishes the latent network conduits of information and influence, which Granovetter refers to, from the relations of obligation at the core of *guanxi*.

Although widely used, the concept of influence is infrequently specified in the literature; it is sometimes regarded as distinct from power, sometimes seen as overlapping with power, and sometimes regarded as a form of or synonymous with power (see Dahl 1957; Lasswell and Kaplan 2017: 71; Lenski 1966: 57; Lukes 2005: 21, 36). In the present context interpersonal influence is loosely understood as a form of power that affects another's behaviour or outlook in the absence of either authoritative or coercive means. It can be noted that Edward Banfield (2009: 4) and Robert Merton (1968: 473), in contradistinction to the position outlined here, hold that authority and coercion are forms or means of influence. Authority and coercion are distinguished from influence in the present discussion, however, because they are forms of power that can be explained in their own terms without recourse to 'influence'. Authority typically is associated with externally enforceable legitimate sanctions and coercion is associated with means that preclude independent action for those subject to it. Influence, on the other hand, is generally understood to lead to an unimpeded acceptance of previously untried or unthought possible behaviour or orientation on the part of the influenced.

In the simplest terms, a person's change of behaviour or outlook that is not affected by command or force but by persuasion through the provision of information or regard can be understood as the result of 'influence'. The information and regard that serves to influence a person may be honestly or truthfully provided, or they may be manipulative or fraudulent; the hallmark of influence is simply that it results from a mobilization of resources that do not derive from authority or coercion and which leads to changes in the behaviour and outlook of the recipient. 'Information', in this context, may refer to knowledge or advice which clarifies what is possible or desirable; 'regard', on the other hand, includes affection, concern, respect, sympathy, and similar factors that would lead the influenced person to behave differently in order to please or gratify the source of influence. The relevance of the notions of *renqing, ganqing,* and, perhaps more remotely, *xinyong,* to the concept of influence will be obvious in this description.

In an extensive discussion of 'influence' the classical American sociologist Talcott Parsons (1969) argues that it is a characteristically 'generalized medium', which is to say that its purpose is achieved with indifference to its subjects, that it has the quality of 'mutual acceptability' and operates in a unit or field of 'common membership...through which influence may flow from one group to the other' (Parsons 1969: 409, 434). The various mechanisms which permit influence to possess the quality of a generalized medium all depend, says Parsons (1969: 415) 'on the institutionalization of attitudes of trust', by which he means that there is a relevant group acceptance of the credibility or dependability of the means of influence in question. Parsons (1969: 419–27) distinguishes four types of influence: first, political influence, a generalized persuasion without coercion or threat designed to affect the goals or purposes of collectives; second, fiduciary influence, directed to the allocation of resources in a collective; third, influence that appeals to differential loyalties; and finally, influence directed to the interpretation of norms.

The type of influence mentioned by Parsons which comes closest to the affective form of interpersonal influence, that operates through an endeavour to gratify the source of influence, is the third type, in which the commitments available to a social actor include the possibility of a particular commitment in contradistinction to a generalized commitment (Parsons 1969: 424). But whereas interpersonal influence may relate to a particular loyalty, in Parsons's discussion the loyalty in question could only influence, in the form of a generalized medium, if the loyalty in question were to a set of values, socially dispersed or generalized, but not to a person or persons. Action resulting from an appeal to loyalty to another person requires a prior commitment that stands apart from influence as a generalized medium.

The influence that may operate in a *guanxi* network, according to Bian's account, is the influence of obligation. 'Obligation', like 'influence', can be described as a poly-semantic term; one meaning relates to duty, possibly enforceable duty, in the sense that a person is obliged to obey laws, comply with authority, and so on. *Guanxi* obligation, on the other hand, is not general in the sense that all who are subject to formal authority are obliged to conform to its requirements. Rather, it is an interactively formed obligation particular to the individuals who participate in it, typically by virtue of favour exchange limited to the participants in question (see Barbalet 2020). The obvious link between interpersonal influence and *guanxi* obligation is through the element in the former of what was above described as 'regard', for the affective components of interpersonal influence almost directly map onto *ganqing*, essential to *guanxi* ties, as well as *renqing*.

The obligations through which *guanxi* relations are structured in fact distort or may even prevent the flow of influence as a generalized medium through networks and collectives, as evidenced in the way in which *guanxi* practices are indifferent to legal and formal regulation. The idea that *guanxi* may 'influence' the decision of a participant in a *guanxi* relation is redundant given prior obligatory expectations. *Guanxi* generates opacity, a lack of transparency, that confounds the flows typical of the network forms assumed by standard network analysis. In terms of the formal properties of relations, the obscurity of *guanxi* arises from its non-transitivity as a result of the particularity of relations between participants, such that provision of a favour and the obligations that arise from it are exclusive to the persons within a given dyad. Additionally, *guanxi* is asymmetric in so far as its structure is different for each of its members, although this is likely to be a feature of networks in general even if more intense in *guanxi*. Finally, there is significant non-reflexivity in *guanxi* exchanges because resources lack equivalence between participants. As shown elsewhere, in the indirect connections of *guanxi* the provision of a job, say, may be a favour in which the recipient is not employed, and also employment for someone who is not a direct recipient of the pertinent favour (Barbalet 2015: 1044–6). In terms of the formal properties of relations, the non-transitivity, asymmetry, and non-reflexivity of *guanxi* enforce opacity with regard to influence in the relevant networks.

What has been called the 'opacity' and 'obscurity' of *guanxi* relations, which result from the highly particularistic nature of the obligations underpinning them, means that the social solidarity between participants is not derived from a volitional provision of trustfulness, of accepting the vulnerability of depending on another prior to knowing the outcome of such a commitment to trust. Nor can it be characterized in terms of the trust implicit in strong ties, derived from familial roles or the loyalties of pre-given contacts. Rather, the trustworthiness of each member of the dyadic couple constituting a *guanxi* comes from a detailed knowledge of the other person, resulting from repeated and close interaction and the assurance of the other's reliability through the sanction of face and the desire of each *guanxi* participant to avoid losing face. A loss of face is necessarily a public disclosure of unreliability, the occurrence of which will preclude access to future favour from any of the members of the *guanxi* network concerned as well as their associates.

Conclusion

This chapter began with a description of research which purported to demonstrate the centrality of trust to *guanxi* and an associated claim that the Chinese term for trust is as ambiguous as the English-language equivalent.

It has been shown that the place of trust in *guanxi* is not well represented in the literature and that the understanding of trust and also trustworthiness as they relate to *guanxi* in particular and Chinese cultural practices and meanings in general require much closer attention that they are usually given. A sub-theme that runs through this chapter is the nature of social networks, especially as they relate to trust relations as well as the nature of trust, and also the ways in which *guanxi* networks have characteristics that distinguish them from the standard form of network that occupies the attention of researchers.

The notion of trust is extensively drawn on by sociologists of different persuasions to account for a multiplicity of social effects. Trust is widely seen as fundamental to sociality itself. The pervasive application of trust to explanation of a variety of social situations, including social order, political stability, professional competency, financial certainty, ontological security, coping with complexity, to mention only some obvious candidates, suggests that the term is best thought of as an umbrella under which sit a number of distinct although possibly, but not always, overlapping concepts. Certainly, in examining the notion of 'trust' in *guanxi*, analytically separate concepts have been identified and the influence of cultural meanings and distinctions have been shown to generate additional variation and divergence in what loosely passes as 'trust'. If these discernments are not acknowledged then the account to which the notion of trust is applied fails to be convincing.

As the notion of trust is complex rather than simple, so that its application in social analysis cannot be executed without regard to its pitfalls and the traps they contain, so sensitivity to the impact of cultural factors on the analysis of social practices, including *guanxi*, cannot itself provide useful results in the absence of independent assessment. The risks of 'going native' are real if cultural sensitivity alone determines the analysis, rather than providing support to it. In this chapter and the previous two, awareness of cultural factors was crucial to our appreciating the nature of *guanxi* and such cultural awareness and sensitivity served the analysis of *guanxi*. A consideration of the cultural context of *guanxi* is considered in the following chapter, but there the concern is to avoid distortion in the analysis which comes from an acceptance of what might be called 'folk categories' as explanatory concepts.

6

Guanxi, Three Forms or One

The term 关系 *guanxi*, according to one author, has a 'complicated and rich meaning' (King 1991: 68). Another writer, who does not necessarily disagree with this point of view, holds that the term 'has lost its analytic usefulness, for it simultaneously refers to too many things and smooths over the distinctions in *guanxi* practice among the different identity categories' (Evasdottir 2004: 27). Such an acknowledgement, that *guanxi* is not a unified concept, is expounded by yet another writer who welcomes the idea that there 'are different categories of *guanxi*, each with its own different behavioral and moral standards' (Luo 2011: 330). It will be shown in this chapter that if this last proposition is accepted then we shall have to agree that the term *guanxi* may indeed be without 'analytic usefulness'.

Preceding chapters have challenged various conventions concerning how *guanxi* is frequently presented. The supposed Confucian lineage of *guanxi* was critically assessed in Chapters 2 and 3, and the idea that *guanxi* should be understood in terms of the trust between participants was in Chapter 5 qualified with regard to differences between the English-language term 'trust' and Chinese 信 *xin* terms, as well as through acknowledgement of the distinction between trust as a dyadic relation and assurance as triadic. These discussions concerned the meaning of *guanxi* in terms of associative concepts, that is, attention was given to the way in which *guanxi* acquired meaning through its relation with distinct categories that clarify its character and identity. In this chapter, the focus is on the question of ambiguity in the category of *guanxi* itself, namely whether the notion of *guanxi* points to phenomena that might be coherently covered by this single term. This is a matter of whether a category, such as *guanxi*, operates within a unitary explanatory frame or whether more than one frame attaches to it, leading to multiple and discordant meanings (Chliova *et al.* 2020: 1019–22).

There is a widely accepted view, which will be discussed in what follows, that there are three variant forms of *guanxi*, loosely described here as family *guanxi*, friendship *guanxi,* and acquaintance *guanxi* (Bian 2018: 603–4; Bian 2019:142–7; Chen and Chen 2004: 308–9; Fan 2002: 551–3; Fu *et al.* 2006; Guo and Miller 2010; Hwang 1987; Luo 2011; Luo *et al.* 2016;

The Theory of Guanxi *and Chinese Society.* Jack Barbalet, Oxford University Press (2021). © Jack Barbalet.
DOI: 10.1093/oso/9780198808732.003.0007

Wank 1996: 826–8; Yan 1996: 99–100). It will be argued that the notion of 'family *guanxi*' is redundant in so far as family connections comprise closed relations universally understood to entail implicit support between members on the basis of perceived need without expectation of a return provision. Additionally, it will be shown in this chapter that the distinction between friendship *guanxi* and acquaintance *guanxi* is best treated as referring to different phases of a broadly single form of engagement rather than discrete categories of analysis or dissimilar forms. *Guanxi*, it will be shown here, is best conceived as a volitionally formed and therefore open relationship, without formal restriction on membership, encouraged by exchanges of various kinds. Another point at issue concerns a widely accepted idea that family *guanxi* and friendship *guanxi* are possibly linked through 'pseudo-family' bonds. This widely accepted assumption will also be critically assessed in discussion. The purpose here is to provide a distinctive sociological statement of what constitutes *guanxi*.

The discussion will begin with the nature of family associations and relationships, and why they must be regarded as distinct from *guanxi*, even though most accounts of *guanxi* assume that its structure is elementally familial. Next will be considered an associated idea, namely that in order to achieve efficacy *guanxi* relations must somehow mimic familial relations, which is achieved through practices of fictive kinship. Fictive kinship, then, or pseudo-family relations as they are often called, will be considered in the next section of the chapter. In the third section, it will be shown that friendship and acquaintance do not produce different types of *guanxi* but rather are continuous or connected variations of association within a single social form. Finally, the sources of confusion that lead to a merging of the closed relations of family with the open relations of *guanxi*, and the radical separation of friendship and acquaintance, will be identified and examined.

Family *Guanxi*

A hallmark proposition in the standard literature is that the strongest type and archetypical representation of *guanxi* is its familial form, a *guanxi* based on family bonds or ties of kinship (Bian 2019: 2–11; King 1991: 67–8, 75; Lin 2001: 154–5; Luo 2011: 332–3; Yang 1994: 111–14). A defining characteristic of family *guanxi* is the provision of support in the absence of a favour in return. Such a relationship is based on what Hwang (1987) describes as the 'needs rule', that one is obliged to assist a family member on the basis of their need, not in expectation of what they might do in return at some future time, as in the case of Hwang's 'equity rule', nor on the basis of a quid pro quo of direct exchange, as with Hwang's 'equality rule'. David Wank (1996: 826–7) appropriately describes familial *guanxi* as an 'endowed' form which is 'ascriptive and produced by birth' involving directly related kin, namely parents and offspring, brothers, and also possibly patrilineal cousins. He notes that it is 'forthcoming with little or no need to offer material reward' because 'intimacy can be more or less taken for granted' and there is therefore no need 'to spend resources on deepening the ties' so that there is 'a lack of explicit reciprocity… [between] endowed ties' (Wank 1996: 826, 828).

There is a fundamental qualitative distinction between the obligations that obtain between close kin on the one hand and non-kin on the other. *Guanxi* obligations between the latter derive, first, from exchanges which arise either through shared experiences of friendship, through the provision of favours, or, secondly, in recognition of a common interest facilitated through the exchange of gifts, which are called respectively 'savings' *guanxi* and 'investment' *guanxi* (Wank 1996: 826–7), corresponding with what is descriptively called here 'friendship *guanxi*' and 'acquaintance *guanxi*'. Although the terminology varies in different accounts, the general framework of what is described here is more or less consistent in the literature.

The idea that kinship, between parents and offspring and also between siblings, is a sufficient basis from which instrumental support may be forthcoming, and therefore that a favour or gift is unnecessary between them in securing assistance, does not mean that family members do not exchange favours and gifts, as of course they may frequently do so. The point here, though, is that such exchanges are not the basis of support between family members whereas support between non-kin typically requires such favour exchange. The notion of family obligation without reference to *guanxi* has been found to be a continuing feature of social practice and commitment in China. The 'structure of Chinese families continues to be one of mutual dependence rather than independence [and] economically, socially and emotionally Chinese family relationships tend to be close and inwardly directed' (Qi 2015: 151). While this pattern may be associated historically with Confucian norms, 'from which it draws its imagery', its basis today is in the current structure of legal and administrative institutions and practices (Qi 2015: 157). As a result of the absence of alternative arrangements in China, including the reluctance of banks to provide start-up finance to small business, the lack of comprehensive state-provided aged care, and other social goods, such services and support are largely provided by close family members. Under these circumstances it is not surprising that high levels of commitment to principles of family obligation are consistently reported in China (Fuligni and Zhang 2004; Lin and Yi 2013; Whyte 2005).

The strength of needs-based support between close kin is demonstrated by Chinese rural-to-urban migrant workers who remit significant portions of their earning to their immediate family. Internal migration in China is 'underpinned by the pre-existing values of…family loyalty' (Murphy 2002: 216; see also Guo *et al.* 2012). The purpose of migration in the vast majority of cases is to repatriate remittances to the family that stays behind, as remittances 'represent one dimension of family ties and demonstrate high degrees of interaction between migrants and families at home' (Cai 2003: 472). Migrant workers will endure personal deprivation in order to increase the size of the remittance they send home (Huang and Zhan 2008: 235–6). The vast majority of migrant workers remit; a widely accepted estimate is that approximately 75 per cent of them do so. Those who do not remit typically have employers who withhold wages (Cheng *et al.* 2013), while a growing minority of migrant workers have no need to remit as they relocate with family members (*China Daily* 2014; Hu *et al.* 2011; Qi 2018).

The sense of a needs-based family obligation is manifest in a concept of masculinity, 'respectable manhood', developed by migrant workers in contrast to what they regard as the 'moneyed manhood' of wealthy urban entrepreneurs (Choi and Peng 2016: 100–1). Respectable manhood is 'a sense of masculinity based on the effort a man makes to fulfill his responsibility to provide and care for his family' in contrast with 'rich city entrepreneurs' who they regard as 'corrupted by money' as well as prone to 'marital infidelity' (Choi and Peng 2016: 101–2). In light of this assessment it is of particular interest that money-driven and adulterous entrepreneurs are themselves shown to adhere to the principle and practice of family obligation. In his ethnography of the new rich in the city of Chengdu, John Osburg (2013: 67) shows that, for these men, 'the domestic (*jiali*) was a realm of responsibility…measured not by "quality time" and fidelity, but by the conditions their families lived under'. The importance of 'responsibility (*zerengan*) to his family' remained high to these entrepreneurs (Osburg 2013: 72), just as it did for poor rural migrants who pride themselves on possessing 'respectable manhood'.

While there is agreement about the prevalence of support between family members there are divergent views regarding its basis. In his classic treatment of the Chinese family, which we examined in Chapter 2, Fei Xiaotong (1992: 73–5) holds that ethical norms govern relations between family members, in particular, the 'ethical values' of 'filial piety and fraternal duty' (Fei 1992: 74). This notion is echoed by others who hold that moral codes and family ethics secure the obligatory satisfaction of one family member's need by another (Luo 2011: 331; Luo *et al.* 2016: 651). Other writers, though, have referred instead to emotions. Fan (2002: 548–9) effectively distinguishes between the three types of *guanxi* in terms of three different emotions that 'vary in both nature and intensity', namely '*qinqing* (affection to the loved ones), *ganqing* (emotion to friends) and *renqing* (human debt to acquaintances)'.

While the tripartite forms of *guanxi* may be considered to operate through three distinct emotions respectively, the particular emotions in question vary. Guo and Miller (2010: 274) write that the 'core circle' of family *guanxi* is based 'on *ganqing* (affection)-based *guanxi* ties', while an 'intermediary circle' of non-kin ties is based on '*renqing* (reciprocity-based)' feelings and a 'periphery circle' of non-kin is based on '*jiaoqing* (acquaintance-based) *guanxi* ties'. The difference between Fan (2002) and Guo and Miller (2010) in relation to the emotional basis of family *guanxi* is summarized in the table.

Table: Types of *guanxi* distinguished by different **emotions.**

	Fan (2002)	Guo and Miller (2010)
Family *guanxi*	*Qinqing*	*Ganqing*
Friendship *guanxi*	*Ganqing*	*Renqing*
Acquaintance *guanxi*	*Renqing*	*Jiaoqing*

The differences between the emotions indicated here are significant. First, 亲情 *qinqing* simply means 'family feeling' whereas 感情 *ganqing*, usually translated as affection or emotional commitment, has been widely regarded as the emotional basis of friendship (Fried 1953; Jacobs 1979; Smart 1999), although the term can be used to describe affection between family members, not in general but with regard to instances of affection between particular individuals. It is of interest, though, that Fei (1992: 88) explicitly rejects any role for *ganqing* in 'stabilizing social relationships', preferring instead 'understanding (*liaojie*)' of status mutuality and therefore distinction, essential in traditional kin relations. The linguistic shift indicated in this case, from ethics terms to emotions terms, suggests that Fei's analysis derives from possibly antiquated Confucian notions, as we saw in Chapter 2, and at the same time suggests how in China today emotions tend to displace ethics in characterizing relationships, a supposition loosely proposed by Mark Elvin (1991) in a chapter concerned with the 'modernization' of emotions in Chinese society.

The third term referred to by Guo and Miller above, 交情 *jiaoqing*, indicates feelings between acquaintances that emerge from contact between people and the exchanges in which they participate. In these terms the feelings in question may not be the basis but rather the outcome of such contacts. Nevertheless, once it appears, *jiaoqing* will consolidate a feeling of affection between friends who share a sense of pragmatic obligation (Chen and Chen 2004: 314; Guo and Miller 2010: 280). Finally, 人情 *renqing* is not particularly useful in distinguishing between the elements of tripartite *guanxi* because it can apply to any of them. Fei (1992: 124–5) associates *renqing* with both family life and relations between friends and implies that it has customary and ritual dimensions (Fei 1992: 126–7); indeed, it can be taken to mean the etiquette of exchange. As we saw in Chapters 2 and 3, *renqing* can also be understood as the emotions inherent in 'natural' human relations, especially those of family life; more usually, though, the term can be used to refer to feelings associated with appropriate action, proportionate expectation, as well as normative patterns that run through social interactions and a person's sensibility to such norms. *Renqing* therefore also includes such feelings as sympathetic regard and respect for others as well as properly acknowledging a favour received or a debt incurred. *Renqing* thus captures a broad spectrum of feelings concerning what is culturally appropriate for a given situation involving persons occupying particular roles. Failure to express appropriate emotions and to behave according to custom, propriety, and social etiquette is likely to lead to withdrawal of approval and therefore to loss of face. *Renqing* is thus an inadequate index of distinction between the three forms of *guanxi* indicated in the present discussion because it can be reasonably associated with any of them.

The purpose here is not to legislate on usage but to indicate the difficulty in providing simple rules for distinguishing the elements of tripartite *guanxi* on the basis of a culturally informed emotions terminology. Any particular sense of obligation, including that which underlies each of the distinct forms comprising tripartite *guanxi*, will have an ethical as well as an emotional element, one relating to its rationale, justification, or explanation and the other to its experiential manifestation. In a sociological discussion of family obligation in modern Britain both moral commitment and emotional feelings are indicated as necessary. Why close kin relations have power over individuals is explained sociologically by Janet Finch (1994) in terms of a number of factors. First, a family of origin is the source of an 'irrevocable membership' which 'places each person in series of two-way relationships with a number of individuals' (Finch 1994: 234), especially a parent, sibling, and offspring. These relationships are both socially visible and enduring, thus providing such irrevocable membership with special responsibilities that derive from 'emotional ties and the history of relationships in which they are embedded' (Finch 1994: 235).

Given the lifetime interaction between kin and its emotional significance to them there is an inherent dynamic that reinforces 'the social definition of kin as people whom you treat differently' (Finch 1994: 235). Another aspect of the lifelong interaction between kin noted by Finch is that kin relations have a 'negotiated element' in so far as they operate as 'a necessary mechanism for continually recreating and sustaining a sense of social identity' (Finch 1994: 235). Out of all of this, Finch (1994: 236) says, people form a 'sense of the "ideal norm" of kinship obligations', which provides them with an inescapable moral quality. The moral quality of kinship relations, Finch (1994: 236) goes on to add:

> can only be understood with reference to the sense which it enables people to make of their own position in the social world, rather than a fixed set of prescriptive rules which people follow. When it stops giving meaning and shape to the social world, the power of the moral imperative is reduced considerably, as it is when it conflicts with material self-interest.

These are important qualifications which explain the compelling power of kinship over its participants and at the same time the possibility that the obligations 'inherent' in kinship may under specified circumstances be ignored.

The moral imperatives of kinship within the framework of Confucian ethics are definitional, and therefore departure from them is more or less unconscionable within its ideological framework. This is a different perspective from the one provided by Finch, in which the idea of the moral quality of kinship corresponds to a means which 'enables people to make [sense] of their own position in the social world, rather than a fixed set of prescriptive rules which people follow'. The difference here, though, is between a philosophical outlook and a sociological one, rather than between Chinese and Western understandings. In China as elsewhere, expectations of kinship may indeed be ignored and abrogated under certain circumstances. Possibly because of the strength of a culturally based conceptualization of the Chinese family, as both central and enduring, respondents who acknowledge a weakening of their sense of family obligation tend to qualify or downplay the reduction of its moral imperative, as in the case reported by Yang (1994: 112–13) of a young woman whose feelings for her mother were 'not very "deep"'. In an unusually detailed account Chang (2009: 385–90) provides summaries of a number of cases of family rupture in which kinship, at best, operates as a cleavage of hostility.

While kinship bonds are universally taken to imply an unconditional obligation of support for family members on the basis of need without regard to recompense, this does not mean that support will be forthcoming. Fei (1992:

125) reports that family intimacy 'may turn into resentment'. A respondent reported by Guo and Miller (2010: 276), who held that communication with family members 'does not always guarantee that you will get support from them', was not expressing a unique experience. Indeed, expected familial obligation cannot be taken for granted (Guo and Miller 2010: 270; Fried 1953: 91, 139–42).

To summarize this part of the discussion: family ties may lead to the provision of support between kin as a result of an obligatory sense based on irrevocable membership of a closed relation. A notable feature of this relationship is that support is provided between its constituents without requirement of recompense or acquisition of a debt. At the same time relations between family members may not necessarily meet the expectation implicit in this construction; as Finch indicates, it is always possible that the obligations of kinship may 'stop giving meaning and shape to the social world' in which case 'the power of [its] moral imperative is reduced considerably'. In the present context these two aspects of family obligation are taken as grounds for reassessing the idea that a *guanxi* relationship is involved in the case of family relations. The claim here is that the notion of *guanxi* is simply redundant in the case of family obligation because the family relationship itself is sufficient to characterize and explain the provision of support of one family member to another. There is no need to introduce an additional explanatory category, *guanxi*, which in fact better serves in the characterization of non-kin obligatory relations.

It must be noted that in the present context 'kinship' refers to parent–child and sibling relations rather than to extended kinship. This qualification is important as the term 'kinship' in the discussion of Chinese society, and *guanxi* in particular, is frequently used to refer to same-name lineage. This leads to a confusion that has been incorporated into much of the discussion of *guanxi*. In his classic account of the basis of Chinese society, Fei (1992: 74) says that the relations between family members, parents and children on the one hand and siblings on the other, are based on ethically informed obligations of filial piety and fraternal duty. He goes on to say, though, that 'the unity of the intimate [kinship] group depends on the fact that each member owes countless favors to the other members' (Fei 1992: 124). It can be seen that Fei thus effectively invokes two distinct principles of organization, one pertaining to the immediate family and the other to extended kinship; these may be called respectively 'role obligations' and 'exchange obligations', as we saw in Chapter 2, a distinction developed in more general terms elsewhere (Barbalet 2020). Indeed, what distinguishes family relations from *guanxi* relations is that the former are closed to outsiders, given that they are based on obligations pertaining to lifelong familial roles, as indicated above, whereas the latter is an open-ended relationship based on the obligations that arise from the exchange of favours and are negotiated and constructed by the participants.

Proponents of a tripartite *guanxi*, however they themselves characterize this notion, which includes a family variant, will not necessarily disagree with the understanding of family bonds presented here. Such agreement, however, does not lead to the conclusion drawn in the present discussion because of a related assumption which in effect covers over and ignores the difference between solidarity based on familial role obligations, on the one hand, and solidarity derived from the expectations of reciprocity founded on exchanges of favour, on the other. The assumption in question is that the closed relations of kinship and the open relations of friendship can be bridged and integrated through transitions in the latter to a 'pseudo-family' form. It is therefore necessary to consider the notion of fictive kinship as it relates to the formation of *guanxi*.

Fictive Kinship

Corresponding with the supposition that the family is the primary institution of Chinese society, and of the 'inclusiveness' of Chinese kinship, it is assumed in much of the published discussion of *guanxi* that non-kin social relationships may imitate the kinship form so that they become functionally equivalent to kinship and may merge with it in the constitution of family *guanxi*. According to Luo *et al.* (2016: 651) a 'family tie' in the context of Chinese particularism includes 'real- and pseudo-family ties' through which are maintained 'loyalty...unlimited...[and] complete and unbreakable responsibility to each other'. This statement echoes the supposition that persons construct *guanxi* out of either 'kinship or fictive kinship bases' (King 1991: 68). Similarly, Guo and Miller (2010: 270) hold that, while family ties 'are characterized by unconditional loyalty and involve social obligations that are not based on reciprocity...people cannot solely rely on family in dealing with everyday life, and therefore, *guanxi* serves as a mechanism by which "quasifamilial" relations can be created to cultivate trust among non-kin'. In this way, they continue, '*guanxi* ties with non-kin can be viewed as an extension of *guanxi* ties inherent in family members'. Such an argument is given a classical form through the Confucian notion of 伦 *lun* or cardinal relation, as when Luo (2011: 331) claims that 'the concept of *lun* is not applied to only familial members...[as the] five elements of Confucian *lun* also include loyalty between emperor and subordinates, and friendship'. It does not follow, even though Luo and others assume that it does, that familial ties may therefore 'include patron-client, adoptive, and blood-brother relations' because they take a 'pseudo-familial' form (see also Bian 2018: 604; Chen and Chen 2004: 307–8; King 1991: 65–8).

Sociologically, the formation of fictive-kinship bonds can be understood in terms of two distinct processes, one is adoption of kinship terms of address between persons who do not share kin ties. This practice typically emerges out of a growing intensity of feelings that result from close and frequent interaction. Such interactions arise in structured circumstances or environments, as occur among classmates, neighbours, workmates, or through the sharing of common interests, including recreational, vocational, or political interests. The other possibility, which generally requires this first as its precondition, is achieved through a ritualized ceremony which in the Chinese context is typically described as 结拜兄弟 *jiebai xiongdi*, 'sworn brotherhood', a practice reported as early as the fourteenth century in the classic novels *The Water Margin*, attributed to Shi Naian, and *Romance of Three Kingdoms*, by Luo Guanzhong. The discussion to follow will examine sworn brotherhood first, followed by a treatment of the use of kinship terms of address between persons who in fact do not share a kinship link.

Bian (2019: 8) characterizes sworn brotherhood and other forms of 'ritualized kin' as the 'conversion of a non-kin tie into a kin tie through a ritualized ceremony' (see also Baker 1979: 164). While it is appropriate to describe sworn brotherhood as a form of fictive kinship it does not follow that a functional equivalent of a kin tie will emerge through it. This is because the 'fictive quality' of sworn brotherhood 'remains vibrantly in the consciousness of the participants, and no attempt is made to forget the artificiality of its creation' (Jordan 1985: 233). This latter point has been reinforced in a more recent discussion of a particular type of sworn brotherhood practised in south China (Santos 2008). Santos argues that the practice of sworn brotherhood does not principally draw attention to the overarching significance of kinship in social life, but instead it paradoxically points to the importance of friendship. It is indicated that friendship is a 'key form of human relatedness' consisting of alliances 'marked by frequent voluntary displays of mutual generosity and trust with varying degrees of affection and practicality as well as instrumentality' (Santos 2008: 536–7). These qualities may be found in kin relations, certainly, but friendship possesses them unencumbered by considerations of procreation or generational succession that more centrally defines kinship. Indeed, friendship serves to provide a basis of non-kin alliance that is free of the competitive elements of Chinese kin relations, in which tensions between generations and laterally between siblings have been a traditional and also persisting feature of Chinese family life (Chang 2009: 385–90; Freedman 1979: 236–7; Newell 1985; Redding 1993: 104–7, 215).

Unlike the compulsory bonds of kinship, the obligations of friendship are voluntary and therefore may be felt to be vulnerable to the demands and exigencies of kin. It is out of this circumstance that sworn brotherhood arises. Persons who deem friendship particularly significant may embark on the ceremonies of sworn brotherhood as a 'way of protecting and reinforcing their relation of close friendship and allowing it to become longer-lasting' (Santos 2008: 543; see also Jordan 1985: 233, 236–7). Indeed, Jordan (1985: 238–9) shows that sworn brotherhood is a means of protecting close friendship from challenges by kin, so that sworn brothers may devote resources between themselves against the otherwise prior claims of kin, in this way 'the kinship idiom in which [financial] assistance is phrased overcomes the argument that a person is helping his friend at the expense of his natural family, since his sworn brother may arguably constitute part of his family' (Jordan 1985: 238). Sworn brotherhood, then, draws on the kinship form as a means of defence against its obligatory demands. It indicates strengthened friendship, even though its ritualized form superficially suggests adoption of kinship protocols, which it effectively subverts. It is perhaps for this reason that Jacobs (1979: 249) sees sworn brotherhood as entirely secondary in considerations of *guanxi* even though it is widespread among his informants; its importance is 'to symbolize an extant *kuan-hsi* (*guanxi*) which the parties wish to make closer'.

In addition to ritualized kinship 'very close friends are likely to become pseudo-kin by addressing each other as brothers or sisters' (Bian 2019: 8). The role of 'kinship addresses' (Yang 1994:114) is widely considered to be responsible for the formation of fictive kinship or pseudo-family ties. It is assumed that 'family-like sentiments' will emerge when participants 'address each other in kinship terms, such as brothers, sisters, aunts and uncles' (Bian 2018: 604). Lin (2001: 154) argues that 'the Chinese extend their relations beyond their families by constructing pseudofamilies' through the engagement of two types of social relationships. 'First, there is a sharing of life experiences' so that 'shared identities can be forged even if the two persons involved attended the same school or worked in the same unit years or decades apart. It is the intersection of individuals in the same social space that counts.' On this basis the possibility of a second factor arises, namely such persons 'may choose to make their relationship closer by calling each other "old so and so" and eventually "old brother" (*laoxun*) or "old younger brother" (*laodi*)' and so on (Lin 2001: 154). Lin (2001: 155) is clear, though, that it is necessary to 'differentiate these pseudo-relations from real familial relations' as they form parallel rather than integrated networks. The majority of scholars, though, who discuss pseudo-familial relations, tend to ignore this cautionary qualification. It will be shown here that even the weaker version of the pseudo-family argument on the basis of familial address-term usage is overdrawn.

Use of kinship terms of address has an obvious role in affecting the structure and depth of relations between addressee and addressor. In the Chinese context strangers and acquaintances may use kinship terms in addressing each other as a means of indicating politeness, of generating familiarity or closeness, and inculcating a sense of intimacy. In polite exchanges kinship terms are frequently invoked. It is reported that 'the kinship term *a-sao* ("sister-in-law") was used strategically by sales persons in privately owned stores in South China to claim familiarity with the customer as a way to show politeness and to persuade the customer' (Pan and Kádárb 2011: 1534). Indeed, the 'use of such terms in address is mandatory for the closest relationships; it is preferable for medium-distance ones; and it is usable even with strangers, such as old women from whom one wishes to ask directions' (Blum 1997: 361). The use of kinship terms between persons who have no kin relationship is an extension outward of a kinship vocabulary rather than incorporation of persons into a kinship form of relation. The purpose is not to extend kinship but to achieve an extrinsic purpose, in Chinese 'this is known as *tao jinhu* "to try to win someone's friendship" or "to butter someone up"' (Wu 1990: 86–7).

The use of kin terms between non-kin persons draws on a vocabulary significantly more limited than that used by kin. Chinese kinship terminology is extremely complex although it has become simpler in recent times. Drawing on classical sources Chen and Shryock (1932: 631–8) identify 176 distinct kinship terms pertaining to father's clan, sixteen terms used by the husband for his wife's clan (Chen and Shryock 1932: 639), eight terms used by the wife for her husband's clan (Chen and Shryock 1932: 640), and seventy terms for mother's clan (Chen and Shryock 1932: 640–3). Confining himself to mid-twentieth-century usage Chao (1956: 230–33) identifies a total of 114 distinct kinship terms. Wu (1990: 66–7), on the other hand, in considering post-1978 reform China, indicates ten distinct kinship terms relevant to father's family, six regarding mother's family, and twenty-two regarding one's own family. Approximately half of these terms 'can be used to address non-kin although they have different distributions: some of them are used for strangers, some for acquaintances and some can be used for both situations... [the different terms also distinguish] different degrees of familiarity in terms of the personal relations between speaker and addressee' (Wu 1990: 66).

Although such usage is subject to certain linguistic restrictions the employment of kinship terms to address non-kin is 'one of the typical characteristics of Chinese [language]' which provides extensions of social familiarity between the parties of a conversational dyad, but does not provide access to the kin of the addressee (Wu 1990: 62, 85):

> The use of kinship address forms gives the impression of warmth and intimacy. This corresponds to the typical neighborhood situation in China. Neighbors help each other and treat each other as 'family members'. A Chinese proverb *Yuanqin bu ru jinlin* 'Remote kin cannot compare with close neighbors' is a good indication of how Chinese people attach importance to the relationship among neighbors...By using kinship address forms, polite and close interpersonal relations can be established.   (Wu 1990: 86)

The idea that the use of kin terms between non-kin inculcates sociologically meaningful 'fictive kinship' or 'pseudo-family' ties requires careful qualification. As Wu (1990: 86) puts it: 'By using kinship terms, for example in order to ask a favour of an addressee or to sell something to him/her, the speaker attempts to establish a temporary solidarity like that between family members.'

The idea that the use of kin terms by non-kin may 'establish a temporary solidarity *like* that between family members' has been taken by various writers to imply that the resulting fictive-kin or pseudo-family appellation bridges the gap between kin and non-kin and provides non-kin persons with access to the opportunities and resources associated with kinship. It has been shown here that this is not merely an exaggeration but it distorts the actual consequences of the use of kin address terms between non-kin individuals. In his classic study of the economic structure and social relations of Kaixiangong village in eastern China, Fei (1939: 90) notes that a limited range of kinship terms were used for addressing fellow villagers: '[The] purpose [of] this extended use of relationship terms... [is to] attach certain psychological attitudes corresponding to the intimate relationships for which they were initially devised. These emotional attitudes may, by the extended use of the term, be taken up to persons not actually standing in such an intimate relationship.' Fei (1939: 91) goes on to say that: 'the extension of such emotional attitudes to persons not actually related as the terms would imply does not necessarily involve an extension of specific privileges and obligations. It does not imply a real extension of kinship relation.' This indicates not an incorporation of non-kin persons into relations between kin but on the contrary points to a clear disjuncture between authenticity and mimicry, effectively acknowledged by the tactical use of kin terminology.

Friendship and Acquaintance in *Guanxi*

In addition to the notion of 'family *guanxi*' there is a broad consensus in the literature that there are two further types or forms of *guanxi*, descriptively identified as 'friendship *guanxi*' and 'acquaintance *guanxi*'. These can be distinguished in terms of the particular configurations of obligation and sentiment that underlie each of them. In terms of the processes through which friendship and acquaintance operate, however, they can be described as different phases in a process of *guanxi* formation rather than as distinct and alternate kinds of *guanxi*. This is because there are no inhibiting factors that would prevent acquaintance developing into friendship or friendship weakening to mere acquaintance. On this basis, then, rather than distinct types of *guanxi* these may best be conceptualized as stages of *guanxi* formation.

Guanxi has been distinguished in terms of 'the different types of people with whom the *guanxi* is formed' (Fu *et al.* 2006: 2); the distinction between '*shuren* (acquaintances or familiar persons such as neighbors, or people from the same village, friends, colleagues, or classmates) and *shengren* (strangers)', entails that one 'type' of person may become another. This is because Fu *et al.* (2006: 5) argue that, as well as denoting strangers, '*shengren* also implies a yet-to-be-discovered *guanxi* created by common social identities shared by two parties', including a common birthplace, workplace, educational institution, or a third person known to each of them. In this case, then,

> *shengren*-based *guanxi* exists between two people who are connected by a yet-to-be-discovered tie, such as a common social identity or a common third party…[so that] two strangers (*shengren*) may establish a strong rapport as soon as they discover a common identity [or] shared values or interests after they meet and exchange information about each other…the two could feel like old friends in a matter of minutes because of the obligations, expectations, as well as social norms, embedded in the newly-discovered tie

so that '*shengren*-based *guanxi* could change into a *shuren*-based relationship in a short time'.

It can be noted that the transformation of one type of *guanxi* into another may be in either direction, not only from 生人 *shengren* to 熟人 *shuren*, but also from *shuren* to *shengren*, if one of the parties involved defaults on the relationship in some way (Fu *et al.* 2006: 7; see also Luo 2011: 345). These different stages of *shengren*, one existing prior to a transition to *shuren* and the other arising out of a spoiled *shuren*, are clearly not qualitative equivalents in so far as one indicates expansive potential while the other indicates contraction and 丢面子 *diu mianzi*, loss of face. But it is in the nature of *guanxi* that neither of these qualitatively distinct stages of *shengren* is final or terminal. Face may be lost, but lost face may be regained or recovered (Hwang 1987: 961–2; Qi 2017a: 9–10). *Guanxi* cultivation as an agentic engagement is necessarily multidirectional.

The distinction between friendship *guanxi* and acquaintance *guanxi* as well as the possibility of one converting to or merging with the other is widely accepted. This raises conceptual issues, though, that are seldom addressed. The first issue to be noted is that non-comparable qualities are used to identify each of these supposed forms of *guanxi*. Friendship *guanxi* is typically characterized in terms of the means employed in achieving it, such as identity markers of various kinds including an emotional attachment. The particular emotion in question may vary, most frequently it is either *ganqing* (Fan 2002: 549; Fu *et al.* 2006: 7; Jacobs 1979: 261–5; Kipnis 1997; Wank 1996: 826) or *renqing* (understood as feelings underlying proportionate relational expectation) (Hwang 1987; Luo 2011: 331–2; Yan 1996). Acquaintance *guanxi*, on the other hand, is typically characterized not in terms of its means but of its goal or purpose, whether that purpose is characterized as instrumental or as a debt-payment nexus, sometimes rendered as *jiaoqing* and—confusingly—*renqing* (understood as acknowledging a favour and repaying a debt) (Fu *et al.* 2006: 7; Guo and Miller 2010: 280–1; Wank 1996: 826–7). The distinction between 'friendship *guanxi*' and 'acquaintance *guanxi*' thus arises from different ways of identifying each rather than anything intrinsic to them.

The basis of this use of non-comparable qualities in distinguishing friendship and acquaintance *guanxi* has its source in another distinction also frequently mentioned in discussion of *guanxi*, namely the distinction between expressivity, on the one hand, and instrumentality, on the other. If these are taken as alternatives, as they frequently are in discussion of *guanxi* (Gold 1985: 659; Hwang 1987: 949–53; Yan 1996: 226–9), then confusion will result. Expressivity and instrumentality are different but they are not alternatives; they coexist in the practice of *guanxi* by each contributing to its possibility or occurrence (Barbalet 2015: 1040). Even when the instrumental aspect is at a premium, as with business *guanxi*, favours can be exchanged only if there is expressivity realized as bonding feelings (*ganqing*) between participants (Osburg 2013: 42–5).

A tripartite characterization of *guanxi* is further supported by a notion widespread among *guanxi* researchers that has not yet been treated directly although it is implicit in much of the discussion above, namely the necessity of *guanxi* bases in the formation of *guanxi* (Chen and Chen 2004: 311–12; Chen *et al.* 2013: 171–2; Jacobs 1979: 243–56; Tong and Yong 1998; Yang 1994: 111–19). As shown in previous chapters, *guanxi* bases can be characterized in a number of ways, but they are essentially made of elements that correspond with the forms of *guanxi* commonly identified in the literature, including family and kinship and the various sources of friendship and acquaintance, including common locality or birthplace, education, employment, and so on. While *guanxi* bases are widely regarded as necessary in the formation of *guanxi* relations they are typically not regarded as sufficient.

In his classic statement concerning *guanxi* bases Jacobs (1979) provides the qualification that the mobilization of any given *guanxi* base requires engagement of a particular 'affective component', namely *ganqing* (senti-mental attachment) that is achieved through 'two dynamic processes: (1) social interaction and (2) utilization and helping' (Jacobs 1979: 259). Indeed, in his discussion of the political party activists that are the subject of his study Jacobs shows that the level and type of activity in which they are engaged determines which *guanxi* base is relevant to their purposes and therefore which particular *guanxi* base they cultivate in establishing their relations with others. In this sense, then, *guanxi* bases are not determinative of *guanxi* relations and therefore do not produce *guanxi* in and of them-selves. Rather, *guanxi* bases are selected strategically by individuals enabling the formation of relations to achieve their purposes or intentions. The rela-tionship, then, between a supposed *guanxi* base and the actual practice of *guanxi* may be entirely contingent, as indicated in discussion of *guanxi* bases since Jacobs's seminal contribution.

Chen and Chen (2004: 311–12) distinguish three types of *guanxi* bases: first, common social identity, typically based on shared birthplace, educa-tional institution, and workplace, second, triangular relations in which a third party links two otherwise unconnected persons, particularly useful for foreign business persons seeking a *guanxi* connection with a Chinese counterpart (see Luo 2007: 159–209), and, finally, what they call an 'antici-patory' base of future intention to form a *guanxi* relation:

In social and business interactions, individuals who do not share common social identification can still initiate a *guanxi* by creating potential future bases through expressing an intention or even a promise to engage in future exchanges, collaborations, or joint ventures. These *guanxi* intentions hence become *guanxi* bases for further interactions. Notice that potential *guanxi* partners often also share similar aspirations, ideals, or values but it is not similarity itself but the expressed intention of *guanxi* exchanges that constitute an anticipatory *guanxi* base.   (Chen and Chen 2004: 311–12; see also Chen *et al.* 2013: 172, 182)

The concept of an 'anticipatory' *guanxi* base effectively indicates that the generic notion, '*guanxi* base', is in fact misleading. Rather than bases in the sense of something on which *guanxi* rests or which provides bottom-up support for *guanxi* practices, these elements are instead resources which individuals may draw upon in creating a sense of common identity with another for their mutual benefit. If it is anything a *guanxi* base is not a foundation or structural property but rather an opportunity for agentic engagement.

Guanxi always exists as a connection between individuals who cultivate it in order to achieve their purposes. Those purposes will necessarily be compound, including securing and enhancing *mianzi*, their social standing or face, so that their reliability and therefore their availability for and appeal as prospective *guanxi* partners will be realized. As well as building their social resources another purpose of a *guanxi* relation includes the mobilization of these resources to acquire materially beneficial goods or preferment in opportunities for acquiring such goods. The cultivation of *guanxi* requires a sense of shared identity or commonality of purpose which provides focus to the participants in cultivating their *guanxi* and also a sense of common commitment, achieved by emotional attachment to their association. *Guanxi* is not an emergent outcome of latent structures, then, that can be found in a pre-existing 'base'; rather it is necessarily an open-ended relation that requires the time and resources to discover a (prospective) partner's tastes and purposes and how they may be matched to the initiator's own requirements and abilities in forging an enabling relationship that is *guanxi*, as we saw in Chapter 1. In terms of the qualities outlined here *guanxi* is necessarily unlike the closed and compulsory relations of intimate kinship that form from a prior structure into which a person is born. A contact provided by either friendship or acquaintance may be recruited for the purpose of cultivating *guanxi*. Not all friendships and acquaintances will lead to a *guanxi* relationship but no *guanxi* can be cultivated in the absence of such an initial social contact. Out of these contacts the persons involved cultivate a *guanxi* connection.

Sources of Category Ambiguity

As a category employed in social analysis the term *guanxi* has an established presence and meaning, even though the content of that meaning operates in a wide penumbra because in many ways it remains sociologically unresolved. Nevertheless, it is possible to locate frequently sourced definitions in the literature that converge on some particular and arguably necessary characteristics. To confine ourselves to a small number of obvious cases (Bian 2006: 312; 2018: 603; 2019: 6; Chen and Chen 2004: 306; Gold 1985: 661; King 1991: 69) there is agreement that *guanxi* is an informal and particularistic dyadic connection, built or cultivated by the participants involved through a sense of common identity and sentiment, involving reciprocity and exchange generative of obligation, and with the potential of application to achieve purposive or instrumental outcomes. Beyond this summary account agreement is difficult to locate.

As I have indicated, there is a broad consensus that a core form of *guanxi* exists between family members even though family *guanxi* is understood to occur in the absence of a requirement of exchange, based on a compulsion sufficient in itself to satisfy another's need. It is also widely assumed, as we have seen, that fictive-kinship or pseudo-family ties assimilate non-kin into family or family-like *guanxi*, even though firm evidence for such a prospect is absent. It has also been shown that the widespread conceptualization of distinct and separate *guanxi* forms based respectively on friendship and acquaintance can more meaningfully be characterized not as residual categories or states but rather as variable phases of non-kin relations. The confusion that has been identified here can be explained in terms of three distinct factors of language, culture, and method. Each will be considered in turn.

Vernacular or everyday language usage tolerates, indeed encourages the idea that *guanxi* might apply to both kin and non-kin connections. The literal meaning of the term *guanxi* is much broader than the sociological renditions. In Chinese language *guanxi* is a multiplex term that can refer to any type of relationship, not only between persons, and the quality of the relationship indicated is also variable. The first character, *guan*, means to close, shut, or form a barrier, while the second character, *xi*, means to fasten or link, as when systems or serial entities are formed. Together the characters indicate a relationship or a connection; that is all. The relationship in question may be causal, 因果关系 *yinguo guanxi*, or mathematical, 数学关系 *shuxue guanxi*; it may be a hostile relationship, 敌对关系 *didui guanxi*, or a family relationship 家庭关系 *jiating guanxi*. The relationship may be sexual, either innocent love, 肯定关系 *kending guanxi*, literally, 'to confirm the relationship', or an illicit relationship, 乱搞男女关系 *luan gao nannu guanxi*, literally, 'disorderly relations between a man and a woman'. *Guanxi* may also refer to an evaluative relationship, as in 没有关系 *meiyou guanxi*, literally, 'not having concern', indicating that something 'doesn't matter'. It also, of course, may mean a social relationship, 社会关系 *shehui guanxi*. It goes without saying that social relationships may be of many types.

The type of relationship that is implied in the social science discussion of *guanxi* is generally a dyadic relation, based on sentiment or affection, and involving exchanges of favour or reciprocal benefit. When Chinese people in conversation refer to *guanxi* they may not necessarily have any one of these particular meanings in mind, but some other; and if they do refer to the type of relationship discussed in social science treatments of *guanxi* they may use a term other than *guanxi*, such as 人脉 *renmai*, literally, 'human mountain range' or 'vascular system', indicating expansive connections, referring to sustaining contacts or networks, or 勾兑 *goudui*, literally 'blend', implying relationship cultivation, or they may refer to some other construction.

By its nature sociological discussion inevitably draws on everyday terms, namely categories based on direct experience of social participation that are used to refer to such experiences by those involved. This is not to suggest that sociology is devoid of technical terms, but in treating aspects of relationships and social organization the words that social participants themselves employ frequently inform more formal characterizations of events and processes and thus effectively play a dual role, as vernacular labels and also technical terms. Recognition of the problematic nature of this dual aspect of natural language words in sociological discourse is not new. It has, however, not led to acknowledgement of limitations in the social science discussion of *guanxi*, let alone attempts to rectify such problems. The caution indicated by Robert Merton (1968: 145, 168–9), that sociological explanation requires not only empirical investigation but also 'conceptual analysis' and conceptual 'clarification', can be applied to how the vernacular concept of *guanxi* is sociologically employed. Concepts 'constitute the definitions (or prescriptions) of what is to be observed; they are the variables between which empirical relationships are to be sought' so that the 'function of conceptual analysis…is to maximize the likelihood of the comparability…of data which are to be included in the research' (Merton 1968: 143, 145).

When the same common-language term, *guanxi*, is applied in sociological analysis to both close family or kin connections and non-kin connections which provide support to participants, even though one is based on closed relations not requiring a return favour and the other on open relations in which such return favours are routine and necessary, then the comparability of data will be jeopardized. In such situations the discussion is rationalized in ways that led Arthur Stinchcombe (1968: 41), for instance, to say that when 'natural variables' are seen to have 'multiple causes', then the 'researcher is trying to explain the wrong thing'. More recently it has been acknowledged that 'If the everyday meaning is used, the research will have difficulty in creating a sociological analysis and may instead end up with one that is based on folk wisdom' (Swedberg 2020: 435). This is a situation that arguably emerges when it is supposed that *guanxi* derives its meaning from a Confucian basis of Chinese society or has a more general traditional lineage, as discussed in Chapter 3 and elsewhere.

It is held to be axiomatic in a significant section of the *guanxi* literature that China is a 'Confucian society' (Bian 2019: 9–12; Fu *et al.* 2006: 17; Guo and Miller 2010: 270; Wang and Rowley 2017: 102–4), a view encouraged by official and semi-official sources since the 1980s (Makeham 2008) and given explicit sociological endorsement (Kang 2013). But this proposition requires careful examination. The ideological dominance of Confucianism was attempted after 戊戌变法 *Wuxu Bianfa*, the Hundred Days Reform of 1898, when, in an endeavour to preserve the Qing court during a period of political, economic and military turmoil, Confucian literati sponsored the suppression of Buddhism, Daoism, and local cults, newly designated as 'superstitions' (Goossaert 2006). This was in contravention of the established view, that had operated from the sixth century, that Chinese culture is based on the harmonious combination of 三教 *san jiao*, 'three teachings', namely Confucianism, Daoism, and Buddhism, which together inform Chinese cultural and social practices and orientations. As we saw in Chapter 4 the social bearers of Confucianism, 绅士 *shenshi*, the gentry, constituted only a small portion of the population of China at the end of the Qing dynasty (Michael 1955: 422; Yang 1959: 255). The vast majority of the population, peasants excluded from both governance and privilege, had little knowledge of or interest in Confucianism. Their gods were local and domestic rather than imperial, they worshipped ancestors, certainly, feared ghosts on the basis of vague beliefs, and were familiar with Daoist and Buddhist rather than Confucian ideas and practices (Eastman 1988: 42–59; Granet 1975: 144–56). With the collapse of the Qing Dynasty through the advent of Republican China in 1911, Confucianism was itself disembedded from its social and political base.

In reaction to the anti-traditional New Culture Movement (1913–17), conservative scholars and gentry elements during the period from the 1920s until the late 1940s attempted to reassert Confucian social doctrine, as we saw in Chapter 2. Two late Republican Confucian thinkers in particular,

Liang Shuming and Fei Xiaotong, developed an idealized Confucian model of Chinese society that has informed the theoretical framework of many *guanxi* studies. Indeed, late Republican Confucianism was the source of the idea that the 'most important relationship' in Chinese society is kinship (Fei 1992: 63) and that the Chinese family as lineage has a permanency and structural flexibility that the merely conjugal family lacks and therefore that the 'Chinese family is a medium through which all activities are organized' (Fei 1992: 84). These ideas underpin the conception of *guanxi* expressed in leading sections of the sociological literature, as we have seen. The presentation of the Chinese family that continues to run through a good deal of the present-day conceptualization was subject to significant sociological critique during the late Republican period (Cheng 1939; Hsu 1943; Lee 1949), sources unfortunately neglected in recent discussion.

It was shown in Chapter 2 that, in addition to kinship bases of social support, anthropologist William Skinner (1964: 35–9) demonstrated that the networks of Chinese rural society involved extensive and important connections among non-kin. Similarly, on the basis of extensive fieldwork, carried out during 1947–8 in Zhu Xian within Anhui Province, Morton Fried (1953: 230) shows that the 'complex design of Chinese society becomes more comprehensible when systematic study of extra-familial relations is added to the research on Chinese familial organization'. Fried's study demonstrates that the structure of relations is not exhausted by kinship and that other forms of relationships, summarized in large part as non-kin friendship, operate alongside it. Friendship, Fried (1953: 67) says, 'at times...serves as a complement to pre-existing kinship rights and obligations [though] it often challenges kinship for prior loyalty...[when it] furnishes avenues by which familial pressures may be avoided and introduces elements which are potentially subversive of familial unity'. Fried insists, therefore, that a comprehensive and meaningful understanding of Chinese society, both rural and urban, requires that due regard is given to non-kin relationships in their own right. Second, he identifies an independent basis of non-kin relations in *ganqing*, prefiguring the later treatment of *guanxi*. This important corrective to the revivalist Confucianism of Fei (1992) and others is overlooked or simply misunderstood, as when it is claimed that: 'Fried's study of a county seat in Anhui province before 1949 confirms that the web of familial and kinship obligations indeed extended into and became the "fabric" of the economic, political and social organizations of the county seat before the 1949 Communist revolution' (Bian 2001: 276). Fried (1953) in fact shows the opposite. The point here is not to suggest that kinship is without importance in Chinese society but rather that the Confucian ideological elevation of kinship as both socially dominant and an archetypical form to which other types of relations are subject is not supported by the evidence.

Finally, a tripartite *guanxi* formation with family *guanxi* at its core tends to be a favoured conceptualization when social network analysis (SNA) is chosen as the method for data-gathering and explanation. This is because tie strength enjoys explanatory privilege in SNA. It is not necessary to fully develop an argument concerning departures of *guanxi* networks from the network form assumed by SNA as it is provided in the previous chapter and elsewhere (Barbalet 2015, 2020: 10–13). In the present context, it is sufficient to show that difficulties for the study of *guanxi* become apparent when tie strength is the basis of analysis, as indicated in the following account:

> a friend should be categorized as a weak tie if the definition follows the kinship method, but the job seeker may have frequent interactions with this friend and they may share many homogenous personal characteristics. Hence, there is a strong relationship between the job seeker and the friend, and this so-called weak tie can be much stronger than a strong tie relative with whom the job seeker has infrequent contact.   (Weng and Xu 2018: 72)

Consideration concerning *guanxi*, as implicitly indicated in this quotation, signifies that through *guanxi*, weak ties become strong ties and strong ties may become weak. The observation that the 'art of *guanxi* involves the strategic strengthening of weak into strong ties' may encourage the idea 'that weak and strong ties are not permanently distinct categories' (Smart 1998: 561). More importantly, as we have seen in other chapters, it leads to a questioning of why these categories are used at all in attempts to understand *guanxi*, and how *guanxi* connections may be more adequately theorized in other terms.

As a cultivated practice the predictors of *guanxi* cannot be social ties embedded in latent structures. *Guanxi* comprises agentic practices volitionally constructed or created by the participants in their interaction and the ties between participants are therefore never fixed. It is necessary, then, to distinguish a *guanxi* connection from a network tie (Wu and Wall 2019). The construction of *guanxi* connections requires mutual long-term monitoring and surveillance as well as personal disclosure and shared activities of various sorts, as described by ethnographic accounts (e.g. Osburg 2013; Wank 2009). The strength of any *guanxi* connection is always and necessarily a work in progress, never final, and always capable of being increased as well as decreased through the activities of those involved, in terms of their strategic considerations.

Conclusion

Guanxi is a form of particularistic tie integral to social connections based on affective bonds generated or maintained by favour exchange and mobilized in order to achieve the purposes of its participants. The study of *guanxi* has attracted growing attention in the social sciences since the early 1980s. While research on *guanxi* was originally conducted primarily by anthropologists and sociologists, today the largest single research constituency focused on *guanxi* is business and marketing academics (Liu and Mei 2015). Researchers, who favour a tripartite model of *guanxi* as discussed in the present chapter, are drawn from the full range of social science disciplines. This testifies to the broadness of the appeal of the idea that family *guanxi*, friendship *guanxi*, and acquaintance *guanxi* are distinct forms of *guanxi* subject to different types of obligation.

If the study of *guanxi* is to continue to act as a platform from which meaningful knowledge of social relations in Chinese society is provided, then conceptual refinement and increased theoretical sophistication are required. Such a task inevitably includes challenging those assumptions that underlie current research and examining suppositions inherent in established linguistic practices and cultural beliefs which are not the foundation of social scientific refinement but its impediment. The issue here is not entirely the one Lewis Carroll addressed, in *Through the Looking-Glass*, captured by a conversation between Humpty Dumpty, an anthropomorphic egg, and Alice, a young girl who visits an impossible world:

> 'When *I* use a word', Humpty Dumpty said, in rather a scornful tone, 'it means just what I choose it to mean—neither more nor less'.
>
> 'The question is', said Alice, 'whether you *can* make words mean so many different things'.
>
> 'The question is', said Humpty Dumpty, 'which is to be master—that's all'.

The meaning of terms in arguments concerning *guanxi* does not necessarily reflect the arbitrary power of a Humpty Dumpty. The case under consideration highlights instead the risks in the acquiescence of social scientists to the overarching influence of everyday language, cultural stereotypes, and inappropriate or limited methods. These conventional powers, rather than the power of persons, overdetermine the ways in which *guanxi* is understood in the social science literature. Theoretically robust research can proceed only on the basis of conceptual refinement. The contribution of the present chapter is to show that the notion of *guanxi* is in need of such refinement. A way in which the conceptual refinement of *guanxi* in sociological treatments may be achieved is also indicated here.

In particular, it has been shown that, if the widely accepted core notion of *guanxi* as a 'personalized tie between two persons affectively connected and engaged in an exchange of favours' is taken as basic, then a number of things follow. First, the obligations of reciprocity that derive from *guanxi* exchanges must be distinguished from the role obligations that typically underpin the support provided by a parent to an adult child, for instance, by a child to a parent, and between siblings. This distinction in forms of obligation is fundamental, as indicated in the difference between 'a social structure of positions in relation' and a 'social structure of relations among persons' (Coleman 1990: 427–8). In the first of these, Coleman goes on to say, persons 'take on the obligations and expectations…associated with their positions', whereas in the second the obligations arise out of mutually beneficial trans-actions that exist in exchanges as 'self-contained pairwise relations'. It was shown above how these distinct bases of relations, one associated with the closed affinities of immediate family and the other with the open possibilities of non-kin acquisitions of esteem, social standing, or face through a volun-tary provision appreciated by another (Blau 1964; Brennan and Pettit 2005), are obscured when family or kin relations are defined broadly and also taken to incorporate non-family members through the means of fictive kinship.

A second thing that follows from the core statement of *guanxi*, then, is that assumptions related to the mechanisms of sworn brotherhood and the use of familial names in bridging kin and non-kin ties cannot be taken for granted or at their face value. It was shown that the practices of fictive kinship can encourage a sense of psychological closeness without providing access to the resources of kinship, in the case of the use of familial names, and also that sworn brotherhood in fact intensifies friendship bonds by adopting familial forms in order to protect participants from the intrusive demands of kinship that may detract from a friendship connection and its commitments. Both of these findings encourage the view that the basic content of *guanxi* connections derive from the friendship form rather than the kinship form. This is a conclusion quite contrary to the dominant understanding in the current literature. Finally, the distinction between friendship *guanxi* and acquaintance *guanxi* was shown to be phasal rather than definitive. By its nature *guanxi* is both open in the possibilities of membership or association and flexible in its operation, subject to the intention of its participants and the utility of its provision, both of which are context-given and subject to volitionally driven change and variation. In this sense, then, acquaintance and friendship as proxy terms for *guanxi* episodes are each ever likely to be variably dominant, and therefore variably recessive, depending on the changing needs, resources, and broader situation of participants.

It has also been shown that inhibition around the findings presented in this chapter can be readily understood as derived from an over-reliance on everyday terms in sociological analysis, acceptance rather than critical assessment of cultural assumptions in social reasoning, and insufficient reflexivity in adoption of research methods. Advances in the sociological study of *guanxi* have been cumulative over the past forty or so years. At the same time, the practices of *guanxi* have changed as the society to which they are attached change, and the transformation of China since the onset of economic marketization in the early 1980s has been unprecedented. The present chapter contributes to the continuing reflections on *guanxi* by applying principles of systematic sociological analysis to certain widely held assumptions in the sociology of China, in order to better appreciate the nature of *guanxi* and the distinctions within it.

Conclusion

The Persistence and Diverse Application of a Changing Form

In the preceding six chapters 关系 *guanxi* has been analysed and contextualized. It has been shown that the term, applied to practices of instrumental particularism, became widely used from the 1980s. In earlier times, as we have seen, other terms referred to similar or at least related practices, and today people who wish to avoid the odious association of 拉关系 *la guanxi*, pulling or self-interested *guanxi*, might refer to such practices with the terms 人脉 *renmai*, 勾兑 *goudui*, or 往来 *wanglai*. *Guanxi* is rather like those intricately carved balls, fashioned from a block of ivory, jade, or wood, in which one hollow sphere sits inside another, and within that another, and so on, so that as many as a dozen balls or more are reticulated in a descending nested order. Such artefacts, which have a long history in China's craft traditions, are known as 鬼工球 *gui gong qiu*, devil's work ball, because it might be thought that human hands could not reasonably fashion such intricate and complex objects. It could be similarly said of *guanxi*, a social practice that arises from strategic alliances which sit inside so many other engagements. Known by different names over the course of historical time, we have seen that, whatever it is called, instrumental particularism manifests the attributes of an affective bond serving participants' 面子 *mianzi*, face, and that such participants are obligated to serve the interests or needs of their associates, with whom they exchange favour. In concluding this discussion of *guanxi* it can be asked what is its general significance for an understanding of China today and its future.

In writing this book the purpose was not simply to provide an exposition of the notion and practice of *guanxi*, but also to treat *guanxi* and the way in which it has been understood in the relevant literature as a prism through which Chinese society, including aspects of its history and cultural background, could be displayed and thereby meaningfully apprehended. There is a general sense that *guanxi* is a uniquely Chinese cultural artefact. This is a matter of perspective, however. While *guanxi* is pervasive in Chinese

The Theory of Guanxi *and Chinese Society.* Jack Barbalet, Oxford University Press (2021). © Jack Barbalet.
DOI: 10.1093/oso/9780198808732.003.0008

behaviour, in many respects it shares a number of attributes found in relationships and commitments located in quite different societies. If the purpose of inquiry is to examine, say, 'patrons, clients, and friends' across a range of different societies, then the Chinese incidence of 感情 *ganqing* may exist alongside comparable manifestations in thirty or more national or regional cases (Eisenstadt and Roniger 1984: 139–45). In this light *guanxi* has been compared, for instance, to Russian *blat* (Ledeneva 2008; Michailova and Worm 2003), Middle Eastern *wasta* (Hutchings and Weir 2006; see also Ali and Weir 2020; Cunningham and Sarayrah 1993), and Korean *yongo* (Horak and Taube 2016; see also Bian and Ikeda 2016). It could also be compared to Indian *jaan-pehchaan* (Berger *et al.* 2020), for example, Brazilian *jeitinho* (Duarte 2006; Park *et al.* 2018), or Azerbaijanian *tapsh* (Aliyev 2017). In terms of its elemental properties and functions, *guanxi* displays similarities with informal relationships across a range of different societies. But what determines the details of its particular character and operation is the social context in which *guanxi*, or Russian *blat*, Arabic *wasta*, Korean *yongo*, Indian *jaan-pehchaan*, Brazilian *jeitinho*, or Azerbaijanian *tapsh* actually reside—and it is here that the differences lie.

In considering the relevance of *guanxi* for understanding Chinese society and its future it might be asked what role *guanxi* plays today in economic and social relations. There is a consensus that, while remaining politically socialist, China's economy is capitalist. It is true that at the Twelfth National Party Congress in 1982, paramount leader Deng Xiaoping argued that the introduction of market incentives, including the retention of profits by enterprises and the provision of performance bonuses for workers, was no more nor less than 'socialism with Chinese characteristics'. By 2001, however, through joining the World Trade Organization, China was subject to a number of conditions, including the liberalization of its service, banking, and financial sectors, as well as insurance and telecommunications, all of which were now opened to foreign investment (Branstetter and Lardy 2008). Through these and associated changes, it became difficult to doubt that the economy was anything but capitalist, even if with Chinese characteristics. As we are now used to the idea that there are varieties of capitalism (Hall and Soskice 2001), it can be asked which variety is China's capitalism? There are a number of possibilities, including state capitalism (Y. Huang 2008; Naughton and Tsai 2015), neo-liberal capitalism (Harvey 2005), state neo-liberal capitalism (So and Chu 2016), and *guanxi* capitalism (Boisot and Child 1996; Chow 1997; McNally 2011; Nitsch and Diebel 2008).

The problem with summary terms, including those which designate the character of China's capitalism, is what they leave out. China's economy retains significant state ownership, in key areas, which exists alongside collectively owned enterprises as well as privately owned firms, ranging from family businesses and small-to-medium enterprises (SMEs) to multinational corporations. The coexistence of these different ownership forms, which are all effectively subject to state management through broadly set directions of the economy, may suggest state capitalism, or possibly even market socialism (Naughton 2017). At the same time, foreign ownership restrictions have been progressively removed in China, with full foreign ownership currently permitted in the banking, insurance, and retail asset management sectors. This arguably provides a neo-liberal dimension to China's economy. Another factor that is important in these considerations is the development in China of legal frameworks and provisions, partly to encourage foreign investment and partly to simplify compliance requirements in a growing economy (Lam 2009; Peerenboom 2002). According to some researchers, these latter developments in the current mix of proclivities and orientations will drive *guanxi* out of the formal economy (Guthrie 1998; Hanser 2002; X. Huang 2008; Wank 2002). As an adjunct to the development of law, the anti-corruption campaign initiated by President Xi in 2012 may also be seen as a force diminishing the prospects for *guanxi* (but see Lee 2018).

In spite of these developments, there are a number of reasons why it is unlikely that in China's economy *guanxi* will be diminished as a continuing force. Implementation of modern business law remains incomplete in China, and more important than law in the official management of business are administrative regulative documents and administrative orders, which are widely employed as means of policy enforcement (Zhao and Qi 2020). Not only are many of these decidedly extra-legal in their form, they are amenable to negotiation and interpretation at the local level of implementation, and therefore implicitly available to be managed through *guanxi* relations, to a higher degree than the judicial process which is itself notably subject to a determination of outcomes through *guanxi* involvement (Li 2018; Zhao 2019). Here *guanxi*, law, and administrative regulation operate in conformity with the metaphor of *gui gong qiu*, a devil's work ball, suggestive of the way in which *guanxi* may persist and adjust within the hollows of insipient institutions and practices. Given the effective facilitation of *guanxi* in legal and administrative arenas, it is likely that newcomers to China's commercial and business practices will accept the lubricative efficiency of *guanxi*. Indeed, in a study of foreign bankers in China it is shown that a significant portion of Western managers, in working with local businesses and officials, accept the prevailing ethos and not only accommodate to *guanxi* practices but initiate, facilitate, and encourage them (Nolan 2011).

It would be an error, however, to assume that the continuing relevance of *guanxi* to the Chinese economy is incidental and a result of social inertia. The political framework governing China's economic advancement effectively encourages the continuing role of *guanxi*. The development of China's market economy as a consequence of the Deng reforms of the late 1970s involved both central direction and local innovation, a combination which continues to the present day. In the early stage of the reforms, property rights were not protected and financial institutions were directed to servicing only state-owned enterprises. In these circumstances 'it was the development and use of innovative informal arrangements within networks of like-minded economic actors that provided the necessary funding and reliable business norms' (Nee and Opper 2012: 9), which is to say *guanxi* played a necessary role from the beginnings of marketization. The contribution to China's GDP of this bottom-up, *guanxi*-organized private economy quickly became too significant to be ignored by central authorities, and its competitive pressure on state-owned enterprises led to a relative decline in the latter's market share. This contribution of *guanxi* was significantly enhanced through progressive fiscal decentralization, begun in the 1990s, which had a positive impact on economic outcomes (Ding *et al.* 2019).

Among other things, the fiscal reforms from the late 1990s, through which regional government could retain a portion of tax revenue, generated 'incentives for local government officials to do what they could to assure that local firms prospered' so that 'local and provincial government [was led] to accommodate entrepreneurial endeavors, particularly if state-owned sources of income were insufficient to support local government activities' (Nee and Opper 2012: 228). Regional administrative agencies enhance business activities principally through the mechanism of *guanxi*, 'personal connections' between cadres and entrepreneurs which linked profit generation and political administration in a nexus that enhances the benefits of both. This particular *guanxi* has a number of consequences in addition to increased marketization and economic growth, which has been remarkable, including the formation of privileged associations, significant regulatory distortion, and corruption (Ang 2016: 29–33; see also Paik and Baum 2014; Sun *et al.* 2014). The endemic corruption that is a consequence of a development strategy based on *guanxi* between regional cadres and entrepreneurs, while not impeding growth (Wedeman 2012), has given rise to significant numbers of 群体性事件 *qunti xing shijian*, mass incidents, involving Chinese citizens mobilized against the excesses of privileged extraction at the expense of villagers and townspeople. Such collective actions, typically 'spontaneous' and short-lived, are organized and supported through the *guanxi* of those involved, not only between citizens but also between citizens and journalists as well as academics (Qi 2017b: 115–20). It is of particular interest that state suppression of such mass incidents is also achieved by *guanxi*. In response to outbreaks of protest against corruption and administrative excesses, local officials establish 'work teams' comprising persons who have *guanxi* with individual protesters, which is then deployed to dissuade them from continued involvement in dissent (Deng and O'Brien 2013: 537–41).

This summary confirms the observation, made in Chapter 1, that *guanxi* is sufficiently versatile to be applied in the acquisition of quite different resources, including social goods as well as private values. This summary also supports the proposition, again indicated in Chapter 1, that *guanxi* is sufficiently flexible to become a suitable means for providing service in achievement of a purpose where it had not previously been used, that as conditions change *guanxi* may be successfully applied and, by the same token, it may be less useful in other areas of social life if its viability as an instrument of purposeful acquisition is reduced as a result of other changes in its context and the circumstances of those who engage it. It was shown in Chapter 4 that under different names instrumental particularism has a long history in Chinese society, and that while there has been variation in how and where it has been practised, and the social reach of its availability, its potential value is high for those who have access to facilitating others and the social resources to bond with them in the provision of favour that is both mutual and supportive. Developments in China since the 1950s and even more so since the 1980s have meant that the demographic reach of potential *guanxi* use and users is now extensive, more than it has ever been. A survey conducted in Shanghai and an adjacent rural county during 1987 involving 2,000 adults revealed how extensive was acceptance of *guanxi* and its use at this time. Respondents were asked what importance they attached to *guanxi*; nearly 43 per cent reported that it was 'very important' and a further 27 per cent agreed that it was 'important', with only 5 per cent of respondents reporting that it was 'not very important' and 2.5 per cent saying that it was 'not at all important' (Chu and Ju 1993: 151). When asked about the actual use of *guanxi* 72 per cent of respondents reported that they would use *guanxi* rather than other means, whereas only 20 per cent reported that they would first try 'normal channels', with the remainder saying that they were undecided (Chu and Ju 1993: 152). It is of particular interest that younger respondents saw *guanxi* as both more important and more useful than older respondents, and that the 'greater the Western cultural influence [on respondents], the higher the percentage endorsing the importance of network connections' and reporting that they would 'first try using' *guanxi* rather than other approaches (Chu and Ju 1993: 151, 152). It is likely that broadly similar findings may be reported today in most locations in China.

It is difficult to doubt the continuing importance of *guanxi* for understanding social relations in China. Indeed, rather than simply saying 'the continuing importance of *guanxi*' it is more meaningful to refer to the 'prevalence and the increasing significance of *guanxi*', to borrow from the title of a recent publication (Bian 2018). We have seen why this situation, including the findings of Chu and Ju (1993) concerning the increased appeal of *guanxi* to younger generations of Chinese and those exposed to Western cultural influence, should lead to a re-evaluation of ideas concerning the cultural basis of *guanxi*, including its supposed Confucian foundation, discussed extensively in Chapters 2, 3, and 6. The present book, then, in recognizing the importance of *guanxi* for an understanding of China today and its prevalent use in many areas of Chinese society, has taken the opportunity to properly situate *guanxi* historically and culturally and to suggest the need in researching *guanxi* to respect its form and nature in theoretical exposition and methodological exploration. The increasing significance of *guanxi* in present-day China, and thus in its future prospects, encourages a broad scholarly grasp of it in order that continuing research meets the challenge of understanding the changing forms of *guanxi* and providing guidance to new generations of researchers focused on reporting and analysing emergent *guanxi* practices and outcomes.

It is appropriate to close on a note concerning a possible consequence of the developments indicated here for China's future. It has been shown throughout that the social conditions which promote the use of *guanxi* are many. But if there is an overarching factor which encourages the appeal of instrumental particularism today and supports its application, it is no doubt the fact that, as established certainties become fewer, and the complexity of prospect and circumstance in a marketized economy subject to an increasingly hostile external environment becomes greater, then *guanxi* as both personalized and self-fashioned by those who participate in it provides a viable means for reducing the uncertainties prevalent in late-modern China. It has also been shown that, given the relative weakness of legal institutions, the multiple sources of influence on regulatory mechanisms, and the unpredictability of change in political direction, it is entirely rational for those who can to deploy *guanxi* in achieving their purposes.

The other side of this scenario, however, is a probability that, in the circumstances described here, the costs of relying on extended personalism will continue to grow. Such cost increases necessarily impose limiting effects not only on the alliances that are formed, and how and to what they are applied, but also relate to the larger inefficiencies generated through significant deployment of attention and resources to relationship building at the possible expense of substantive engagements. The implications of these factors for China's future in an increasingly unsettled global economy with intensified geopolitical contestation thus links the domain of a decidedly domestic pattern of instrumental particularism with the rapidly evolving transitions in regional and global power. Between these distinct realms there is much that will inevitably change. It may be banal to say that change in these arenas is unavoidable, but that banality is undergirded by the unpredictability of the substance and direction of whatever change occurs, and the pace with which it proceeds. All of this attests to the real-world significance of making sense of *guanxi*. It also reminds us that the work of analysis and theoretical apprehension is never finally done.

References

Ali, Sa'ad, and Weir, David (2020) *Wasta*: Advancing a Holistic Model to Bridge the Micro-macro Divide. *Management and Organization Review,* 16(3): 657–85.

Aliyev, Huseyn (2017) Informal Institutions in Azerbaijan: Exploring the Intricacies of *Tapsh. Europe-Asia Studies,* 69(4): 594–613.

Alsen, Jonas (1996) An Introduction to Chinese Property Law. *Maryland Journal of International Law,* 20(1): 1–60.

Ames, Roger T. (2011) *Confucian Role Ethics: A Vocabulary.* Hong Kong: Chinese University Press.

Ames, Roger T., and Rosemont, Henry (2014) Family Reverence (*xiao* 孝) in the *Analects.* Pp. 117–36 in Amy Olberding (ed.), *Dao Companion to the Analects.* New York: Springer.

Ang, Yuen Yuen (2016) *How China Escaped the Poverty Trap.* Ithaca, NY: Cornell University Press.

Arkush, R. David (1981) *Fei Xiaotong and Sociology in Revolutionary China.* Cambridge, MA: Harvard University Press.

Arrow, Kenneth J. (1974) *The Limits of Organization.* New York: Norton.

Aspers, Patrik (2011) *Markets.* Cambridge: Polity Press.

Baier, Annette (1986) Trust and Antitrust. *Ethics,* 96(2): 231–60.

Baker, Hugh D. R. (1979) *Chinese Family and Kinship.* New York: Columbia University Press.

Balazs, Etienne (1964) *Chinese Civilization and Bureaucracy: Variations on a Theme.* New Haven: Yale University Press.

Banfield, Edward C. (2009) *Political Influence.* New Brunswick, NJ: Transaction Books.

Barbalet, Jack (2009) A Characterization of Trust, and its Consequences. *Theory and Society,* 38(4): 367–82.

Barbalet, Jack (2013) Self-Interest in Chinese Discourse and Practice: Temporal Distinctions of Self. *Sociological Review,* 61(4): 649–66.

Barbalet, Jack (2014) Greater Self, Lesser Self: Dimensions of Self-Interest in Chinese Filial Piety. *Journal for the Theory of Social Behaviour,* 44(2): 186–205.

Barbalet, Jack (2015) *Guanxi,* Tie Strength, and Network Attributes. *American Behavioral Scientist,* 59(8): 1038–50.

Barbalet, Jack (2017a) *Confucianism and the Chinese Self.* London: Palgrave/Macmillan.

Barbalet, Jack (2017b) Dyadic Characteristics of *Guanxi* and their Consequences. *Journal for the Theory of Social Behaviour,* 47(3): 332–47.

Barbalet, Jack (2018) *Guanxi* as Social Exchange: Emotions, Power and Corruption. *Sociology,* 52(5): 934–49.

Barbalet, Jack (2019) Trust: Condition of Action or Condition of Appraisal. *International Sociology,* 34(1): 83–98.

Barbalet, Jack (2020) Bases of Social Obligation: The Distinction Between Exchange and Role, and its Consequences. *Distinktion: Journal of Social Theory,* 21(3): 334–49.

Barker, Martin (1980) Kant as a Problem for Weber. *British Journal of Sociology,* 31(2): 224–45.

Bedford, Olwen (2011) *Guanxi*-Building in the Workplace: A Dynamic Process Model of Working and Backdoor *Guanxi. Journal of Business Ethics,* 104(1): 149–58.

Berger, Peter L. (1966) *Invitation to Sociology: A Humanistic Perspective.* London: Penguin.

Berger, Ron, Barnes, Bradley R., Konwar, Ziko, and Singh, Ramendra (2020) Doing Business in India: The Role of *Jaan-pehchaan*. *Industrial Marketing Management*, 89: 326–39.

Berger, Ron, Herstein, Ram, Silbiger, Avi, and Barnes, Bradley R. (2018) Is *Guanxi* Universal in China? Some Evidence of a Paradoxical Shift. *Journal of Business Research*, 86(C): 344–55.

Bian, Yanjie (1994) *Guanxi* and the Allocation of Urban Jobs in China. *The China Quarterly*, 140: 971–99.

Bian, Yanjie (1997) Bringing Strong Ties Back: Indirect Ties, Network Bridges, and Job Searches in China. *American Sociological Review*, 62(3): 366–85.

Bian, Yanjie (2001) *Guanxi* Capital and Social Eating in Chinese Cities. Pp. 275–95 in Nan Lin, Karen Cook, and Ronald S. Burt (eds), *Social Capital: Theory and Research*. New Brunswick, NJ: Transaction.

Bian, Yanjie (2002) Institutional Holes and Job Mobility Processes: *Guanxi* Mechanisms in China's Emergent Labor Markets. Pp. 117–35 in Thomas Gold, Doug Guthrie, and David Wank (eds), *Social Connections in China: Institutions, Culture, and the Changing Nature of Guanxi*. Cambridge: Cambridge University Press.

Bian, Yanjie (2006) *Guanxi*. Pp. 312–14 in Jens Beckert and Milan Zafirovski (eds), *International Encyclopedia of Economic Sociology*. London: Routledge.

Bian, Yanjie (2018) The Prevalence and the Increasing Significance of *Guanxi*. *The China Quarterly*, 235: 597–621.

Bian, Yanjie (2019) *Guanxi: How China Works*. Cambridge: Polity Press.

Bian, Yanjie, and Ikeda, Ken'ichi (2016) East Asian Social Networks. In Reda Alhajj and Jon Rokne (eds), *Encyclopedia of Social Network Analysis and Mining*. New York: Springer. https://doi.org/10.1007/978-1-4614-6170-8_60.

Blau, Peter M. (1964) *Exchange and Power in Social Life*. New York: Wiley.

Blomqvist, Kirsimarja (2005) Trust in a Dynamic Environment: Fast Trust as a Threshold Condition for Asymmetric Technology Partnership Formation in the ICT Sector. Pp. 127–41 in Katinka Bijlsma-Frankema and Rosalinde Klein Woolthuis (eds), *Trust under Pressure: Empirical Investigations of Trust and Trust Building in Uncertain Circumstances*. Cheltenham: Edward Elgar.

Blum, Susan D. (1997) Naming Practices and the Power of Words in China. *Language in Society*, 26(3): 357–79.

Blum, Susan D. (2007) *Lies that Bind: Chinese Truth, Other Truths*. Lanham, MD: Rowman & Littlefield Publishers.

Boisot, Max, and Child, John (1996) From Fiefs to Clans and Network Capitalism. *Administrative Science Quarterly*, 41(4): 600–28.

Bonnin, Michael (2013) *The Lost Generation: The Rustication of China's Educated Youth (1968–1980)*. Hong Kong: Chinese University Press.

Bourdieu, Pierre (1992) *The Logic of Practice*. Cambridge: Polity.

Branstetter, Lee, and Lardy, Nicholas R. (2008) China's Embrace of Globalization. Pp. 633–81 in Loren Brandt and Thomas G. Rawski (eds), *China's Great Economic Transformation*. Cambridge: Cambridge University Press.

Brennan, Geoffrey, and Pettit, Philip (2005) *The Economy of Esteem: An Essay on Civil and Political Society*. Oxford: Oxford University Press.

Brook, Timothy (1997) Profit and Righteousness in Chinese Economic Culture. Pp. 27–44 in Timothy Brook and Hy V. Luong (eds), *Culture and Economy: The Shaping of Capitalism in Eastern Asia*. Ann Arbor, MI: University of Michigan Press.

Burt, Ronald S., and Burzynska, Katarzyna (2017) Chinese Entrepreneurs, Social Networks, and *Guanxi*. *Management and Organization Review*, 13(2): 221–60.

Burt, Ronald S., Bian, Yanjie, and Opper, Sonja (2018) More or Less *Guanxi*: Trust is 60% Network Context, 10% Individual Difference. *Social Networks*, 54: 12–25.

Cai, Qian (2003) Migrant Remittances and Family Ties: A Case Study in China. *International Journal of Population Geography*, 9(6): 471–83.

Calvin, John (2002 [1559]) *Institutes of the Christian Religion*. Grand Rapids, MI: Christian Classics Ethereal Library.

Celarent, Barbara (2013) Review of *Peasant Life in China* by Fei Xiaotong and *Earthbound China* by Fei Xiaotong and Zhang Zhiyi. *American Journal of Sociology*, 118(4): 1153–60.

Chan, Anita, and Unger, Jonathan (1982) Grey and Black: Rural China's Hidden Economy. *Pacific Affairs*, 55(3): 452–71.

Chan, Cheris Shun-ching (2012) *Marketing Death: Culture and the Making of a Life Insurance Market in China*. Oxford: Oxford University Press.

Chan, Cheris Shun-ching, and Yao, Zelin (2018) A Market of Distrust: Toward a Cultural Sociology of Unofficial Exchanges between Patients and Doctors in China. *Theory and Society*, 47(6): 737–72.

Chang, Xiangqun (2009) *Guanxi or Li Shang Wanglai? Reciprocity, Social Support Networks, and Social Creativity in a Chinese Village*. Taipei: Airiti Press.

Chao, Yuen Ren (1956) Chinese Terms of Address. *Language*, 32(1): 217–41.

Chen, Hon Fai (2018) *Chinese Sociology*. London: Palgrave/Macmillan

Chen, Chao C., Chen, Xiao-Ping, and Huang, Shengsheng (2013) Chinese *Guanxi*: An Integrative Review and New Directions for Future Research. *Management and Organization Review*, 9(1): 167–207.

Chen, T. S., and Shryock, J. K. (1932) Chinese Relationship Terms. *American Anthropologist*, 34(4): 623–64.

Chen, Xiao-Ping, and Chen, Chao C. (2004) On the Intricacies of the Chinese *Guanxi*: A Process Model of *Guanxi* Development. *Asia Pacific Journal of Management*, 21(3): 305–24.

Cheng, Ch'eng-K'un (1939) The Chinese Large Family System and its Disorganization. *Social Forces*, 17(4): 538–45.

Cheng, L., and So, A. (1983) The Reestablishment of Sociology in the PRC. *Annual Review of Sociology*, 9: 471–98.

Cheng, Zhiming, Nielsen, Ingrid, and Smyth, Russell (2013) Determinants of Wage Arrears and their Implications for the Socioeconomic Wellbeing of China's Migrant Workers. *Department of Economics Discussion Paper*, 50/13, Monash University.

Chiang, Yung-Chen (2001) *Social Engineering and the Social Sciences in China, 1919–1949*. Cambridge: Cambridge University Press.

China Daily (2014). Summary of China's Migrant Population Report for 2013. *China Daily*, 16 May. Available at: www.chinadaily.com.cn/m/chinahealth/2014-05/16/content_17514058.htm

Chliova, Myrto, Mair, Johanna, and Vernis, Alfred (2020) Persistent Category Ambiguity: The Case of Social Entrepreneurship. *Organization Studies*, 41(7): 1019–42.

Choi, Sang-Chin, and Han, Gyuseog (2008) Immanent Trust in a Close Relationship: A Cultural Psychology of Trust in South Korea. Pp. 79–104 in Ivana Marková and Alex Gillespie (eds), *Trust and Distrust: Sociocultural Perspectives*. Charlotte, NC: Information Age Publishing.

Choi, Susanne Y. P., and Peng, Yinni (2016) *Masculine Compromise: Migration, Family and Gender in China*. Oakland, CA: University of California Press.

Chow, Gregory C. (1997) Challenges of China's Economic System for Economic Theory. *American Economic Review*, 87(2): 321–7.

Chow, Tse-tsung (1960) *The May Fourth Movement: Intellectual Revolution in Modern China*. Cambridge, MA: Harvard University Press.

Chu, Godwin, C., and Ju, Yanan (1993) *The Great Wall in Ruins: Communication and Cultural Change in China*. Albany, NY: State University of New York Press.

Chu, Wan-wen (2011) Entrepreneurship and Bureaucratic Control: The Case of the Chinese Automotive Industry. *China Economic Journal*, 4(1): 65–80.

Chun, Allen (2012) From Sinicization to Indigenization in the Social Sciences. Pp. 255–82 in Arif Dirlik, Guannan Li, and Hsiao-Pei Yen (eds), *Sociology and Anthropology in Twentieth-Century China*. Hong Kong: Chinese University Press.

Coleman, James S. (1990) *Foundations of Social Theory*. Cambridge, MA: Harvard University Press.

Cornell, John B. (1976) Review of *The Cultural Ecology of Chinese Civilization: Peasants and Elites in the Last of the Agrarian States* by Leon Stover. *Social Science Quarterly*, 57(2): 479–80.

Croll, Elizabeth (2006) The Intergenerational Contract in the Changing Asian Family. *Oxford Development Studies*, 34(4): 473–91.

Cunningham, Robert B., and Sarayrah, Yasin K. (1993). *Wasta: The Hidden Force in Middle Eastern Society*. Westport, CT: Praeger.

Dahl, Robert A. (1957) The Concept of Power. *Behavioral Science*, 2(3): 201–15.

DeGlopper, Ronald R. (1995) *Lukang: Commerce and Industry in a Chinese City*. Albany, NY: SUNY Press.

Deng, Yanhua, and O'Brien, Kevin J. (2013) Relational Repression in China: Using Social Ties to Demobilize Protesters. *The China Quarterly*, 215: 533–52.

Ding, Yi, McQuoid, Alexander, and Karayalcin, Cem (2019) Fiscal Decentralization, Fiscal Reform, and Economic Growth in China. *China Economic Review*, 53(1): 152–67.

Duarte, Fernanda (2006) Exploring the Interpersonal Transaction of the Brazilian *Jeitinho* in Bureaucratic Contexts. *Organization*, 13(4): 509–27.

Dunbar, R. I. M. (2017) Breaking Bread: The Functions of Social Eating. *Adaptive Human Behavior and Physiology*, 3: 198–211.

Durkheim, Emile (1972) *Suicide: A Study in Sociology*. London: Routledge & Kegan Paul.

Durkheim, Emile (2014) *The Division of Labour in Society*. New York: Free Press.

Eastman, Lloyd E. (1988) *Family, Fields and Ancestors: Constancy and Change in China's Social and Economic History, 1550–1949*. New York: Oxford University Press.

Eisenstadt, S. N., and Roniger, L. (1984) *Patrons, Clients and Friends: Interpersonal Relations and the Structure of Trust in Society*. Cambridge: Cambridge University Press.

Eliaeson, Sven (2002) *Max Weber's Methodologies*. Oxford: Polity.

Elvin, Mark (1973) *The Pattern of the Chinese Past*. Stanford, CA: Stanford University Press.

Elvin, Mark (1996) The Last Thousand Years of Chinese History: Changing Patterns in Land Tenure. Pp. 1–19 in his *Another History: Essays on China from a European Perspective*. Honolulu: University of Hawaii Press.

Elvin, Mark (1991) In What Sense is it Possible to Speak of a 'Modernization' of the Emotions in Chinese Society? Pp. 105–64 in Chang Yü-fa (ed.), *Symposium on the Modernization in China, 1860–1949*. Taipei: Institute of Modern History, Academia Sinica.

Emerson, Ralph Waldo (1950) Gifts. Pp. 402–5 in Brooks Atkinson (ed.), *The Complete Essays of Ralph Waldo Emerson*. New York: Random House.

Emirbayer, Mustafa, and Goodwin, Jeff (1994) Network Analysis, Culture, and the Problem of Agency. *American Journal of Sociology*, 99(6): 1411–54.

Ermisch, John, and Gambetta, Diego (2010) Do Strong Family Ties Inhibit Trust? *Journal of Economic Behavior and Organization*, 75(3): 365–76.

Evasdottir, Erika E. S. (2004) *Obedient Autonomy: Chinese Intellectuals and the Achievement of Orderly Life*. Honolulu: University of Hawai'i Press.

Fairbank, John K. (1976) Review of *The Cultural Ecology of Chinese Civilization: Peasants and Elites in the Last of the Agrarian States* by Leon Stover. *American Political Science Review*, 70(1): 266–7.

Fan, Ying (2002) Questioning *Guanxi*: Definition, Classification and Implications. *International Business Review*, 11(5): 543–61.

Farmer, Edward L. (1974) Review of *The Cultural Ecology of Chinese Civilization: Peasants and Elites in the Last of the Agrarian States* by Leon Stover. *The Annals of the American Academy of Political and Social Sciences*, 414: 170–1.

Faure, David (1986) *The Structure of Chinese Rural Society*. Hong Kong: Oxford University Press.

Fei, Hsiao T'ung (1939) *Peasant Life in China: A Field Study of County Life in the Yangtze Valley*. London: Routledge & Kegan Paul.

Fei, Hsiao-Tung (1946) Peasantry and Gentry. *American Journal of Sociology*, 52(1): 1–17.

Fei, Hsiao-tung (1953) *China's Gentry: Essays in Rural-Urban Relations*, ed. Margaret Park Redfield. Chicago: University of Chicago Press.

Fei, Xiaotong (1992) *From the Soil: The Foundations of Chinese Society*, tr. Gary G. Hamilton and Zheng Wang. Berkeley, CA: University of California Press.

Fei, Hsiao-Tung, and Chang, Chih-I. (1948) *Earthbound China: A Study of Rural Economy in Yunnan*. London: Routledge & Kegan Paul.

Feng, Han-Yi (1937) The Chinese Kinship System. *Harvard Journal of Asiatic Studies*, 2(2): 142–275.

Feuchtwang, Stephen (2015) Social Egoism and Individualism. *Journal of China in Comparative Perspective*, 1(1): 128–45.

Finch, Janet (1994) *Family Obligations and Social Change*. Cambridge: Polity.

Foa, Edna B., and Foa, Uriel G. (2012) Resource Theory of Social Exchange. Pp. 15–32 in K. Törnblom and A. Kazemi (eds), *Handbook of Social Resource Theory: Theoretical Extensions, Empirical Insights, and Social Applications*. New York: Springer.

Folsom, Kenneth E. (1968) *Friends, Guests and Colleagues: The Mu-fu System in the Late Ch'ing Period*. Berkeley, CA: University of California Press.

Freedman, Maurice (1979) *The Study of Chinese Society*. Stanford, CA: Stanford University Press.

Freeman, Linton C. (2004) *The Development of Social Network Analysis: A Study in the Sociology of Science*. Vancouver: Empirical Press.

Freitag, Markus, and Traunmüller, Richard (2009) Spheres of Trust: An Empirical Analysis of the Foundations of Particularised and Generalised Trust. *European Journal of Political Research*, 48(6): 782–803.

Fried, Morton H. (1953) *Fabric of Chinese Society: A Study of the Social Life of a Chinese County Seat*. New York: Praeger.

Fu, Ping Ping, Tsui, Anne S., and Dess, Gregory G. (2006) The Dynamics of *Guanxi* in Chinese Hightech Firms: Implications for Knowledge Management and Decision Making. *Management International Review*, 46(3): 1–29.

Fukuyama, Francis (1995) *Trust: The Social Virtues and the Creation of Prosperity*. London: Hamish Hamilton.

Fuligni, Andrew J., and Zhang, Wenxin (2004) Attitudes toward Family Obligation among Adolescents in Contemporary Urban and Rural China. *Child Development*, 74(1): 180–92.

Fung, Edmund S. K. (2010) *The Intellectual Foundations of Chinese Modernity: Cultural and Political Thought in the Republican Era*. Cambridge: Cambridge University Press.

Fung, Yu-Lan (1952) *A History of Chinese Philosophy*, vol. 1. Princeton: Princeton University Press.

Fung, Yu-Lan (1998a) The Philosophy at the Basis of Traditional Chinese Society. Pp. 632–9 in his *Selected Philosophical Writings of Fung Yu-lan*. Beijing: Foreign Languages Press.

Fung, Yu-Lan (1998b) A Short History of Chinese Philosophy. Pp. 193–567 in *Selected Philosophical Writings of Fung Yu-Lan*. Beijing: Foreign Languages Press.

Gambetta, Diego (1990) Can we Trust Trust? Pp. 213–37 in Diego Gambetta (ed.), *Trust: Making and Breaking Cooperative Relations*. Oxford: Blackwell.

Gardner, Daniel K. (2007) *The Four Books: The Basic Teachings of the Later Confucian Tradition*. Indianapolis: Hackett Publishing Co.

Gates, Hill (1996) *China's Motor: A Thousand Years of Petty Capitalism*. Ithaca, NY: Cornell University Press.

Giddens, Anthony (1990) *The Consequences of Modernity*. Stanford, CA: Stanford University Press.

Girardot, Norman J. (2002) *The Victorian Translation of China: James Legge's Oriental Pilgrimage*. Berkeley, CA: University of California Press.

Gold, Thomas B. (1985) After Comradeship: Personal Relations in China since the Cultural Revolution. *The China Quarterly*, 104: 657–75.

Gold, Thomas, Guthrie, Doug, and Wank, David (eds) (2002) *Social Connections in China: Institutions, Culture, and the Changing Nature of Guanxi*. Cambridge: Cambridge University Press.

Goldin, Paul R. (2008) When Zhong 忠 does Not Mean 'Loyalty'. *Dao*, 7(2): 165–74.

Goldin, Paul R. (2014) *Confucianism*. London: Routledge.

Goossaert, Vincent (2006) 1898: The Beginning of the End for Chinese Religion. *Journal of Asian Studies*, 65(2): 307–36.

Gouldner, Alvin W. (1960) The Norm of Reciprocity: A Preliminary Statement. *American Sociological Review*, 25(2): 161–78.

Granet, Marcel (1975 [1922]) *The Religion of the Chinese People*, tr. with an Introduction by Maurice Freedman. Oxford: Basil Blackwell.

Granovetter, Mark (1973) The Strength of Weak Ties. *American Journal of Sociology*, 78(6): 1360–80.

Granovetter, Mark (1985) Economic Action and Social Structure: The Problem of Embeddedness. *American Journal of Sociology*, 91(3): 481–510.

Gransow, Bettina (2001) 'Nontranslatable': Indigenous Concepts in Social Science Research on China. *Asian Journal of Social Science*, 29(1): 262–84.

Greif, Avner (2006) *Institutions and the Path to the Modern Economy: Lessons from Medieval Trade*. Cambridge: Cambridge University Press.

Guan, Shanshan, and James, Fiona (2020) Staying Afloat via *Guanxi*: Student Networks, Social Capital and Inequality in Chinese Adult Higher Education. *British Journal of Educational Studies*, 68(3): 349–64.

Guo, Chun, and Miller, Jane K. (2010) *Guanxi* Dynamics and Entrepreneurial Firm Creation and Development in China. *Management and Organization Review*, 6(2): 267–91.

Guo, Man, Chi, Iris, and Silverstein, Merril (2012) The Structure of Intergenerational Relations in Rural China: A Latent Class Analysis. *Journal of Marriage and Family*, 74(5): 1114–28.

Guo, Xuezhi (2001) Dimensions of *Guanxi* in Chinese Elite Politics. *The China Journal*, 46: 69–90.

Guthrie, Douglas (1998) The Declining Significance of *Guanxi* in China's Economic Transition. *The China Quarterly*, 154: 254–82.

Hall, Peter A., and Soskice, David W. (2001) *Varieties of Capitalism: The Institutional Foundations of Comparative Advantage*. Oxford: Oxford University Press.

Hamilton, Gary G. (2015) What Western Social Scientists Can Learn from the Writings of Fei Xiaotong. *Journal of China in Comparative Perspective*, 1(1): 107–27.

Hamilton, Gary G., and Wang, Zheng (1992) Introduction: Fei Xiaotong and the Beginnings of a Chinese Sociology. Pp. 1–34 in Fei Xiaotong, *From the Soil: The Foundations of Chinese Society*. Berkeley, CA: University of California Press.

Hansen, Valerie (1995) *Negotiating Daily Life in Traditional China: How Ordinary People Used Contracts, 600–1400*. New Haven: Yale University Press.

Hanser, Amy (2002) Youth Job Searches in Urban China: The Use of Social Connections in a Changing Labor Market. Pp. 137–61 in Thomas Gold, Doug Guthrie, and David Wank (eds), *Social Connections in China: Institutions, Culture, and the Changing Nature of Guanxi*. Cambridge: Cambridge University Press.

Hardin, Russell (1993) The Street-Level Epistemology of Trust. *Politics and Society*, 21(4): 505–29.

Hardin, Russell (1996) Trustworthiness. *Ethics*, 107(1): 26–42.

Harvey, David (2005) *A Brief History of Neoliberalism*. Oxford: Oxford University Press.

He, Xin, and Ng, Kwai Hang (2017) 'It Must Be Rock Strong!' Guanxi's Impact on Judicial Decision Making in China. *American Journal of Comparative Law*, 65(4): 841–71.

Heilmann, Sebastian, and Melton, Oliver (2013) The Reinvention of Development Planning in China, 1993–2012. *Modern China*, 39(6): 580–628.

Herrmann-Pillath, Carsten (2016) Fei Xiaotong's Comparative Theory of Chinese Culture. *Copenhagen Journal of Asian Studies*, 34(1): 25–57.

Ho, David Yau-fai (1976) On the Concept of Face. *American Journal of Sociology*, 81(4): 867–84.

Horak, Sven, and Taube, Markus (2016) Same But Different? Similarities and Fundamental Differences of Informal Social Networks in China (*guanxi*) and Korea (*yongo*). *Asia Pacific Journal of Management*, 33(3): 595–616.

Hsu, Francis L. K. (1943) The Myth of Chinese Family Size. *American Journal of Sociology*, 48(5): 555–62.

Hsu, Francis L. K. (1948) *Under the Ancestors' Shadow: Chinese Culture and Personality*. New York: Columbia University Press.

Hsu, Francis L. K. (1954) Review of *Fabric of Chinese Society* by Morton H. Fried. *American Anthropologist*, 56(3): 515–17.

Hu, Angang (2013) The Distinctive Transition of China's Five-Year Plans. *Modern China*, 39(6): 629–39.

Hu, Feng, Xu, Zhaoyuan, and Chen, Yuyu (2011) Circular Migration, or Permanent Stay? Evidence from China's Rural–Urban Migration. *China Economic Review*, 22(1): 64–74.

Hu, Hsien Chin (1944) The Chinese Concepts of 'Face'. *American Anthropologist*, 46(1): 45–64.

Hu, Hsien Chin (1948) *The Common Descent Group in China and its Functions*. New York: Viking Fund Publications.

Hu, Hsien Chin (1949) Emotions, Real and Assumed, in Chinese Society. Unpublished manuscript, Margaret Mead Papers and South Pacific Ethnographic Archives, Box G29, folder 4. Manuscript Division, Library of Congress.

Huang, Ping, and Zhan, Shaohua (2008) Migrant Workers' Remittances and Rural Development in China. Pp. 221–45 in Josh DeWind and Jennifer Holdaway (eds), *Migration and Development within and across Borders*. New York: Social Science Research Council.

Huang, Xianbi (2008) Guanxi Networks and Job Searches in China's Emerging Labour Market: A Qualitative Investigation. *Work, Employment and Society*, 22(3): 467–84.

Huang, Yasheng (2008) *Capitalism with Chinese Characteristics: Entrepreneurship and the State*. Cambridge: Cambridge University Press.

Hutchings, Kate, and Weir, David (2006) Guanxi and Wasta: A Comparison. *Thunderbird International Business Review*, 48(1): 141–56.

Hwang, Kwang-kuo (1987) Face and Favor: The Chinese Power Game. *American Journal of Sociology*, 92(4): 944–74.

Jacobs, J. Bruce (1979) A Preliminary Model of Particularistic Ties in Chinese Political Alliances: Kan-ch'ing and Kuan-hsi in a Rural Taiwanese Township. *The China Quarterly*, 78: 237–73.

Jiang, Guoping, Lo, T. Wing, and Garris, Christopher (2012) Formation and Trend of *Guanxi* Practice and *Guanxi* Phenomenon. *International Journal of Criminology and Sociology,* 1: 207–20.

Jiang, Shi-jie, Liu, Xin, Liu, Na, and Xiang, Feiyun (2019) Online Life Insurance Purchasing Intention: Applying the Unified Theory of Acceptance and Use of Technology. *Social Behavior and Personality: An International Journal,* 47(7): e8141.

Jordan, David K. (1985) Sworn Brothers: A Study in Chinese Ritual Kinship. Pp. 232–62 in Jih-chang Hsieh and Ying-chang Chuang (eds), *The Chinese Family and its Ritual Behavior.* Taipei: Institute of Ethnology, Academia Sinica.

Kang, Xiaoguang (2013) Confucianism and Conceiving a Cultural Renaissance in the New Century. *Contemporary Chinese Thought,* 44(2): 61–75.

Kao, Cheng-shu (1996) 'Personal Trust' in the Large Businesses in Taiwan: A Traditional Foundation for Contemporary Economic Activities. Pp. 61–70 in Gary G. Hamilton (ed.), *Asian Business Networks.* New York: Walter de Gruyter.

King, Ambrose Yeo-chi (1985) The Individual and Group in Confucianism: A Relational Perspective. Pp. 57–72 in Donald J. Munro (ed.), *Individualism and Holism: Studies in Confucian and Taoist Values.* Ann Arbor, MI: University of Michigan Press.

King, Ambrose Yeo-chi (1991) *Kuan-hsi* and Network Building: A Sociological Interpretation. *Daedalus,* 120(2): 63–84.

Kipnis, Andrew B. (1997) *Producing Guanxi: Sentiment, Self and Subculture in a North China Village.* Durham, NC: Duke University Press.

Kipnis, Andrew B. (2018) Mediated Agency and Funeral Insurance in China. *PoLAR: Political and Legal Anthropology Review,* 41(2): 319–25.

Komter, Aafke E. (2005) *Social Solidarity and the Gift.* Cambridge: Cambridge University Press.

Komter, Aafke E. (2007) Gifts and Social Relations: The Mechanisms of Reciprocity. *International Sociology,* 22(1): 93–107.

Ku, Hok Bun (2003) *Moral Politics in a South Chinese Village: Responsibility, Reciprocity and Resistance.* New York: Rowman & Littlefield.

Kulp, Daniel Harrison (1925) *Country Life in South China: The Sociology of Familism,* vol. 1. New York: Teachers College, Columbia University.

Kuo, Ya-pei (2008) Redeploying Confucius: The Imperial State Dreams of the Nation. Pp. 65–84 in Mayfair Yang (ed.), *Chinese Religiosities: Afflictions of Modernity and State Formation.* Berkeley, CA: University of California Press.

Lam, Ester (2009) *China and the WTO: A Long March towards the Rule of Law.* Boston: Kluwer Law International.

Langenberg, Eike A. (2007) *Guanxi and Business Strategy: Theory and Implications for Multinational Companies in China.* Heidelberg: Physica-Verlag.

Lasswell, Harold D., and Kaplan, Abraham (2017) *Power and Society: A Framework for Political Inquiry.* London: Routledge.

Lau, D. C. (1979) *Confucius: The Analects.* London: Penguin.

Ledeneva, Alena (2008) *Blat* and *Guanxi*: Informal Practices in Russia and China. *Comparative Studies in Society and History,* 50(1): 118–44.

Lee, Don Y., and Dawes, Philip L. (2005) *Guanxi,* Trust, and Long-Term Orientation in Chinese Business Markets. *Journal of International Marketing,* 13(2): 28–56.

Lee, Rose Hum (1949) Research on the Chinese Family. *American Journal of Sociology,* 54(6): 497–504.

Lee, Tony C. (2018) Pernicious Custom? Corruption, Culture, and the Efficacy of Anti-Corruption Campaigning in China. *Crime, Law and Social Change,* 70(3): 349–61.

Legge, James (1877) *Confucianism in Relation to Christianity: A Paper Read Before the Missionary Conference in Shanghai, on May 11th, 1877.* Shanghai: Kelly & Walsh. London: Trübner & Co.

Legge, James (1880) *The Religions of China: Confucianism and Taoism Described and Compared with Christianity*. London: Hodder & Stoughton.

Legge, James (1885) *The Li Ki, XI–XLVI. The Sacred Books of China: The Texts of Confucianism, Part IV*. Oxford: Clarendon Press.

Legge, James (2001a [1893]) Confucian Analects. Pp. 137–354 in his *The Chinese Classics*, vol. 1. Taipei: SMC Publishing Inc.

Legge, James (2001b [1893]) The Great Learning. Pp. 355–81 in his *The Chinese Classics*, vol. 1. Taipei: SMC Publishing Inc.

Lenski, Gerhard E. (1966) *Power and Privilege: A Theory of Social Stratification*. New York: McGraw-Hill.

Lewis, Steven W., Di, Di and Ecklund, Elaine Howard (2017) The Double-Edged Sword: *Guanxi* and Science Ethics in Academic Physics in the People's Republic of China. *Journal of Contemporary China*, 26(107): 726–40.

Li, Ling (2018) The Moral Economy of *Guanxi* and the Market of Corruption: Networks, Brokers and Corruption in China's Courts. *International Political Science Review*, 39(5): 634–46.

Li, Tian, and Tian, Felicia F. (2020) *Guanxi* and Job Mobility in the Socialist Transformation. *China Review*, 20(2): 183–210.

Liang, Shuming (1949) *Zhongguo wenhua yaoyi* (*The Essence of Chinese Culture*). Shanghai: Luming shudian.

Lin, Ju-Ping, and Yi, Chin-Chun (2013). A Comparative Analysis of Intergenerational Relations in East Asia. *International Sociology*, 28(3): 297–315.

Lin, Nan (2001) *Guanxi*: A Conceptual Analysis. Pp. 153–66 in Alvin Y. So, Nan Lin, and Dudley D. Poston (eds), *The Chinese Triangle of Mainland China, Taiwan and Hong Kong*. Westport, CT: Greenwood Press.

Lin, Nan (2017) Advancing Network Analysis of Chinese Businesses: Commentary on Burt and Burzynska. *Management and Organization Review*, 13(2): 269–74.

Lin, Yutang (1939) *My Country and My People*, revised edition. New York: John Day Co.

Liu, James J. Y. (1961) The Knight Errant in Chinese Literature. *Journal of the Hong Kong Branch of the Royal Asiatic Society*, 1: 30–41.

Liu, James J. Y. (1967) *The Chinese Knight Errant*. London: Routledge & Kegan Paul.

Liu, Li (2008) Filial Piety, *Guanxi*, Loyalty, and Money: Trust in China. Pp. 51–77 in Ivana Marková and Alex Gillespie (eds), *Trust and Distrust: Sociocultural Perspectives*. Charlotte, NC: Information Age Publishing.

Liu, Linqing, and Mei, Shiye (2015) How Can an Indigenous Concept Enter the International Academic Circle: The Case of *Guanxi*. *Scientometrics*, 105(1): 645–63.

Liu, Shao-chi. 1950. *On the Party*. Peking: Foreign Languages Press.

Lovett, Steve, Simmons, Lee C., and Kali, Raja (1999) *Guanxi* versus the Market. *Journal of International Business Studies*, 30(2): 231–48.

Lu, Weiming, and Zhao, Xiaoyu (2009) Liang Shuming's Viewpoint of Chinese and Western Cultures in *The Substance of Chinese Culture*. *Contemporary Chinese Thought*, 40(3): 52–66.

Luhmann, Niklas (1979) *Trust and Power*. Chichester: Wiley.

Lui, Tai-lok (2001) A Brief Note on *Guanxi*. Pp. 385–98 in Richard P. Appelbaum, William L. F. Felstiner, and Volkmar Gessner (eds), *Rules and Networks: The Legal Structure of Global Business Networks*. Oxford: Hart Publishing.

Lukes, Steven (2005) *Power: A Radical View*. 2nd edition. London: Palgrave Macmillan.

Luo, Jar-Der (2005) Particularistic Trust and General Trust: A Network Analysis in Chinese Organizations. *Management and Organization Review*, 1(3): 437–58.

Luo, Jar-Der (2011). *Guanxi* Revisited: An Exploratory Study of Familiar Ties in a Chinese Workplace. *Management and Organization Review*, 7(2): 329–51.

Luo, Jar-Der, and Yeh, Yung-Chu (2012) Neither Collectivism Nor Individualism: Trust in the Chinese *Guanxi* Circle. *Journal of Trust Research*, 2(1): 53–70.

Luo, Jar-Der, Cheng, Meng-Yu, and Zhang, Tian (2016) *Guanxi* Circle and Organizational Citizenship Behavior: Context of a Chinese Workplace. *Asia Pacific Journal of Management,* 33(3): 649–71.

Luo, Xubei, Wang, Yue, and Zhang, Xiaobo (2019) *E-Commerce Development and Household Consumption Growth in China.* Poverty and Equity Global Practice, Policy Research Working Paper 8810. Washington, DC: World Bank.

Luo, Yadong (2007) *Guanxi and Business.* 2nd edition. Singapore: World Scientific Publishing.

McNally, Christopher A. (2011) China's Changing *Guanxi* Capitalism: Private Entrepreneurs between Leninist Control and Relentless Accumulation. *Business and Politics,* 13(2): 1–29.

McNally, Christopher A. (2012) Sino-capitalism: China's Re-emergence and the International Political Economy. *World Politics,* 64(4): 741–76.

Maine, Sir Henry Sumner (1905) *Ancient Law: Its Connection with the Early History of Society and its Relation to Modern Ideas.* London: John Murray.

Makeham, John (2008) *Lost Soul: 'Confucianism' in Contemporary Chinese Academic Discourse.* Cambridge, MA: Harvard University Press.

Mao Zedong (1967a [1927]) Report on an Investigation of the Peasant Movement in Hunan. Pp. 23–59 in *Selected Works of Mao Tse-Tung,* vol. 1. Peking: Foreign Languages Press.

Mao Zedong (1967b [1933]) How to Differentiate the Classes in the Rural Areas. Pp. 137–9 in *Selected Works of Mao Tse-Tung,* vol. 1. Peking: Foreign Languages Press.

Marsden, Peter V., and Campbell, Karen E. (1984) Measuring Tie Strength. *Social Forces,* 63(2): 482–501.

Marsden, Peter V., and Campbell, Karen E. (2012) Reflections on Conceptualizing and Measuring Tie Strength. *Social Forces,* 91(1): 17–23.

Mead, George H. (1934) *Mind, Self and Society: From the Standpoint of a Social Behaviorist.* Chicago: University of Chicago Press.

Merton, Robert K. (1968) *Social Theory and Social Structure,* enlarged edition. New York: Free Press.

Metraux, Rhoda (1980) The Study of Culture at a Distance: A Prototype. *American Anthropologist,* 82(2): 362–73.

Meyerson, Debra, Weick, Karl E., and Kramer, Roderick M. (1996) Swift Trust and Temporary Groups. Pp. 166–95 in Roderick M. Kramer and Tom R. Tyler (eds), *Trust in Organizations: Frontiers of Theory and Research.* London: Sage.

Michael, Franz (1955) State and Society in Nineteenth-Century China. *World Politics,* 7(3): 419–33.

Michailova, Snejina, and Worm, Verner (2003) Personal Networking in Russia and China: *Blat* and *Guanxi. European Management Journal,* 21(4): 509–19.

Mills, C. Wright (1970 [1959]) *The Sociological Imagination.* London: Penguin Books.

Molm, Linda, Takahashi, Nobuyuki, and Peterson, Gretchen (2000) Risk and Trust in Social Exchange: An Experimental Test of a Classical Proposition. *American Journal of Sociology,* 105(5): 1396–1427.

Murphy, Rachel (2002) *How Migrant Labour is Changing Rural China.* Cambridge: Cambridge University Press.

Naughton, Barry (2007) *The Chinese Economy: Transitions and Growth.* Cambridge, MA: MIT Press.

Naughton, Barry (2017) Is China Socialist? *Journal of Economic Perspectives,* 31(1): 3–24.

Naughton, Barry, and Tsai, Kellee S. (eds) (2015) *State Capitalism, Institutional Adaptation, and the Chinese Miracle.* Cambridge: Cambridge University Press.

Nee, Victor, and Opper, Sonja (2012) *Capitalism from Below: Markets and Institutional Change in China.* Cambridge, MA: Harvard University Press.

Newell, William H. (1985) Structural Conflicts within the Chinese Family. Pp. 84–93 in Jih-chang Hsieh and Ying-chang Chuang (eds), *The Chinese Family and its Ritual Behavior.* Taipei: Institute of Ethnology, Academia Sinica.

Nitsch, Manfred, and Diebel, Frank (2008) *Guanxi* Economics: Confucius Meets Lenin, Keynes, and Schumpeter in Contemporary China. *European Journal of Economics and Economic Policies: Intervention,* 5(1): 77–104.

Nolan, Jane (2011) Good *Guanxi* and Bad *Guanxi*: Western Bankers and the Role of Network Practices in Institutional Change in China. *International Journal of Human Resource Management,* 22(16): 3357–72.

Offe, Claus (1999) How Can we Trust our Fellow Citizens? Pp. 42–87 in M. E. Warren (ed.), *Democracy and Trust.* Cambridge: Cambridge University Press.

Oi, Jean C. (1985) Communism and Clientelism: Rural Politics in China. *World Politics,* 37(2): 238–66.

Osburg, John (2013) *Anxious Wealth: Money and Morality among China's New Rich.* Stanford, CA: Stanford University Press.

Pachucki, Mark A., and Breiger, Ronald L. (2010) Cultural Holes: Beyond Relationality in Social Networks and Culture. *Annual Review of Sociology,* 36: 205–24.

Paik, Wooyeal, and Baum, Richard (2014) Clientelism with Chinese Characteristics: Local Patronage Networks in Post-Reform China. *Political Science Quarterly,* 129(4): 675–701.

Pan, Guangdan (2015) *Socio-Biological Implications of Confucianism.* New York: Springer.

Pan, Yuling, and Kádárb, Dániel Z. (2011) Historical vs. Contemporary Chinese Linguistic Politeness. *Journal of Pragmatics,* 43(6): 1525–39.

Park, Camila Lee, Nunes, Mauro Fracarolli, Muratbekova-Touron, Maral, and Moatti, Valérie (2018) The Duality of the Brazilian *Jeitinho*: An Empirical Investigation and Conceptual Framework. *Critical Perspectives on International Business,* 14(4): 404–25.

Parkin, Frank (2002) *Max Weber,* revised edition. London: Routledge.

Parsons, Talcott (1969) On the Concept of Influence. Pp. 405–38 in his *Politics and Social Structure.* New York: Free Press.

Peerenboom, Randall (2002) *China's Long March toward Rule of Law.* Cambridge: Cambridge University Press.

Peng, Yusheng (2004) Kinship Networks and Entrepreneurs in China's Transitional Economy. *American Journal of Sociology,* 109(5): 1045–74.

Perks, Helen, and Halliday, Sue Vaux (2003) Sources, Signs and Signaling for Fast Trust Creation in Organisational Relationships. *European Management Journal,* 21(3): 338–50.

Powell, Walter W. (1990) Neither Market Nor Hierarchy: Network Forms of Organization. *Research in Organizational Behavior,* 12: 259–336.

Putnam, Robert D. (1993) *Making Democracy Work: Civic Traditions in Modern Italy.* Princeton: Princeton University Press.

Qi, Xiaoying (2013) *Guanxi,* Social Capital Theory and Beyond. *British Journal of Sociology,* 64(2): 308–24.

Qi, Xiaoying (2014) *Globalized Knowledge Flows and Chinese Social Theory.* New York: Routledge.

Qi, Xiaoying (2015) Filial Obligation in Contemporary China: Evolution of the Culture-System. *Journal for the Theory of Social Behaviour,* 45(1): 141–61.

Qi, Xiaoying (2017a) Reconstructing the Concept of Face in Cultural Sociology: In Goffman's Footsteps, Following the Chinese Case. *Journal of Chinese Sociology,* 4(19): 1–17.

Qi, Xiaoying (2017b) Social Movements in China: Augmenting Mainstream Theory with *Guanxi. Sociology,* 51(1) 111–26.

Qi, Xiaoying (2018) Floating Grandparents: Rethinking Family Obligation and Intergenerational Support. *International Sociology,* 33(6): 761–77.

Redding, S. Gordon (1993) *The Spirit of Chinese Capitalism.* Berlin: de Gruyter.

Redfield, Robert (1953) Introduction. Pp. 1–16 in Fei Hsiao-tung, *China's Gentry: Essays in Rural-Urban Relations.* Chicago: University of Chicago Press.

Redfield, Margaret Park (1954) Review of *Fabric of Chinese Society* by Morton H. Fried. *American Journal of Sociology,* 59(6): 599.

Robert, L.P. Jr., Dennis, Alan R., and Hung, Yu-Ting Caisy (2009) Individual Swift Trust and Knowledge-Based Trust in Face-to-Face and Virtual Team Members. *Journal of Management Information Systems,* 26(2): 241–79.

Rosemont, Henry (1991) Rights-Bearing Individuals and Role-Bearing Persons. Pp. 71–101 in Mary Bockover (ed.), *Rules, Rituals, and Responsibility.* La Salle, IL: Open Court.

Rousseau, Denise M., Sitkin, Sim B., Burt, Ronald S., and Camerer, Collin (1998) Not So Different After All: A Cross-Discipline View of Trust. *Academy of Management Review,* 23(3): 393–404.

Ruan, Ji (2017) *Guanxi, Social Capital and School Choice in China: The Rise of Ritual Capital.* London: Palgrave Macmillan.

Ruan, Ji (2019) 'Bribery with Chinese Characteristics' and the Use of *Guanxi* to Obtain Admission to Prestigious Secondary Schools in Urban China. *Critical Asian Studies,* 51(1): 120–30.

Ruf, Gregory A. (1998) *Cadres and Kin: Making a Socialist Village in West China, 1921–1991.* Stanford, CA: Stanford University Press.

Sachsenmaier, Dominic (2014) Notions of Society in Early Twentieth-Century China, 1900–25. Pp. 61–74 in Hagen Schulz-Forberg (ed.), *A Global Conceptual History of Asia, 1860–1940.* London: Pickering & Chatto.

Saich, Tony (1994) The Chinese Communist Party and the Anti-Japanese War Base Areas. *The China Quarterly,* 140: 1000–6.

Santos, Gonçalo D. (2008) On 'Same-Year Siblings' in Rural South China. *Journal of the Royal Anthropological Institute,* 14(3): 535–53.

Sasaki, Masamichi (2019) Introduction. Pp. 1–8 in Masamichi Sasaki (ed.), *Trust in Contemporary Society.* Leiden: Brill.

Schurmann, H. F. (1956) Traditional Property Concepts in China. *Far Eastern Quarterly,* 15(4): 507–16.

Schwalbe, Michael L. (1988) Role Taking Reconsidered: Linking Competence and Performance to Social Structure. *Journal for the Theory of Social Behaviour,* 18(4): 411–36.

Selden, Mark (1993) Family Strategies and Structures in Rural North China. Pp. 139–64 in Deborah Davis and Stevan Harrell (eds), *Chinese Families in the Post-Mao Era.* Berkeley, CA: University of California Press.

Silver, Allan (1985) 'Trust' in Social and Political Theory. Pp. 52–67 in Gerald Suttles and Mayer Zald (eds.), *The Challenge of Social Control: Citizenship and Institution Building in Modern Society.* Norwood, NJ: Ablex.

Simmel, Georg (1950) *The Sociology of Georg Simmel,* ed. Kurt H. Wolf. New York: Free Press.

Siu, Helen F. (1989) *Agents and Victims in South China: Accomplices in Rural Revolution.* New Haven: Yale University Press.

Skinner, G. William (1964) Marketing and Social Structure in Rural China: Part I. *Journal of Asian Studies,* 24(1): 3–43.

Smart, Alan (1993) Gifts, Bribes, and *Guanxi*: A Reconsideration of Bourdieu's Social Capital. *Cultural Anthropology,* 8(3): 388–408.

Smart, Alan (1998) *Guanxi*, Gifts and Learning from China: A Review Essay. *Anthropos,* 93(4/6): 559–65.

Smart, Alan (1999) Expressions of Interest: Friendship and *Guanxi* in Chinese Societies. Pp. 119–36 in Sandra Bell and Simon Coleman (eds), *The Anthropology of Friendship.* Oxford: Berg.

Smith, Adam (1979 [1759]) *The Theory of Moral Sentiments.* Oxford: Oxford University Press.

Smith, Arthur H. (1890) *Chinese Characteristics.* Shanghai: North-China Herald.

So, Alvin Y., and Chu, Yin-wah (2016) *The Global Rise of China.* Cambridge: Polity.

So, Ying Lun, and Walker, Anthony (2006) *Explaining Guanxi: The Chinese Business Network.* London: Routledge.

Stinchcombe, Arthur L. (1968) *Constructing Social Theories*. New York: Harcourt, Brace & World.

Stover, Leon E. (1974) *The Cultural Ecology of Chinese Civilization: Peasants and Elites in the Last of the Agrarian States*. New York: Pica Press.

Sun, Xin, Zhu, Jiangnan, and Wu, Yiping (2014) Organizational Clientelism: An Analysis of Private Entrepreneurs in Chinese Local Legislatures. *Journal of East Asian Studies*, 14(1): 1–29.

Swedberg, Richard (2020) On the Use of Definitions in Sociology. *European Journal of Social Theory*, 23(3): 431–45.

Tai, James H-Y. (1975) Vocabulary Changes in the Chinese Language: Some Observations on Extent and Nature. *Journal of Chinese Linguistics*, 3(2/3): 233–44.

Tang, Ling (2020) Gendered and Sexualized *Guanxi*: The Use of Erotic Capital in the Workplace in Urban China. *Asia Pacific Business Review*, 26(2): 190–208.

Tawney, R.H. (1932) *Land and Labour in China*. London: George Allen & Unwin.

Tian, Hailong (2014) Differing Translations, Contested Meanings: A Motor for the 1911 Revolution in China? Pp. 43–60 in Hagen Schulz-Forberg (ed.), *A Global Conceptual History of Asia, 1860–1940*. London: Pickering & Chatto.

Tian, Xiaoli (2018) Escaping the Interpersonal Power Game: Online Shopping in China. *Qualitative Sociology*, 41(4): 545–68.

Tobias, Stephen S. (1976) Review of *The Cultural Ecology of Chinese Civilization: Peasants and Elites in the Last of the Agrarian States* by Leon Stover. *American Anthropologist*, 78(2): 411–12.

Tong, Chee-Kiong (2014) *Chinese Business: Rethinking Guanxi and Trust in Chinese Business Networks*. Singapore: Springer.

Tong, Chee Kiong, and Yong, Pit Kee (1998) *Guanxi* Bases, *Xinyong* and Chinese Business Networks. *British Journal of Sociology*, 49(1): 75–96.

Tsang, Eric W. K. (1998) Can *Guanxi* be a Source of Sustained Competitive Advantage for Doing Business in China? *Academy of Management Executive*, 12(2): 64–73.

Tullberg, Jan (2008) Trust: The Importance of Trustfulness versus Trustworthiness. *Journal of Socio-Economics*, 37(5): 2059–71.

Vogel, Ezra F. (1965) From Friendship to Comradeship: The Change in Personal Relations in Communist China. *The China Quarterly*, 21: 46–60.

Walder, Andrew G. (1986) *Communist Neo-Traditionalism: Work and Authority in Chinese Industry*. Berkeley, CA: University of California Press.

Wang, Barbara Xiaoyu (2019) *Guanxi in the Western Context: Intra-Firm Group Dynamics and Expatriate Adjustment*. London: Palgrave.

Wang, B. X., and Rowley, C. (2017). Business Networks and the Emergence of *Guanxi* Capitalism in China. Pp. 93–118 in J. Nolan, C. Rowley, and M. Warner (eds), *Business Networks in East Asian Capitalisms: Enduring Trends, Emerging Patterns*. London: Elsevier.

Wang, Cheng Lu (2007) *Guanxi* vs. Relationship Marketing: Exploring Underlying Differences. *Industrial Marketing Management*, 36(1): 81–6.

Wang, Jenn-Hwan, and Hsung, Ray-May (eds) (2016) *Rethinking Social Capital and Entrepreneurship in Greater China: Is Guanxi Still Important?* London: Routledge.

Wang, Jenn-Hwan, Chen, Tsung-Yuan, and Hsung, Ray-May (2016) *Guanxi* Matters? Rethinking Social Capital and Entrepreneurship in Greater China. Pp. 1–18 in Jenn-Hwan Wang and Ray-May Hsung (eds), *Rethinking Social Capital and Entrepreneurship in Greater China*. London: Routledge.

Wang, Mingming (2012) South East and South West: Searching for the Link between 'Research Regions'. Pp. 161–90 in Arif Dirlik, Guannan Li, and Hsiao-Pei Yen (eds), *Sociology and Anthropology in Twentieth-Century China*. Hong Kong: Chinese University Press.

Wang, Peng (2016) Military Corruption in China: The Role of *Guanxi* in the Buying and Selling of Military Positions. *The China Quarterly,* 228: 970–91.

Wang, Peng (2020) How to Engage in Illegal Transactions: Resolving Risk and Uncertainty in Corrupt Dealings. *British Journal of Criminology,* 60(5): 1282–1301.

Wank, David L. (1996) The Institutional Process of Market Clientelism: *Guanxi* and Private Business in a South China City. *The China Quarterly,* 147: 820–38.

Wank, David L. (2001) *Commodifying Communism: Business, Trust and Politics in a Chinese City.* Cambridge: Cambridge University Press.

Wank, David L. (2002) Business-State Clientelism in China: Decline or Evolution? Pp. 97–115 in Thomas Gold, Doug Guthrie, and David Wank (eds), *Social Connections in China: Institutions, Culture, and the Changing Nature of Guanxi.* Cambridge: Cambridge University Press.

Wank, David L. (2009) Local State Takeover as Multiple Rent Seeking in Private Business. Pp. 79–97 in Tak-Wing Ngo and Yongping Wu (eds), *Rent Seeking in China.* London: Routledge.

Watson, Ruby S. (2004) Wives, Concubines and Maids: Servitude and Kinship in the Hong Kong Region, 1900–1940. Pp. 169–98 in James L. Watson and Ruby S. Watson, *Village Life in Hong Kong: Politics, Gender and Ritual in the New Territories.* Hong Kong: Chinese University Press.

Weakland, John H. (1950) The Organization of Action in Chinese Culture. *Psychiatry,* 13(3): 361–70.

Weber, Max (1949) *The Methodology of the Social Science.* New York: Free Press.

Weber, Max (1964) *The Religion of China: Confucianism and Taoism.* New York: Free Press.

Wedeman, Andrew (2012) *Double Paradox: Rapid Growth and Rising Corruption in China.* Ithaca, NY: Cornell University Press.

Wellman, Barry, and Wortley, Scot (1990) Different Strokes from Different Folks: Community Ties and Social Support. *American Journal of Sociology,* 96(3): 558–88.

Weng, Yulei, and Xu, Hao (2018) How *Guanxi* Affects Job Search Outcomes in China? Job Match and Job Turnover. *China Economic Review,* 51: 70–82.

Whyte, Martin King (1996) The Chinese Family and Economic Development: Obstacle or Engine? *Economic Development and Cultural Change,* 45(1): 1–30.

Whyte, Martin King (2005) Continuity and Change in Urban Chinese Family Life. *The China Journal,* 53: 9–33.

Wierzbicka, Anna (1997) *Understanding Cultures through their Key Words: English, Russian, Polish, German, and Japanese.* Oxford: Oxford University Press.

Williamson, Oliver (1993) Calculativeness, Trust, and Economic Organization. *Journal of Law and Economics,* 36(2): 453–86.

Wilson, Scott (2002) Face, Norms and Instrumentality. Pp. 163–77 in Thomas Gold, Doug Guthrie, and David Wank (eds), *Social Connections in China: Institutions, Culture, and the Changing Nature of Guanxi.* Cambridge: Cambridge University Press.

Wong, Bernard (1985) Family, Kinship, and Ethnic Identity of the Chinese in New York City, with Comparative Remarks on the Chinese in Lima, Peru and Manila, Philippines. *Journal of Comparative Family Studies,* 16(2): 231–54.

Wong, Man Kong (2005) The Use of Sinology in the Nineteenth Century. Pp. 135–54 in Lee Pui Tak (ed.), *Colonial Hong Kong and Modern China: Interaction and Reintegration.* Hong Kong: Hong Kong University Press.

Wong, Siu-Lun (1979) *Sociology and Socialism in Contemporary China.* London: Routledge.

Wong, Siu-Lun (1996) Chinese Entrepreneurs and Business Trust. Pp. 13–26 in Gary G. Hamilton (ed.), *Asian Business Networks.* New York: Walter de Gruyter.

Wu, Yan, and Wall, Mathew (2019) The Ties that Bind: How the Dominance of WeChat Combines with *Guanxi* to Inhibit and Constrain China's Contentious Politics. *New Media and Society,* 21(8): 1714–33.

Wu, Yongyi (1990) The Usages of Kinship Address Forms amongst Non-Kin in Mandarin Chinese: The Extension of Family Solidarity. *Australian Journal of Linguistics*, 10(1): 61–88.

Yamagishi, Toshio, and Yamagishi, Midori (1994) Trust and Commitment in the United States and Japan. *Motivation and Emotion*, 18(2): 129–65.

Yan, Yunxiang (1996) *The Flow of Gifts: Reciprocity and Social Networks in a Chinese Village*. Stanford, CA: Stanford University Press.

Yan, Yunxiang (2009) *The Individualization of Chinese Society*. Oxford: Berg.

Yan, Yunxiang (2015) Moral Hierarchy and Social Egoism in a Networked Society: The *Chaxugeju* Thesis Revisited. *Korean Journal of Sociology*, 49(3): 39–58.

Yang, C. K. (1959) *A Chinese Village in Early Communist Transition*. Cambridge, MA: MIT Press.

Yang, Lien-sheng (1957) The Concept of *Pao* as a Basis for Social Relations in China. Pp. 291–309 in John K. Fairbank (ed.), *Chinese Thought and Institutions*. Chicago: University of Chicago Press.

Yang, Mayfair Mei-Hui (1989) The Gift Economy and State Power in China. *Comparative Studies in Society and History*, 31(1): 25–54.

Yang, Mayfair Mei-hui (1994) *Gifts, Favors and Banquets: The Art of Social Relationships in China*. Ithaca, NY: Cornell University Press.

Yang, Mayfair Mei-hui (2002) The Resilience of *Guanxi* and its New Deployments: A Critique of Some New *Guanxi* Scholarship. *The China Quarterly*, 170: 459–76.

Yeung, Irene Y. M., and Tung, Rosalie L. (1996) Achieving Business Success in Confucian Societies: The Importance of *Guanxi*. *Organizational Dynamics*, 25(2): 54–65.

Yuan, Samson (2014) Disciplining the Party: Xi Jinping's Anti-Corruption Campaign and its Limits. *China Perspectives*, 3: 41–7.

Zelin, Madeleine (2009) The Firm in Early China. *Journal of Economic Behavior and Organization*, 71(3): 623–37.

Zeng, Qingjie, and Yang, Yujeong (2017) Informal Networks as Safety Nets: The Role of Personal Ties in China's Anti-Corruption Campaign. *China: An International Journal*, 15(3): 26–57.

Zhang, Gupeng, Xiong, Libin, Wang, Xiao, Dong, Jianing, and Duan, Hongbo (2020) Artificial Selection versus Natural Selection: Which Causes the Matthew Effect of Science Funding Allocation in China? *Science and Public Policy*, 47(3): 434–45.

Zhang, Joe (2014) *Party Man, Company Man: Is China's State Capitalism Doomed?* Hong Kong: Enrich Professional Publishing.

Zhang, Mo (2008) From Public to Private: The Newly Enacted Chinese Property Law and the Protection of Property Rights in China. *Berkeley Business Law Journal*, 5(2): 317–63.

Zhang, Nana (2011) The Impact of *Guanxi* Networks on the Employment Relations of Rural Migrant Women in Contemporary China. *Industrial Relations Journal*, 42(6): 580–95.

Zhang, Yongjin, and Buzan, Barry (2012) The Tributary System as International Society in Theory and Practice. *Chinese Journal of International Politics*, 5(1): 3–36.

Zhao, Xiaofan, and Qi, Ye (2020) Why do Firms Obey? The State of Regulatory Compliance Research in China. *Journal of Chinese Political Science*, 25(2): 339–52.

Zhao, Yanrong (2019) Social Connections (*Guanxi*) and Judicial Decision-Making in China. *China: An International Journal*, 17(3): 1–27.

Zmerli, Sonja, and Newton, Ken (2008) Social Trust and Attitudes toward Democracy. *Public Opinion Quarterly*, 72(4): 706–24.

Index of names

For the benefit of digital users, indexed terms that span two pages (e.g., 52–53) may, on occasion, appear on only one of those pages.

Index

For the benefit of digital users, indexed terms that span two pages (e.g., 52–53) may, on occasion, appear on only one of those pages.